LIVY

BOOK XXVII

LIVY

BOOK XXVII

Edited by

S. G. CAMPBELL, M.A.
Fellow and Classical Lecturer of Christ's College and
Lecturer in Classical Epigraphy and Dialects
in the University of Cambridge

Cambridge:
at the University Press
1926

CAMBRIDGE UNIVERSITY PRESS
Cambridge, New York, Melbourne, Madrid, Cape Town,
Singapore, São Paulo, Delhi, Mexico City

Cambridge University Press
The Edinburgh Building, Cambridge CB2 8RU, UK

Published in the United States of America by Cambridge University Press, New York

www.cambridge.org
Information on this title: www.cambridge.org/9781107620025

First edition 1913
First published 1913
Reprinted 1922 (twice), 1923, 1926
First paperback edition 2013

A catalogue record for this publication is available from the British Library

ISBN 978-1-107-62002-5 Paperback

PREFACE

THE text of this edition and the analysis which accompanies it have been printed from the plates of Mr Stephenson's edition of Book XXVII, previously published by the Cambridge University Press. Some alterations, however, have been introduced. In a few places a different reading has been adopted, some misprints have been corrected, and, though I have refrained from substituting *u* for *v* throughout, a number of slight spelling changes have been made. In the Notes on the Text appended to the Commentary the more important variant readings are noted and briefly discussed.

The edition to which I am chiefly indebted in the notes both for explanation and illustration is of course that of Weissenborn. I have also consulted Friedersdorff's commentary and have occasionally quoted a note from Mr Stephenson's edition. Many useful hints have been derived from the editors of other books of Livy in the Pitt Press Series, especially from Professor R. S. Conway, whose edition of Book II seems to me a model of lucidity and freshness.

For textual questions Luchs' edition has been indispensable, and in addition to the critical notes in Madvig and Ussing's edition I have used Madvig's *Emendationes.*

On points of constitutional and political history my chief guides have been Mommsen's *Roman History* and *Römisches Staatsrecht*. The last section of the Introduction gives a brief account of some of the problems connected with the Metaurus. Among the mass of literature that has been written on this campaign I am most deeply indebted to Mr B. W. Henderson's able articles in the *English Historical Review* and to Kromayer's monumental *Antike Schlachtfelder*. The discussion of Livy's sources and narrative in the previous section is based on Soltau's work on the sources of the third decade.

I have to thank my friend Mr W. H. Balgarnie of the Leys for most generous assistance in reading the proofs of the notes and introduction and for valuable suggestions on a number of points. I must also express my gratitude to the readers of the University Press whose lynx-eyed vigilance has saved me from many inconsistencies and not a few mistakes.

S. G. C.

BALLYNATRUA, DERRY,
September 1913.

CONTENTS

INTRODUCTION

I. THE POSITION OF AFFAIRS IN 210 B.C.

§ 1. *Italy*

After Cannae the Italian allies of Rome over a large part of the South of Italy joined Hannibal, and the

216 B.C. Carthaginians secured Apulia, Lucania, Bruttium and most of Samnium, and by winning Capua and a number of the neighbouring towns established themselves also in Campania. In the centre, however, Rome retained as allies most of the tribes—Marsi, Vestini, Picentines, Frentani, Sabines and others; and though the surrounding districts declared for Carthage, the chief towns in S. Italy, Brundisium, Tarentum, Beneventum, Venusia, Luceria, and others were held by Rome, and her garrisons secured also some of the Campanian cities. In the North, in spite of a severe defeat sustained by the praetor, L. Postumius Albinus, at the hands of the Gauls, Rome kept Etruria and Umbria.

The Italian campaigns of the next three years produced no material change in this position. Hannibal's

215 B.C.–213 B.C. most important success was the gain of Tarentum[1], followed by that of Metapontum, Heraclea, Thurii, and Locri. The Romans still held the citadel of Tarentum and Rhegium, but with these exceptions Hannibal had all the south coast. Campania, however, was the main seat of the war and in the following years the dogged persistence of Rome was rewarded. In 211 B.C. after a long siege Capua fell and Campania was lost to Hannibal. After his unavailing attempt

211 B.C. to raise the siege by his famous march to Rome Hannibal retired south to Bruttium.

[1] 212 B.C. according to Polybius.

The consuls elected for 210 B.C. were M. Claudius Marcellus and M. Valerius Laevinus, who had been for several years commander of the fleet and army in Greece. The provinces assigned to them by the Senate were Italy with the war against Hannibal and Sicily with the command of the fleet. The lot gave Marcellus the latter, but owing to the entreaties of the Sicilians, who declared it were better that their island should be sunk in the sea or buried under Etna's fires than have Marcellus again its master[1], an exchange of provinces was brought about—*rapiente fato Marcellum ad Hannibalem.* Each consul had the usual two legions and, in addition to the troops in Spain, Sardinia, and Greece, Rome had armies in Apulia under Cn. Fulvius Centumalus (2 legions), in Capua under Q. Fulvius[2] Flaccus (1 legion), in Etruria under C. Calpurnius Piso (2 legions), in Cisalpine Gaul under C. Laetorius (2 legions), and at Rome (2 urban legions)[3].

210 B.C.

Of the military history of the early part of 210 B.C. we have a somewhat rambling account in cc. 37–40 of Book 26, preceding the lengthy section on Spain with which that book closes. The Roman garrison continued to hold out in the citadel of Tarentum though the fleet was defeated by the Tarentines. In Apulia Marcellus took the town of Salapia[4]. It is at this point that the narrative in Book 27 begins. A brief summary of that narrative so far as it relates to the war in Italy is appended.

[1] 26. 29 *obrui Aetnae ignibus aut mergi freto, satius illi insulae esse, quam velut dedi noxae inimico.*

[2] The frequent occurrence of the name *Fulvius* in the earlier chapters of Bk 27 is rather confusing. Distinguish (1) *Cn. Fulvius Centumalus* (cos. 211 B.C., slain in Apulia 210 B.C.); (2) *Q. Fulvius Flaccus* (cos. 212 B.C. and 209 B.C., dictator 210 B.C.); (3) *C. Fulvius Flaccus* (c. 8. 12); and (4) *Cn. Fulvius Flaccus* (praetor 212 B.C.), brothers of (2).

[3] As evidence that after the fall of Capua Rome felt that the strain might be somewhat relaxed, we may note that the instructions to the consuls for the levy of soldiers definitely limit the number of legions to 21. (26. 28. 13 *neve eo anno plures quam una et viginti legiones Romanae essent.*)

[4] See nn. on c. 1. 1 and c. 28. 6.

210 B.C. Marcellus in Samnium. Cn. Fulvius defeated at Herdonea (c. 1). Marcellus goes to Lucania and fights an indecisive battle with Hannibal at Numistro (c. 2). Q. Fulvius Flaccus at Capua (c. 3).

209 B.C. Marcellus and Hannibal at Canusium; three battles (cc. 12–14). Fulvius in Lucania (c. 15. 1–3). Fabius invests and captures Tarentum (c. 15. 4–c. 16. 9). Hannibal arriving too late to save Tarentum retires to Metapontum (c. 16. 10 f.). Unrest in Etruria (c. 21. 6 f.).

208 B.C. Etruria still unsettled (c. 24). War in S. Italy: Crispinus at Locri; marches to join Marcellus in Apulia (c. 25. 11 f.). Marcellus slain and Crispinus wounded near Venusia (cc. 26–27). Hannibal foiled at Salapia, marches S. and raises siege of Locri (c. 28). Death of Crispinus (c. 35. 6).

207 B.C. News of Hasdrubal's crossing the Alps (c. 39). Plan of campaign (c. 40). Hannibal, repulsed in Calabria, retires to Bruttium (c. 40. 10 f.), thence proceeds N. to Lucania and is defeated by Nero at Grumentum. He gets past into Apulia and, followed by Nero, marches to Venusia, thence S. to Metapontum and again N. to Canusium (cc. 41–2). Nero marches N. with 7000 picked men and effects junction with Livius in Umbria (cc. 43, 45–6). Hasdrubal retreats and is defeated and slain by the two consuls at the Metaurus (cc. 47–49). Nero marches S. again and announces the defeat of Hasdrubal to Hannibal. Hannibal retires to Bruttium (cc. 50–51).

§ 2. *Events at Rome*

The history of home affairs in this book consists very largely of a dull catalogue of the yearly occurrence and expiation of prodigies, the celebration of games and the changes in officials civil and religious. Occasionally the chronicle is enlivened by a disputed election, when we get a glimpse of party wire-pulling and family intrigue. There are a few faint echoes of the social struggle that occupies so large a part of the early books, as for instance in c. 8 when a plebeian is elected *curio maximus*.

We are made to realise the closeness of the tie existing between Rome and her colonies throughout Italy, and at the same time the severity of the burden imposed by the war upon the resources of both, when in chapters 9 and 10 Livy describes the dealings of the consuls and Senate with the deputies of the 12 disaffected and the 18 loyal colonies, and immediately after tells us that Rome decided to use the gold reserve that had been kept *ad ultimos casus*[1].

In chapters 40 and 44 Livy gives an interesting picture of the anxiety at Rome before the Metaurus conflict, and at the close we have a vivid description of the reception in the city of the news of the victory[2].

§ 3. *Sicily*

Previous to 215 B.C. Sicily had been peaceful for a long period. The domain of Hiero of Syracuse, Rome's staunch ally, embraced a considerable strip of territory extending along the East coast. The rest of the island formed the Roman province.

On the death of Hiero, his grandson and successor, Hieronymus, gave up the Roman alliance, but he was murdered after a reign of a few months, and in the struggle of factions that ensued the Roman party in Syracuse for a time gained the ascendancy. However, with the break-up of Hiero's kingdom that took place after his death most of the other cities in it had followed the example of Syracuse in opposing Rome, and the cruel treatment of Leontini by Marcellus in 214 B.C. brought about a counter-revolution in Syracuse. This city was accordingly invested by Marcellus and after a long siege was taken and sacked in 212 B.C. Meanwhile the Carthaginians had sent a considerable armament to Sicily and had established themselves on the south coast, taking Agrigentum, which they made their centre of operations, and winning to their side a number of the inland towns. The Numidian horse under Muttines, a half-bred Carthaginian and a brilliant cavalry general, overran the Roman province.

[1] 209 B.C. [2] cc. 50, 51.

Marcellus left Sicily in 211 B.C. and the work of expelling the Carthaginians and reducing the island was completed by Laevinus in the following year. The story of the concluding campaign in 210 B.C. is told by Livy in Bk 26. c. 40. Through the treachery of Muttines, who had been superseded in the command of the cavalry owing to Hanno's jealousy, Laevinus took Agrigentum, and the other towns were stormed or surrendered and the whole island brought under Roman dominion. In the following years we hear little of Sicily. In Book 27, apart from the regular references[1] to the appointment of praetor or propraetor and the disposition of troops, Livy mentions descents by the Sicilian fleet on Africa in 210 B.C.[2] and 208 B.C.[3], the return of Laevinus to Rome and his report of the subjugation of the province[4], a decree for the despatch of a detachment of the fleet to Tarentum[5], Laevinus' review of the island in 209 B.C. and its renewed prosperity[6], and the despatch of reinforcements to Livius by the praetor C. Mamilius in 207 B.C.[7]

§ 4. *Spain*

The defeat and death of the two Scipios in 211 B.C. after six years compaigning in Spain had left the Carthaginians masters of the country S. of the Ebro, and the Romans held only a strip of coast extending N. from the mouth of that river to the Pyrenees. After the fall of Capua Claudius Nero was sent to Spain as propraetor and, if we may believe Livy's account, met with considerable success[8]. At all events he appears to have kept the Carthaginians at bay and held the Roman territory N. of the Ebro. When Nero's year of command came to an end M. Iunius Silanus was appointed as propraetor to succeed him. At the same time in view of the importance of the war the supreme command in Spain was given to an officer of higher rank and the choice fell upon a young man not yet

[1] c. 7. 12, 13, c. 8. 13, c. 22. 3, 9, c. 36. 11, 12.
[2] c. 5. 1, 8 f.
[3] c. 29. 7, 8.
[4] c. 5. 1–7 *se eam provinciam confecisse.*
[5] c. 7. 15.
[6] c. 8. 18, 19.
[7] c. 38. 12.
[8] See n. on c. 44. 9.

thirty, Publius Scipio, son of the Publius who had been slain in Spain some months before. Scipio and Silanus were given ample troops to reinforce the army in Spain and a considerable fleet with Scipio's friend, C. Laelius, in command. They established themselves at Tarraco, on the coast N. of the mouth of the Ebro. As soon as the season permitted, Scipio, leaving Silanus to hold the northern district, boldly crossed the Ebro and marching with great rapidity reached the Carthaginian capital, New Carthage. This town was of supreme importance to Carthage as her chief arsenal in Spain, and in it were detained a large number of important hostages from the Spanish tribes. Yet it was defended by a surprisingly small garrison and within a few hours of Scipio's first attack the walls were stormed, the citadel surrendered and the town given over to plunder[1].

Immense stores of grain and arms, 18 ships of war and a fleet of merchantmen fell into Scipio's hands. Among the prisoners were a number of important Carthaginians and also some 2000 skilled craftsmen. Laelius was despatched to Rome with the former, the latter Scipio employed in manufacturing arms. After a short time spent in this and in exercising his soldiers and sailors Scipio returned to Tarraco.

At this point the Spanish section of Book 26 closes. In Book 27. c. 7 we have an account of Laelius' arrival and reception in Rome and a reference to the various views about the date of the capture of New Carthage[2]. In c. 17 the detailed account of Scipio's campaign is resumed[3].

He marches S. from Tarraco and inflicts a severe defeat on Hasdrubal at Baecula[4]. Yet in spite of the victory Hasdrubal is allowed to slip past, cross the Pyrenees by the western passes and march towards Italy. Scipio returns to Tarraco and a conference of the Carthaginian leaders in Spain closes the section.

[1] Mommsen calls Scipio's exploit 'one of the boldest and most fortunate *coups de main* that are known in history.'

[2] See notes *ad loc.*

[3] 209 B.C. according to Livy, 208 B.C. according to Polybius.

[4] c. 17.

In the succeeding chapters we have only brief references to Spain: the prorogation of the command of Scipio and Silanus for 208 B.C. and 207 B.C.[1], an order for the despatch of 50 ships from Spain to Sardinia[2], and the statement that according to some authorities Scipio sent reinforcements to Livius[3].

§ 5. *Greece and the East*

Rome first intervened in Eastern affairs in 229 B.C. The Illyrian pirates had become troublesome and she repressed them. Ten years later she found it necessary to repeat the lesson.

After Cannae Philip V of Macedon made an alliance with Hannibal but he did not join in the struggle in Italy, and Rome was too much engrossed in that struggle to take a very active part in what is usually called the First Macedonian War (214 B.C.–205 B.C.). She maintained, however, a fleet in the Adriatic and kept a grip on Apollonia and Corcyra and thus controlled the route to Greece.

Beside Macedon the leading powers in Greece at this time were the two Leagues. The ancient Achaean League when reconstituted in the 3rd century consisted at first of ten cities in the north of the Peloponnese, the most important being Aegium, Dyme, and Patrae. Before long its power extended and it included Sicyon, Corinth, Megara, Argos and indeed almost all the cities in the south of Greece except Sparta. From 221 B.C. onwards it became weaker and was dominated by Macedon, and we find its *strategus* acting under Philip.

The chief rival of Macedon was now the Aetolian League which had become the leading power in South Central Greece. Originally a union of country districts in Aetolia with its centre at Thermum, it had spread far beyond the limits of that country. Peloponnesian states and islands were enrolled in it and even cities as far away as Lysimachea in Thrace.

In the Peloponnese Sparta maintained her independence and was the chief opponent of the Achaean League there. Her government had become a despotism and the ruler at this time

[1] c. 22. 7 and c. 36. 12. [2] c. 22. 7. [3] c. 38. 11.

was Machanidas who made himself tyrant in 210 B.C. Some 20 years later, on the death of Nabis, the successor of Machanidas, Sparta passed into the power of the Achaean League[1].

Of the other states, Athens retained her independence but had sunk to an unimportant position. Boeotia also was powerless, and Euboea and Thessaly were completely under Macedonian domination. To the west of Thessaly lay the small but independent kingdom of Athamania[2].

At the date at which Book 27 begins Rome was in alliance with the Aetolians, Eleans, and Sparta against Philip and the Achaeans. An important power on the side of the allies was Rome's faithful friend, Attalus I, king of Pergamum[3], who in 210 B.C. was honorary *strategus* of the Aetolian League. His rival, Prusias of Bithynia, was an ally of Philip[4].

In Book 27 Livy has an excursus of four chapters on affairs in Greece[5]. It deals with the struggle between Philip and the Aetolians and we hear occasionally of the activity of the Roman armament under Sulpicius Galba[6].

II. LIVY'S SOURCES AND THE NARRATIVE OF BOOK 27

For writing the history of the Second Punic War Livy had at his disposal very ample materials. In the first place a mass of public and private documents were within his reach. He might consult such important original sources as the *annales maximi*, a brief record of each year's events kept by the *pontifex maximus*, the *libri lintei* containing lists of magistrates written on linen and preserved in the temple of Juno Moneta, and the registers and commentaries of various officials—censors,

[1] See n. on c. 31. 10.

[2] Mentioned by Livy c. 30. 4 and very frequently in the later books.

[3] c. 29. 10. [4] c. 30. 16. [5] c. 29. 9–c. 33. 5.

[6] c. 30. 2 1000 troops on the Aetolian side, c. 30. 11 fleet at Naupactus, c. 31. 1 repulsed by P. near Corinth, c. 32. 2 at Elis with Aetolians and Eleans, c. 33. 4, 5 at Aegium.

pontiffs, augurs. There were extant tablets of stone and bronze recording laws and treaties, and a multitude of other inscriptions, both public and private, in temples and other public buildings, on tombs, on family busts and on all manner of movable objects. In the family archives too were kept genealogical lists and funeral orations recording the deeds and offices of ancestors. Livy, however, was not a scientific historian in the modern sense, and it is highly unlikely that he investigated or consulted any of these original sources. There is positive evidence in more than one place in his writings that in general he quite neglected archaeological evidence. In an interesting passage at the beginning of the Sixth Book, where he is speaking of the difficulty of writing the early history of Rome[1] owing to the loss of documents when the city was burnt by the Gauls in 390 B.C., he declares that literary records are *una custodia fidelis memoriae rerum.*

In the second place Livy was preceded by a long series of writers of annals, who drew their materials from some or all of the sources of evidence enumerated above. It is probable, however, that Livy did not go directly to the works of the earliest of these annalists, but contented himself with consulting them at second hand in the writings of their successors. For the history of the last quarter of the 3rd century B.C. this neglect is the more remarkable, since Q. Fabius Pictor and L. Cincius Alimentus both lived in this period. The latter, praetor in 210 B.C. and frequently mentioned in Book 27, wrote an account of the Second Punic War, in which he himself took part. Livy refers to this contemporary account in Book 21[2], but, as we have said, he does not appear to have used it at first hand.

Before writing the history of a particular year or incident Livy probably read through several accounts given by the later annalists and possibly made excerpts from them. When writing his ordinary practice apparently was to follow closely one particular author at a time, but he seldom mentions the name of

[1] *res vetustate nimia obscuras.*

[2] 38. 3 *L. Cincius Alimentus, qui captum se ab Hannibale scribit, maxime auctor me moveret, nisi confunderet numerum* etc.

this author. Not infrequently he adds further details on the authority of other writers. Where he finds conflicting accounts he often records the fact without expressing an opinion himself. Occasionally he gives reasons for preferring one or the other; sometimes he counts heads and follows the majority; more than once he gives a combination of contradictory accounts. Book 27 illustrates his practice quite well. Thus we find c. 1. 13 *cum alibi...alibi inveniam*, c. 7. 5 *contuli multis auctoribus*, c. 27. 12, 13 *variant auctores...Coelius edit*, c. 33. 6 *alii...alii...tradunt*, c. 38. 12 *auctores sunt*.

As Livy is our leading authority for the events with which Book 27 deals the question of the trustworthiness of his narrative is one of great importance. The investigations of Dr Soltau[1] have made it probable that for the campaigns of the Hannibalic War Livy used as his main sources Coelius Antipater and Claudius Quadrigarius, and for events in Rome in the same period Calpurnius Piso and Valerius Antias.

L. Coelius Antipater, mentioned by Livy in 27. 27. 13 and frequently in the 3rd decade, lived in the time of the Gracchi and wrote *annales* in which he seems to have made careful use of earlier writers. That he consulted the funeral oration pronounced on Marcellus by his son is clear from the passage in c. 27 just cited.

Q. Claudius Quadrigarius wrote in the time of Sulla. He seems to have modelled his style on the Greek historians and represented the rhetorical school of history to which Cicero is attached[2]. In the descriptions of battles he appears to have romanced freely, and to have coloured his narrative for family reasons, seeking in particular to magnify the exploits of the Claudii and the Cornelii Scipiones[3]. Thus in cc. 41–2 and cc. 46–50, which give an account of Claudius Nero's success against Hannibal in the S. and his famous march N. to join Livius, Soltau thinks that Livy is following Claudius Quadrigarius

[1] *Livius' Geschichtswerk* and *Livius' Quellen in der III Dekade.*

[2] *opus unum oratorium maxime.*

[3] Soltau speaks of his history as 'das romanhafte Geschichtswerk dieses Rhetors.'

directly. Again it has been conjectured that the story of Marcellus' campaigns in cc. 1–2 and cc. 12–14 comes from the same source.

In the latter of these passages we have an account of three battles between Hannibal and Marcellus in 209 B.C. Grave doubt has been cast upon the truth of this narrative, and there are certainly elements in the story which make it look like the invention of a partisan annalist. After an indecisive fight on the first day, Marcellus is defeated on the second, but on the third wins a great victory. No less than 8000 of the enemy are slain, while barely half that number fall on the Roman side. But Marcellus was entirely unable to follow up his success and remained inactive at Venusia for the rest of the season, and the reason given by Livy (*prohibuit multitudo sauciorum*) is dismissed by modern critics as inconsistent with the account of the battle. Again in c. 20. 9 f. we find Marcellus in bad repute at Rome *superquam quod primo male pugnaverat, quia vagante per Italiam Hannibale media aestate Venusiam in tecta milites abduxisset.* It is urged that a defeat followed by a brilliant victory could hardly be a cause of loss of reputation and that the failure of the attack on Marcellus was due to the strong family interest he possessed in Rome and not to his achievements against Hannibal in the field[1].

Another section in which the influence of Claudius Quadrigarius has been plausibly assumed is the Spanish extract (cc. 17–20[2]). The central portion of this section gives an account of the battle of Baecula in which Hasdrubal sustains a severe defeat at the hands of the Romans. Here again, though this time Livy's account is supported by Polybius, modern critics have contended that the victory of Scipio is a myth started by Scipio and Laelius and passed on to Polybius. "That Scipio," it is argued, "after inflicting such a defeat on Hasdrubal should, with all the means of information he had at his command, allow the defeated general to leave Spain unmolested, and that the latter should arrive in Italy with what Livy himself calls *ingens*

[1] Polybius declares that up to Zama Hannibal was undefeated (16. 5 τὸν πρὸ τοῦ χρόνου ἀήττητος ὤν).

[2] See n. on c. 7. 5.

exercitus, is simply incredible[1]." It seems pretty clear at all events that we have not got the whole truth from Livy; whether the account he gives contains a large amount of falsehood is not so certain.

Of the two annalists whom Soltau sets down as Livy's authorities for the events at Rome in these years, L. Calpurnius Piso wrote about the time of the Gracchi, and it appears from the surviving fragments and from other indications that his *annales* were a dry record reflecting the style of the yearly records compiled by the pontifex maximus. Valerius Antias is not mentioned in Book 27 but is very frequently referred to by Livy. Like Quadrigarius he wrote in the time of Sulla. His *annales* also seem to have been based on the pontifical year-book, but he amplified and embellished the narrative of Piso. In the third and later decades Livy used this historian with caution, as he realised his untrustworthy character, especially in the matter of numbers[2]. Thus among the sections dealing with the city chronicles Soltau thinks that the account of the prodigies in c. 4 and of the priestly changes and games at the end of c. 6 are from Piso, while the dispute about the dictatorship in cc. 5–6 is based on Antias. Again he would derive the account of Livius in c. 34 from the fuller history of Antias and assign to Piso the notes on the armies and on prodigies in the following chapters.

For the history of events outside Italy, Livy had a trustworthy authority in the Greek historian Polybius[3]. It was formerly held that throughout the third decade Livy took straight from Polybius the numerous sections dealing with Sicilian, Greek, Spanish and African events, but it appears likely that the direct use of the Greek historian does not begin

[1] Stephenson.

[2] cp. 26. 49. 3 *adeo nullus mentiendi modus est*, 30. 19. 11 *impudenter ficta*, 33. 10. 8 *si Valerio qui credat omnium rerum immodice numerum augenti*.

[3] cp. 33. 10. 10 where L., after mentioning several Roman writers, says *Polybium secuti sumus, non incertum auctorem cum omnium Romanarum rerum tum praecipue in Graecia gestarum*.

till Book 26[1]. These *excursus* were evidently inserted by Livy in his narrative after the composition of the books in which they occur. More than once they are misplaced. The *excursus* on affairs in Greece in cc. 29–33 may be taken as an illustration. That Livy is using Polybius is betrayed by the fact that he puts the Greek events a year too late. The practice of the Greek historian is to equate the Roman official year with the Olympiad beginning half a year earlier. For instance, 216 B.C. is made equivalent to Ol. 140. 4, which began August 217 B.C., and Greek events of 141. 1 (=216 B.C.–215 B.C.) are put parallel with Roman of 215 B.C. Now in c. 30. 17 Livy puts the Nemean Games of 209 B.C. under 208 B.C., and in c. 35. 3 the Olympian Games of 208 B.C. are assigned to 207 B.C.[2] Furthermore, the first events mentioned in this *excursus* belong to 210 B.C. and this points to the fact that the section is a later insertion, stuck in between the mention of the illness of Crispinus and his naming of a dictator just before his death.

III. THE CAMPAIGN OF THE METAURUS

§ 1. *The Carthaginian plan of campaign*

In spite of the victories which Livy attributes to Marcellus and the thousands he would have us believe Hannibal lost in the various battles, the general impression that one gets of the campaigns of 210 B.C.–207 B.C. from reading the first 35 chapters of Book 27 may be summed up in Livy's phrase *res nunc secundae nunc adversae*[3]. With the arrival of Hasdrubal in Italy we feel that the war has entered upon a new phase.

The campaigns of the past years must have made it clear to Hannibal that little more was to be gained in S. Italy. In Central Italy, as we have seen, the influence of Rome had been undisputed, and Hannibal had proved unable to loosen her hold on

[1] See also n. on c. 7. 5.

[2] cp. 28. 7. 14.

[3] c. 3. 8, cp. c. 40. 3 *adversa secundis pensando rem ad id tempus extractam esse.*

these districts. His one chance now was to make a supreme attempt on Central Italy, and the unrest in Etruria[1], and the state of feeling shown two years before in a number of the Latin colonies in the central district[2], seemed to offer a prospect of success if the war were carried further north. To make this attempt was apparently what Hannibal planned in 207 B.C. He and Hasdrubal were to meet in Umbria, where a successful junction might enable them to strike a paralysing blow at Rome by winning over the districts that had been her chief resource.

Although Livy passes lightly over the serious mistake made by P. Scipio in allowing Hasdrubal to leave Spain, he at once emphasises the importance of the campaign of 207 B.C.[3], and in the concluding chapters of the book makes it clear that the Metaurus is indeed the turning-point of the struggle.

At various points in the narrative we hear of the progress of Hasdrubal. In c. 19 he is marching towards the Pyrenees; in c. 36. 1 news arrives from Massilia in the winter of 208 B.C. that he has passed into Gaul and would cross the Alps in the following spring. Then comes Porcius' despatch[4] from Cisalpine Gaul that the crossing is taking place.

The passage proved swift and easy and Hasdrubal was at Placentia earlier than either Hannibal or the Romans anticipated. He wasted some time in a vain attempt to take this town before proceeding on his march towards Umbria. In the South Hannibal after the engagement with Nero at Grumentum marched into Apulia and waited at Canusium ready to march north when he should receive Hasdrubal's despatch announcing his progress and the point of meeting.

§ 2. *The distribution of the Roman troops*

In 207 B.C. there were, according to Livy[5], 15 legions in Italy. Of these 7 were in the South—2 under Nero, 2 under Fulvius Flaccus in Lucania, 2 under Claudius Flaccus at Tarentum and

[1] c. 21. 6, c. 24. [2] c. 9.
[3] c. 35. 5 *periculosissimus annus*, c. 40.
[4] c. 39. 1. [5] See c. 35. 10 f., 36. 12 f.

DISTRIBUTION OF THE

210 B.C.	no. of legions	209 B.C.	no. of legions
Italy: cos. army (1) Marcellus	2[1]		
Lucania and Bruttii:		cos. army (2) Q. Fulvius Flaccus [c. 7 9]	2
Apulia: Cn. Fulvius Centumalus	2	(Venusia) Marcellus [c. 7 11]	2
Tarentum:		cos. army (1) Fabius [c. 7 9]	2
Capua: Q. Fulvius Flaccus	1[2]	T. Quinctius Crispinus [c. 7 10]	1
Etruria: C. Calpurnius Piso	2[3]	C. Calpurnius Piso [c. 7 10]	2
Gallia: C. Laetorius	2[4]	L. Veturius Philo [c. 7 8]	2
Rome: urban legions (*novae*)	2	[c. 8 11] (*novae*)	2
Sicily: cos. army (2) fleet } Laevinus	2	Laevinus (fleet, *Cannenses* and remains of Apulian army) [c. 7 12]	
praetor L. Cincius	2	Cincius	2
Sardinia: P. Manlius Vulso	2	C. Aurunculeius [c. 7 14]	2
Spain: Scipio and Silanus	4	Scipio and Silanus [c. 7 17]	4
	21		21
Greece: P. Sulpicius Galba (fleet)	1	P. Sulpicius Galba [c. 7 15] (fleet)	1

[1] 214 B.C.—211 B.C. Gallia.

[2] 214 B.C. urban,

[4] 212 B.C. urban, 211 B.C. Apulia, 210 B.C.—203 B.C. Gallia.

[6] moved to Rome [c. 43 8].

LEGIONS 210 B.C.—207 B.C.

208 B.C.	no. of legions	207 B.C.	no. of legions
cos. army (1) T. Quinctius Crispinus [c. **22** 2, c. **25** 6]	2	cos. army (1) Claudius Nero	2
		Bruttii: Q. Fulvius Flaccus [c. **35** 12, 13]	2
cos. army (2) Marcellus [c. **22** 2, c. **25** 10]	2		
Q. Claudius Flamen [c. **22** 3]	2	Q. Claudius Flamen [c. **36** 13]	2
Q. Fulvius Flaccus [c. **22** 3]	1	C. Hostilius Tubulus [c. **35** 14]	1 [6]
C. Hostilius Tubulus [c. **22** 4]	2 (*a*)	C. Terentius Varro (*a*) (*b*) (*c*) [c. **35** 10, 11]	2
		cos. army (2) M. Livius (*a*) (*b*) (*c*) [c. **35** 10, 11]	2
L. Veturius Philo [c. **22** 5]	2 (*b*)	L. Porcius Licinus (*a*) (*b*) (*c*) [c. **35** 10, 11]	2
[c. **22** 10]	2 [5] (*c*)	[c. **35** 12] (*novae*)	2 [7]
Laevinus (fleet) [c. **22** 9]			
Sex. Iulius Caesar [c. **22** 9] (*Cannenses*)	2	C. Mamilius [c. **36** 12]	2
C. Aurunculeius (fleet) [c. **22** 6]	2	A. Hostilius Cato [c. **36** 12]	2
Scipio and Silanus [c. **22** 7]	4	Scipio and Silanus	4
[c. **22** 11]	21	[c. **36** 12]	23
P. Sulpicius Galba [c. **22** 10] (fleet)	1	P. Sulpicius Galba (fleet)	1

13 B.C.—211 B.C. Campania. [3] 211 B.C. urban.
[5] C. Terentius Varro leads 1 urban legion to Arretium [c. **24** 6 f.]. to Narnia [c. **43** 9].

1 under Hostilius Tubulus at Capua. In the North there were 6 legions—2 under Livius, 2 under Porcius in Cisalpine Gaul and 2 in Etruria under Terentius Varro—and in addition 2 urban legions available at Rome.

Thus if we take the regular strength of a legion including the allies to have been at this period about 10,000[1], there should have been some 80,000 men for the defence of the north against Hasdrubal. In c. 43. 11 Livy tells us that Nero selected from his army 6000 foot and 1000 horse when he started north to join Livius. That he should have undertaken the march with this force when there were already so many soldiers in the north, and that the transference of so comparatively small a part of the southern armies should have created such a sensation at Rome and should have produced the decisive result related by Livy in the succeeding chapters, is at first sight very puzzling. It leads us to consider the whole question of the strength of the Roman armies during the campaigns of these years. The first point to be noted is that in spite of the regular mention by Livy of a large number of legions in Italy each year, we hear little or nothing about the activity of many of these legions, and the actual campaigning seems to have been confined to the two consular armies or at most to three armies. It has been actually held[2] that these elaborate accounts of the armies given by Livy are a fiction of the annalists, and that in the years following Cannae there were never more than two consular armies of two legions each in Italy.

A much more plausible theory[3] is that while the field armies each year were of full strength the other so-called legions were really only small bodies of garrison troops. But a glance at the table on the opposite page giving the history of the individual legions reveals a serious objection to this solution of the difficulty. It appears that the legions which were on this 'garrison duty' in one year might become one of the consular armies of the following year. Thus we see that the legions raised in 211 B.C., which were in Etruria in 210 B.C., formed Fabius' army at Tarentum in

[1] Say 4400 citizens and 6000 socii.

[2] Beloch, *Die Bevölkerung Italiens im Altertum*.

[3] Delbrück's.

209 B.C. Again in 210 B.C. the army of Marcellus was the same that had done 'garrison duty' in Cisalpine Gaul from 214 B.C. to 211 B.C. It seems, however, quite certain that the legions other than the field armies were regularly weaker. In cases where a number of years had elapsed since enrolment, the numbers must have been considerably less, and the vacancies would not be filled up, as those in the consular armies frequently were, by a levy *in supplementum*. Furthermore the inactivity of legions stationed in districts like Etruria or Cisalpine Gaul might in large measure be explained by the fact that owing to the state of these districts the troops had to be split up into small bodies to garrison different points.

Returning to the case of 207 B.C., we find the weakness of the northern legions emphasised by Livy. In c. 38. 7 he says *Livius cunctabatur parum fidens suarum provinciarum exercitibus*. Livius contrasts the armies of the north with the *consulares egregii exercitus* at the disposal of Nero. Varro's legions had been enrolled in 210 B.C. and had remained in Etruria for three years. Porcius' army was the urban legions of 212 B.C. After a year in Apulia in 211 B.C., they had been in Gaul continuously and they remained there till 203 B.C.

It becomes clear therefore how important and welcome Nero's 7000 picked men[1] would be as an addition to the reinforcements that Livius could hope for from the armies in Etruria and Cisalpine Gaul.

§ 3. *Nero's march*

In recent times there has been a great deal of controversy about the famous march of Nero and a number of German and Italian scholars have rejected the whole tale as an invention of the annalists. Polybius' account of the events preceding the battle of the Metaurus is lost, but in his account of the battle we have no mention of the march back to Canusium which took place immediately after. There is no reason, however, to suppose that Polybius did not, like Livy, mention it after his

[1] Augmented too by numbers of veterans who joined them on the march.

description of the arrival of the news of the victory in Rome, the point at which the fragment we possess stops. In addition to Livy's narrative we have several brief accounts of the march in later writers. The only real difficulty about the story as we have it in Livy is the pace at which the journey was performed. The other arguments advanced against the probability of it have been shown to be valueless[1].

The distance from Canusium to Sena Gallica is 230 miles, and from Canusium to the Metaurus 241 miles. Livy tells us[2] that Nero started on the return march the night after the battle and marching *citatiore quam inde venerat agmine* reached his camp at Canusium on the sixth day. If we select from among the various sites suggested for the battle the one nearest Canusium[3] the distance is 245 miles, i.e. the rate of marching was 41 miles a day. Again if we suppose that the march north to Sena Gallica occupied a day more than the return march, the pace would be 33 miles a day for seven consecutive days. This is generally regarded as incredible and it is certainly far in advance of anything recorded of modern armies. Fifteen to twenty miles a day seems to be the limit for continuous marching. Nor is it altogether satisfactory to suppose that Livy has exaggerated simply in the matter of the time occupied, for every day that we add makes it more difficult to understand Hannibal's continued inaction at Canusium. It must, however, be remembered that all the conditions of the march were the most favourable possible. The soldiers were picked men[4] and they were entirely unencumbered by baggage. They had a straight and level road and were cheered and encouraged all along the route. Food was everywhere provided and horses and vehicles put at the disposal of the weary[5]. Under these exceptional circumstances the feat may well have been accomplished.

[1] See especially B. W. Henderson in *Eng. Hist. Rev.* 1898, p. 427 f.

[2] c. 50. 1. In the other accounts of the march no indication of the time occupied is given.

[3] S. Angelo.

[4] c. 43. 11 *de toto exercitu civium sociorumque quod roboris erat delegit.*

[5] c. 43. 10.

§ 4. *The movements preceding the battle*

Many attempts have been made to identify the actual scene of the battle of the Metaurus. These may be divided into two main classes. The first class includes those who think that the battle took place on the left bank (i.e. on the N. side) of the Metaurus, and that Hasdrubal's march to the river previous to the fight was not a retreat north but a movement S.W. and an attempt to get round the Roman forces, strike the *via Flaminia* and proceed S. to join Hannibal[1]. According to the other view the battle was on the right bank (on the S. side) of the river, the first position was in the neighbourhood of Sena Gallica, S. of the Metaurus, and the march of Hasdrubal was a retreat to the north.

The traditional account is certainly in favour of the second theory and it is the one accepted by most modern historians. Livy's description (cc. 46–49) is our main source[2]. According to his narrative Livius was encamped near Sena with Hasdrubal less than half a mile distant. A river flowed close to the camps, probably between them. The praetor L. Porcius Licinus and his army had been engaged in harassing the march of Hasdrubal[3] and were now encamped alongside Livius. Nero joined his colleague in the night and at the council of war on the next day the Roman generals resolved on battle. Hasdrubal having recognised the addition to the enemies' forces, refused to fight

[1] cp. his dispatch c. 43. 8 *cum in Umbria se occursurum Hasdrubal fratri scribat*. It should be noted that Narnia is not mentioned, and the fact that Nero urged the dispatch of the urban legions to Narnia is not a sufficient ground for assuming that the projected meeting-point of the two Carthaginian generals was in W. Umbria or that Hasdrubal meant to take the *via Flaminia*. On the contrary it is urged that Nero's taking the coast road implies that the information at his disposal did not lead him to think that Hasdrubal would choose the *via Flaminia* in preference to the coast road.

[2] There is also a fragment of Polybius (11. 1–3) describing the battle, and we have brief accounts in later writers.

[3] c. 46. 6.

and on the following night marched to the Metaurus[1]. Deserted by his guides, and failing to find a ford, Hasdrubal marched inland along the bank looking for a crossing. The Romans overtook him next day as he was beginning to fortify a camp, and the battle followed.

The decisive point against the left bank theory is Livy's description of the first position as *ad Senam*—i.e. 10 miles S. of the Metaurus. In addition to this we have the statement that one of Hasdrubal's guides hid in a place he had previously fixed on[2], i.e. presumably in a spot already passed on the march South. Further, if Hasdrubal's march was a movement S.W. to get round the Romans, it is strange that Livy does not mention his destination[3].

But it has been contended that the traditional account is not accurate. There were two main routes south for Hasdrubal, (1) the coast road, (2) the *via Flaminia* running down through Umbria[4]. These two roads parted some 15 miles north of Sena Gallica at Fanum Fortunae. If Hasdrubal was to meet Hannibal in Umbria[5] he would, it is argued, naturally take the *via Flaminia*, and a Roman army at Sena Gallica would not cover the *via Flaminia* but only the coast road. Consequently, say the upholders of the left bank, the statement *ad Senam* is incorrect. But on the other hand it is true that while a Roman army at Fanum Fortunae would cover the two main routes just mentioned, it would leave open a number of other routes over the

[1] Livy does not say whither he was bound.

[2] *in destinatis iam animo latebris.* On the other hand the guide who swam across the Metaurus and escaped is used as an argument for the left bank. It is argued (1) that the river must have been near at hand, (2) that the deserter would naturally flee to the enemy's camp, (3) that therefore the Metaurus must have been the river which lay between the two camps. But neither the first nor the second of these inferences seem to me to be necessary.

[3] Zonaras says Gaul, which supports the right bank theory; Appian τῷ ἀδελφῷ συνελθεῖν ἐπειγόμενος ὑπεχώρει, which is not necessarily inconsistent with that theory.

[4] See Map. [5] See n. on preceding page.

Apennines[1]. Hasdrubal was at Placentia in spring. Porcius pushed forward as far as he dared with his legions[2], and, as Hasdrubal moved forward, kept in touch with him, harassing him at every opportunity. It is suggested[3] then that Livius kept his army in the south of Umbria behind the Apennines until he had information from Porcius that Hasdrubal was past the points at which he would turn off to take the other routes, and then pushed forward to Sena Gallica[4]. This meets plausibly the strategic objection mentioned above.

If the general question be decided in favour of the right bank, the site which appears to have the best claims is that of S. Angelo, a hill[5] lying 4 miles[6] from the mouth of the Metaurus on the south side of the river.

[1] Kromayer, *Antike Schlachtfelder* III. 1 p. 436, enumerates a number of possible passes.

[2] c. 39. 2 *invalido exercitu.*

[3] By Kromayer *o.c.* p. 438 f.

[4] Note that Livy says nothing of fighting between Livius and Hasdrubal before Nero's arrival.

[5] cp. c. 48. 2 *in tumulo super fluminis ripam.*

[6] c 47. 11 *quantum a mari abscedebat* implies a site not very far inland.

TITI LIVI

AB URBE CONDITA

LIBER XXVII.

PERIOCHA.

Cn. Fulvius proconsul cum exercitu ab Hannibale ad Herdoneam caesus est. meliore eventu ab Claudio Marcello consule adversus eundem ad Numistronem pugnatum est. inde Hannibal nocte recessit; Marcellus insecutus est et subinde cedentem pressit, donec confligeret. priore pugna Hannibal superior, Marcellus sequenti. Fabius Maximus consul pater Tarentinos per proditionem recepit. Claudius Marcellus T. Quinctius Crispinus consules, speculandi causa progressi e castris, insidiis ab Hannibale circumventi sunt. Marcellus occisus, Crispinus fugit. lustrum a censoribus conditum est. censa sunt civium capita $\overline{\text{CXXXVII}}$ CVIII; ex quo numero apparuit, quantum hominum tot proeliorum adversa fortuna populo Romano abstulisset. in Hispania ad Baeculam Scipio cum Hasdrubale et Hamilcare conflixit et vicit. inter alia captum regalem puerum eximiae formae ad avunculum Masinissam cum donis dimisit. Hasdrubal, qui cum exercitu novo Alpes transcenderat, ut se Hannibali coniungeret, cum milibus hominum LVI caesus est, capta $\overline{\text{V}}$CCC M. Livi consulis ductu, sed non minore opera Claudi Neronis consulis, qui cum Hannibali oppositus esset, relictis castris ita, ut hostem falleret, cum electa manu profectus Hasdrubalem circumvenerat. res praeterea a P. Scipione in Hispania et a P. Sulpicio praetore adversus Philippum et Achaeos gestas continet.

[I—III. B.C. 210. *War in Italy.*]

Hannibal attacks and defeats Cn. Fulvius, proconsul, near Herdonea. Fulvius is killed in the battle, his army almost annihilated. Hannibal's vengeance on the citizens of Herdonea.

1 Hic status rerum in Hispania erat; in Italia consul
Marcellus Salapia per proditionem recepta Mar-
2 moreas et Meles de Samnitibus vi cepit. ad
tria milia militum ibi Hannibalis, quae praesidii causa relicta erant, oppressa. praeda—
et aliquantum eius fuit—militi concessa. tri-
tici quoque ducenta quadraginta milia modium
3 et centum decem milia hordei inventa. ceterum nequaquam inde tantum gaudium fuit,
quanta clades intra paucos dies accepta est
4 haud procul Herdonea urbe. castra ibi Cn. Fulvius proconsul habebat spe recipiendae Herdoneae, quae post
Cannensem cladem ab Romanis defecerat, nec loco satis
5 tuto posita nec praesidiis firmata. neglegentiam insitam
ingenio ducis augebat spes ea, quod labare iis adversus
Poenum fidem senserat, postquam Salapia amissa exces-
6 sisse iis locis in Bruttios Hannibalem auditum est. ea
omnia ab Herdonea per occultos nuntios delata Hannibali
simul curam sociae retinendae urbis et spem fecere incau-
tum hostem aggrediendi. exercitu expedito, ita ut famam
prope praeveniret, magnis itineribus ad Herdoneam contendit et, quo plus terroris hosti obiceret, acie instructa
accessit. par audacia Romanus, consilio et viribus impar,
7 copiis raptim eductis conflixit. quinta legio et sinistra ala
8 acriter pugnam inierunt. ceterum Hannibal signo equitibus
dato, ut, cum pedestres acies occupassent praesenti certamine oculos animosque, circumvecti pars castra hostium
9 pars terga pugnantium invaderent, ipse in Fulviis similitudinem nominis, quia Cn. Fulvium praetorem biennio
ante in isdem devicerat locis, increpans, similem eventum
10 pugnae fore adfirmabat. neque ea spes vana fuit: nam
cum comminus acie et peditum certamine multi Roma-

norum cecidissent, starent tamen ordines signaque, equestris tumultus a tergo simul a castris clamor hostilis auditus
sextam ante legionem, quae in secunda acie posita prior 11
ab Numidis turbata est, quintam deinde atque eos, qui ad
prima signa erant, avertit. pars in fugam effusi, pars in 12
medio caesi, ubi et ipse Cn. Fulvius cum undecim tribunis
militum cecidit. Romanorum sociorumque quot caesa in 13
eo proelio milia sint, quis pro certo adfirmet, cum alibi
tredecim milia, alibi haud plus quam septem inveniam?
castris praedaque victor potitur. Herdoneam quia et de- 14
fecturam fuisse ad Romanos comperit, nec mansuram in
fide, si inde abscessisset, multitudine omni Metapontum
ac Thurios traducta incendit; occidit principes, qui cum
Fulvio colloquia occulta habuisse comperti sunt. Romani, 15
qui ex tanta clade evaserant, diversis itineribus semermes
ad Marcellum consulem in Samnium perfugerunt.

Marcellus nihil admodum tanta clade territus litteras **2**
Romam ad senatum de duce atque exercitu ad
Herdoneam amisso scribit; ceterum eundem 2
se, qui post Cannensem pugnam ferocem victoria Hannibalem contuderit, ire adversus eum,
brevem illi laetitiam, qua exsultet, facturum.
et Romae quidem cum luctus ingens ex prae- 3
terito, tum timor in futurum erat. consul ex 4
Samnio in Lucanos transgressus ad Numistronem in conspectu Hannibalis loco plano,
cum Poenus collem teneret, posuit castra.
addidit et aliam fidentis speciem, quod prior in aciem eduxit; 5
nec detractavit Hannibal, ut signa portis efferri vidit. ita
tamen aciem instruxerunt, ut Poenus dextrum cornu in
collem erigeret, Romani sinistrum ad oppidum applicarent.
ab hora tertia cum ad noctem pugnam extendissent, fessae- 6

Marcellus marches from Samnium into Lucania to oppose Hannibal. An indecisive battle is fought near Numistro. The next day Hannibal retreats towards Venusia. Marcellus overtakes him and dogs his movements.

que pugnando primae acies essent—ab Romanis prima
legio et dextra ala, ab Hannibale Hispani milites et fundi-
tores Baliares, elephanti quoque commisso iam certamine
7 in proelium acti—, diu pugna neutro inclinata stetit. ⟨ut⟩
primae legioni tertia, dextrae alae sinistra subiit, et apud
8 hostes integri a fessis pugnam accepere, novum atque atrox
proelium ex iam segni repente exarsit recentibus animis
corporibusque; sed nox incerta victoria diremit pugnantes.
9 postero die Romani ab sole orto in multum diei stetere in
acie; ubi nemo hostium adversus prodiit, spolia per otium
10 legere et congestos in unum locum cremavere suos. nocte
insequenti Hannibal silentio movit castra et in Apuliam
abiit. Marcellus, ubi lux fugam hostium aperuit, sauciis
cum praesidio modico Numistrone relictis praepositoque
iis L. Furio Purpurione tribuno militum, vestigiis institit
11 sequi. ad Venusiam adeptus eum est. ibi per dies aliquot, cum ab stationibus procursaretur, mixta equitum
peditumque tumultuosa magis proelia quam magna, et
12 ferme omnia Romanis secunda fuere. inde per Apuliam
ducti exercitus sine ullo memorando certamine, cum
Hannibal nocte signa moveret, locum insidiis quaerens,
Marcellus nisi certa luce et explorato ante non sequeretur.

At Capua (cf. xxvi. 34. 11) a conspiracy to set fire to the Roman quarters is discovered. The guilty parties punished and informers rewarded.

3 Capuae interim Flaccus dum bonis principum vendendis,
agro, qui publicatus erat, locando—locavit
autem omnem frumento—tempus terit, ne
deesset materia in Campanos saeviendi, novum in occulto gliscens per indicium pro-
2 tractum est facinus. milites aedificiis emotos,
simul ut cum agro tecta urbis fruenda locarentur, simul metuens, ne suum quoque
exercitum sicut Hannibalis nimia urbis amoenitas emolliret,

[I—III. B.C. 210. *War in Italy.*]

in portis murisque sibimet ipsos tecta militariter coegerat
aedificare. erant autem pleraque ex cratibus aut tabulis 3
facta, alia harundine texta, stramento intecta omnia, velut
de industria alimentis ignis. haec noctis una hora omnia 4
⟨ut⟩ incenderent centum septuaginta Campani principibus
Blossiis fratribus coniuraverunt. indicio eius rei ex familia 5
Blossiorum facto, portis repente iussu proconsulis clausis,
cum ad arma signo dato milites concurrissent, comprehensi
omnes qui in noxa erant et quaestione acriter habita dam-
nati necatique; indicibus libertas et aeris dena milia data.
Nucerinos et Acerranos, querentes, ubi habitarent, non 6
esse, Acerris ex parte incensis, Nuceria deleta, Romam
Fulvius ad senatum misit. Acerranis permissum, ut aedifi- 7
carent, quae incensa erant; Nucerini Atellam, quia id
maluerant, Atellanis Calatiam migrare iussis traducti.

Troops and provisions sent to Tarentum.

Inter multas magnasque res, quae nunc secundae nunc 8
adversae occupabant cogitationes hominum,
ne Tarentinae quidem arcis excidit memoria.
M. Ogulnius et P. Aquilius in Etruriam 9
legati ad frumentum coemendum, quod Tarentum portaretur, profecti, et mille milites de exercitu urbano, par
numerus Romanorum sociorumque, eodem in praesidium
cum frumento missi.

[IV—VII. 6. B.C. 210. *Affairs in Rome.*]

Laevinus recalled from Sicily to hold the consular elections.

Iam aestas in exitu erat, comitiorumque consularium **4**
instabat tempus. sed litterae Marcelli, negantis
e re publica esse vestigium abscedi ab Hannibale, cui cedenti certamenque abnuenti gravis
ipse instaret, curam iniecerant, ne aut consulem tum maxime 2
res agentem a bello avocarent, aut in annum consules

[IV—VII. 6. B.C. 210. *Affairs in Rome.*]

3 deessent. optimum visum est, quamquam extra Italiam
esset, Valerium potius consulem ex Sicilia revocari. ad
eum litterae iussu senatus ab L. Manlio praetore urbano
4 missae cum litteris consulis M. Marcelli, ut ex iis nosceret,
quae causa patribus eum potius quam collegam revocandi
ex provincia esset.

Embassy from Syphax desiring friendship with Rome. A counter-embassy is sent with gifts and assurance of friendship and with orders to conciliate other African chieftains.

5 Eo fere tempore legati ab rege Syphace Romam venerunt, quae is prospera proelia cum Cartha-
6 giniensibus fecisset memorantes. regem nec
inimiciorem ulli populo quam Carthaginiensi
nec amiciorem quam Romano esse adfirma-
bant; misisse eum antea legatos in Hispaniam
ad Cn. et P. Cornelios imperatores Romanos;
nunc ab ipso velut fonte petere Romanam
7 amicitiam voluisse. senatus non legatis modo
benigne respondit, sed et ipse legatos cum donis ad re-
8 gem misit, L. Genucium P. Poetelium P. Popillium. dona
tulere togam et tunicam purpuream, sellam eburneam,
9 pateram ex quinque pondo auri factam. protinus et alios
Africae regulos iussi adire; iis quoque quae darentur, por-
10 tata, togae praetextae et terna pondo paterae aureae. et
Alexandream ad Ptolomaeum et Cleopatram reges M.
Atilius et M'. Acilius legati, ad commemorandam reno-
vandamque amicitiam missi, dona tulere, regi togam et
tunicam purpuream cum sella eburnea, reginae pallam
pictam cum amiculo purpureo.

Prodigies.

11 Multa ea aestate, qua haec facta sunt, ex propinquis
urbibus agrisque nuntiata sunt prodigia: Tus-
culi agnum cum ubere lactenti natum, Iovis aedis culmen
12 fulmine ictum ac prope omni tecto nudatum; isdem ferme
diebus Anagniae terram ante portam ictam diem ac noctem
sine ullo ignis alimento arsisse, et aves ad Compitum

Anagninum in luco Dianae nidos in arboribus reliquisse;
Tarracinae in mari haud procul portu angues magnitudinis 13
mirae lascivientium piscium modo exsultasse; Tarquiniis 14
porcum cum ore humano genitum, et in agro Capenate
ad lucum Feroniae quattuor signa sanguine multo diem ac
noctem sudasse. haec prodigia hostiis maioribus procurata 15
decreto pontificum; et supplicatio diem unum Romae ad
omnia pulvinaria, alterum in Capenati agro ad Feroniae
lucum indicta.

M. Valerius consul litteris excitus provincia exercituque 5
mandato L. Cincio praetori, M. Valerio Mes-
salla praefecto classis cum parte navium in
Africam praedatum simul speculatumque, quae 2
populus Carthaginiensis ageret pararetque,
misso, ipse decem navibus Romam profectus
cum prospere pervenisset, senatum extemplo habuit. ibi 3
de suis rebus gestis commemoravit: cum annos prope
sexaginta in Sicilia terra marique magnis saepe cladibus
bellatum esset, se eam provinciam confecisse; neminem 4
Carthaginiensem in Sicilia esse; neminem Siculum, qui
fugati metu inde afuerint, non esse; omnes in urbes, in
agros suos reductos arare serere; desertam recoli tandem
terram, frugiferam ipsis cultoribus, populoque Romano pace 5
ac bello fidissimum annonae subsidium. exim Muttine et 6
si quorum aliorum merita erga populum Romanum erant
in senatum introductis, honores omnibus ad exsolvendam
fidem consulis habiti. Muttines etiam civis Romanus fac- 7
tus rogatione ab tribuno plebis ex auctoritate patrum ad
plebem lata.

Laevinus represents to the Senate the complete recovery of Sicily. Muttines is made a Roman citizen.

Dum haec Romae geruntur, M. Valerius quinquaginta 8
navibus cum ante lucem ad Africam accessisset, improviso
in agrum Uticensem escensionem fecit; eumque late de- 9

News received from M. Valerius Messalla, *praefectus classis* in Sicily, that Hasdrubal is going to join Hannibal in Italy. It is determined to appoint a dictator. Dispute between Laevinus and the Senate as to the nomination.

populatus multis mortalibus cum alia omnis generis praeda
captis ad naves redit atque in Siciliam tramisit, tertio decumo die, quam profectus inde
10 erat, Lilybaeum revectus. ex captivis quaestione habita haec comperta consulique Laevino
omnia ordine perscripta, ut sciret, quo in
11 statu res Africae essent: quinque milia Numidarum cum Masinissa Galae filio, acerrimo
iuvene, Carthagine esse, et alios per totam
12 Africam milites mercede conduci, qui in Hispaniam ad Hasdrubalem traicerentur, ut is quam maximo
exercitu primo quoque tempore in Italiam transgressus
iungeret se Hannibali; in eo positam victoriam credere
13 Carthaginienses; classem praeterea ingentem apparari ad
Siciliam repetendam, eamque se credere brevi traiecturam.
14 haec recitata a consule ita movere senatum, ut non exspec-
tanda comitia consuli censerent, sed dictatore comitiorum
habendorum causa dicto extemplo in provinciam rede-
15 undum. illa disceptatio tenebat, quod consul in Sicilia
se M. Valerium Messallam, qui tum classi praeesset, dictatorem dicturum esse aiebat, patres extra Romanum agrum
—eum autem in Italia terminari—negabant dictatorem dici
16 posse. M. Lucretius tribunus plebis cum de ea re consuleret, ita decrevit senatus, ut consul, priusquam ab urbe
discederet, populum rogaret, quem dictatorem dici placeret,
eumque, quem populus iussisset, dictatorem diceret; si
consul noluisset, praetor populum rogaret; si ne is quidem
17 vellet, tum tribuni ad plebem ferrent. cum consul se
populum rogaturum negasset, quod suae potestatis esset,
praetoremque vetuisset rogare, tribuni plebis rogarunt,
plebesque scivit, ut Q. Fulvius, qui tum ad Capuam erat,
18 dictator diceretur. sed quo die id plebis concilium futurum

erat, consul clam nocte in Siciliam abiit; destitutique
patres litteras ad M. Claudium mittendas censuerunt, ut
desertae ab collega rei publicae subveniret diceretque,
quem populus iussisset, dictatorem. ita a M. Claudio 19
consule Q. Fulvius dictator dictus, et ex eodem plebis
scito ab Q. Fulvio dictatore P. Licinius Crassus pontifex
maximus magister equitum dictus.

The dictator holds the consular *comitia*, and succeeds in spite of the tribunes in getting Fabius and himself elected.

Dictator postquam Romam venit, C. Sempronium 6
Blaesum legatum, quem ad Capuam habuerat,
in Etruriam provinciam ad exercitum misit in
locum C. Calpurni praetoris, quem, ut Capuae
exercituique suo praeesset, litteris excivit. ipse 2
comitia in quem diem primum potuit edixit;
quae certamine inter tribunos dictatoremque
iniecto perfici non potuerunt. Galeria iuniorum, quae sorte 3
praerogativa erat, Q. Fulvium et Q. Fabium consules dixe-
rat, eodemque iure vocatae inclinassent, ni se tribuni plebis
C. et L. Arrenii interposuissent, qui neque magistratum 4
continuari satis civile esse aiebant, et multo foedioris
exempli eum ipsum creari, qui comitia haberet; itaque 5
si suum nomen dictator acciperet, se comitiis intercessuros;
si aliorum praeterquam ipsius ratio haberetur, comitiis se
moram non facere. dictator causam comitiorum auctoritate 6
senatus, plebis scito, exemplis tutabatur: namque Cn. 7
Servilio consule, cum C. Flaminius alter consul ad Trasumennum cecidisset, ex auctoritate patrum ad plebem latum,
plebemque scivisse, ut, quoad bellum in Italia esset, ex iis,
qui consules fuissent, quos et quotiens vellet, reficiendi
consules populo ius esset; exemplaque in eam rem se 8
habere vetus L. Postumi Megelli, qui interrex iis comitiis,
quae ipse habuisset, consul cum C. Iunio Bubulco creatus
esset, recens Q. Fabi, qui sibi continuari consulatum, nisi

9 id bono publico fieret, profecto numquam sisset. his ora-
tionibus cum diu certatum esset, postremo ita inter dictatorem ac tribunos convenit, ut eo, quod censuisset senatus,
10 staretur. patribus id tempus rei publicae visum est, ut per
veteres et expertos bellique peritos imperatores res publica
11 gereretur; itaque moram fieri comitiis non placere. con-
cedentibus tribunis comitia habita; declarati consules Q.
Fabius Maximus quintum Q. Fulvius Flaccus quartum.
12 praetores inde creati L. Veturius Philo T. Quinctius
Crispinus C. Hostilius Tubulus C. Aurunculeius. magistratibus in annum creatis Q. Fulvius dictatura se abdicavit.

Attacks on Sardinia by the Carthaginian fleet.

13 Extremo aestatis huius classis Punica navium quadraginta cum praefecto Hamilcare in Sardiniam
traiecta Olbiensem primo, dein, postquam ibi
14 P. Manlius Volso praetor cum exercitu apparuit, circumacta inde ad alterum insulae latus, Caralitanum
agrum vastavit et cum praeda omnis generis in Africam
redit.

Appointment of religious officials.

15 Sacerdotes Romani eo anno mortui aliquot suffectique:
C. Servilius pontifex factus in locum T. Otacili
Crassi, Ti. Sempronius Ti. f. Longus augur
factus in locum T. Otacili Crassi; decemvir
item sacris faciundis in locum Ti. Semproni C. f. Longi
16 Ti. Sempronius Ti. f. Longus suffectus. M. Marcius rex
sacrorum mortuus est et M. Aemilius Papus maximus
curio; neque in eorum locum sacerdotes eo anno suffecti.

Two censors appointed, but one dies and the other resigns.

17 Et censores hic annus habuit, L. Veturium Philonem et
P. Licinium Crassum, maximum pontificem.
Crassus Licinius nec consul nec praetor ante
fuerat quam censor est factus; ex aedilitate

gradum ad censuram fecit. sed ii censores neque senatum 18
legerunt neque quicquam publicae rei egerunt: mors diremit L. Veturi; inde et Licinius censura se abdicavit.
aediles curules L. Veturius et P. Licinius Varus ludos 19
Romanos diem unum instaurarunt. aediles plebei Q. Catius
et L. Porcius Licinus ex multaticio argento signa aenea ad
Cereris dedere, et ludos pro temporis eius copia magnifice
apparatos fecerunt.

C. Laelius reports the capture of *Nova Carthago* and confirms the news sent by Valerius. A *supplicatio* of one day is decreed.

Exitu anni huius C. Laelius legatus Scipionis die quarto 7
et tricensimo quam a Tarracone profectus
erat, Romam venit; isque cum agmine capti-
vorum ingressus urbem magnum concursum
hominum fecit. postero die in senatum intro- 2
ductus captam Carthaginem, caput Hispaniae,
uno die, receptasque aliquot urbes, quae defecissent, novasque in societatem adscitas exposuit. ex 3
captivis comperta iis fere congruentia, quae in litteris
fuerant M. Valerii Messallae. maxime movit patres Hasdrubalis transitus in Italiam, vix Hannibali atque eius
armis obsistentem. productus et in contionem Laelius 4
eadem edisseruit. senatus ob res feliciter a P. Scipione
gestas supplicationem in unum diem decrevit; C. Laelium
primo quoque tempore cum quibus venerat navibus redire
in Hispaniam iussit. Carthaginis expugnationem in hunc 5
annum contuli multis auctoribus, haud nescius
quosdam esse, qui anno insequenti captam
tradiderint, quod mihi minus simile veri visum 6
est annum integrum Scipionem nihil gerundo in Hispania
consumpsisse.

Some authorities place this capture in the next year.

[VII. 7—XI. B.C. 209. *Affairs in Rome. The disaffected Colonies.*]

Arrangements for the campaign. The soldiers of Cn. Fulvius (cf. c. 1) are punished in the same way as the soldiers of Cannae and those of the *praetor* Cn. Fulvius (cf. xxvi. 1. 10).

7 Q. Fabio Maximo quintum Q. Fulvio Flacco quartum
consulibus idibus Martiis, quo die magistratum
inierunt, Italia ambobus provincia decreta,
regionibus tamen partitum imperium: Fabius
ad Tarentum, Fulvius in Lucanis ac Bruttiis
8 rem gereret. M. Claudio prorogatum in annum imperium. praetores sortiti provincias,
C. Hostilius Tubulus urbanam, L. Veturius
Philo peregrinam cum Gallia, T. Quinctius
9 Crispinus Capuam, C. Aurunculeius Sardiniam. exercitus
ita per provincias divisi: Fulvio duae legiones, quas in
Sicilia M. Valerius Laevinus haberet, Q. Fabio, quibus in
10 Etruria C. Calpurnius praefuisset; urbanus exercitus ut in
Etruriam succederet; C. Calpurnius eidem praeesset provinciae exercituique; Capuam exercitumque, quem Q.
11 Fulvius habuisset, T. Quinctius obtineret; C. Hostilius
ab C. Laetorio propraetore provinciam exercitumque, qui
tum Arimini erat, acciperet. M. Marcello, quibus consul
12 rem gesserat, legiones decretae. M. Valerio cum L. Cincio
—iis quoque enim prorogatum in Sicilia imperium—Cannensis exercitus datus, eumque supplere ex militibus, qui
13 ex legionibus Cn. Fulvi superessent, iussi. conquisitos
eos consules in Siciliam miserunt; additaque eadem
militiae ignominia, sub qua Cannenses militabant quique
ex praetoris Cn. Fulvi exercitu ob similis iram fugae missi
14 eo ab senatu fuerant. C. Aurunculeio eaedem in Sardinia
legiones, quibus P. Manlius Volso eam provinciam obtinu-
15 erat, decretae. P. Sulpicio eadem legione eademque classe
Macedoniam obtinere iusso prorogatum in annum imperium.
triginta quinqueremes ex Sicilia Tarentum ad Q. Fabium
16 consulem mitti iussae; cetera classe placere praedatum in
Africam aut ipsum M. Valerium Laevinum traicere aut

mittere seu L. Cincium seu M. Valerium Messallam vellet.
nec de Hispania quicquam mutatum, nisi quod non in 17
annum Scipioni Silanoque, sed donec revocati
ab senatu forent, prorogatum imperium est.
ita provinciae exercituumque in eum annum
partita imperia.

The command of Scipio and Silanus in Spain is extended *donec revocati ab senatu forent.*

Dispute over the election of *Curio maximus.* A plebeian elected. C. Valerius Flaccus, *flamen dialis,* reasserts the right of the *flamines* to sit in the Senate.

Inter maiorum rerum curas comitia maximi curionis, cum 8
in locum M. Aemili sacerdos crearetur, vetus
excitaverunt certamen, patriciis negantibus 2
C. Mamili Atelli, qui unus ex plebe petebat,
habendam rationem esse, quia nemo ante eum
nisi ex patribus id sacerdotium habuisset.
tribuni appellati ad senatum ⟨rem⟩ reiecerunt; 3
senatus populi potestatem fecit: ita primus ex
plebe creatus maximus curio C. Mamilius Atellus. et 4
flaminem Dialem invitum ⟨in⟩augurari coegit P. Licinius
pontifex maximus C. Valerium Flaccum; decemvirum sacris
faciundis creatus in locum Q. Muci Scaevolae demortui
C. Laetorius. causam inaugurari coacti flaminis libens 5
reticuissem, ni ex mala fama in bonam vertisset. ob
adulescentiam neglegentem luxuriosamque C. Flaccus flamen captus a P. Licinio pontifice maximo erat, L. Flacco
fratri germano cognatisque aliis ob eadem vitia invisus.
is ut animum eius cura sacrorum et caerimoniarum cepit, 6
ita repente exuit antiquos mores, ut nemo tota iuventute
haberetur prior nec probatior primoribus patrum, suis
pariter alienisque, esset. huius famae consensu elatus ad 7
iustam fiduciam sui rem intermissam per multos annos ob
indignitatem flaminum priorum repetivit, ut in senatum
introiret. ingressum eum curiam cum L. Licinius praetor 8
inde eduxisset, tribunos plebis appellavit. flamen vetustum
ius sacerdotii repetebat: datum id cum toga praetexta et

9 sella curuli ei flaminio esse. praetor non exoletis vetustate
annalium exemplis stare ius, sed recentissimae cuiusque
consuetudinis usu volebat: nec patrum nec avorum me-
10 moria Dialem quemquam id ius usurpasse. tribuni rem
inertia flaminum obliteratam ipsis, non sacerdotio damno
fuisse cum aequom censuissent, ne ipso quidem contra
tendente praetore magno adsensu patrum plebisque flaminem in senatum introduxerunt, omnibus ita existimantibus,
magis sanctitate vitae quam sacerdotii iure eam rem flaminem obtinuisse.

Levying of supplementary soldiers, and disposition of troops in Italy and Sicily.

11 Consules priusquam in provincias irent, duas urbanas
legiones, in supplementum quantum opus erat
12 ceteris exercitibus militum scripserunt. urbanum veterem exercitum Fulvius consul C.
Fulvio Flacco legato—frater hic consulis
erat—in Etruriam dedit ducendum, et legiones quae in
13 Etruria erant Romam deducendas. et Fabius consul
reliquias exercitus Fulviani conquisitas—fuere autem ad
quattuor milia trecenti quadraginta quattuor—Q. Maximum
filium ducere in Siciliam ad M. Valerium proconsulem
iussit atque ab eo duas legiones et triginta quinqueremes
14 accipere. nihil eae ductae ex insula legiones minuerunt
15 nec viribus nec specie eius provinciae praesidium. nam
cum praeter egregie suppletas duas veteres legiones trans-
fugarum etiam Numidarum equitum peditumque magnam
vim haberet, Siculos quoque, qui in exercitu Epicydis aut
16 Poenorum fuerant, belli peritos viros, milites scripsit. ea
externa auxilia cum singulis Romanis legionibus adiunxisset,
17 duorum speciem exercituum servavit: altero L. Cincium
partem insulae, qua regnum Hieronis fuerat, tueri iussit;
altero ipse ceteram insulam tuebatur, divisam quondam
Romani Punicique imperii finibus, classe quoque septua-

ginta navium partita, ut omni ambitu litorum praesidia orae
maritumae essent. ipse cum Muttinis equitatu provinciam 18
peragrabat, ut viseret agros cultaque ab incultis notaret et
perinde dominos laudaret castigaretque. ita tantum ea 19
cura frumenti provenit, ut et Romam mitteret, et Catinam
conveheret, unde exercitui, qui ad Tarentum aestiva acturus
esset, posset praeberi.

Ceterum transportati milites in Siciliam—et erant 9
maior pars Latini nominis sociorumque—
prope magni motus causa fuere: adeo ex
parvis saepe magnarum momenta rerum pen-
dent. fremitus enim inter Latinos sociosque 2
in conciliis ortus, decimum annum dilectibus,
stipendiis se exhaustos esse; quotannis ferme
clade magna pugnare; alios in acie occidi, 3
alios morbo absumi; magis perire sibi civem,
qui ab Romano miles lectus sit, quam qui ab
Poeno captus: quippe ab hoste gratis remitti
in patriam, ab Romanis extra Italiam in exilium verius
quam in militiam ablegari. octavum iam ibi annum sene- 4
scere Cannensem militem, moriturum ante, quam Italia
hostis, quippe nunc cum maxime florens viribus, excedat.
si veteres milites non redeant in patriam, novi legantur,
brevi neminem superfuturum. itaque, quod propediem res 5
ipsa negatura sit, priusquam ad ultimam solitudinem atque
egestatem perveniant, negandum populo Romano esse. si 6
consentientes in hoc socios videant Romani, profecto de
pace cum Carthaginiensibus iungenda cogitaturos; aliter
numquam vivo Hannibale sine bello Italiam fore. haec
acta in conciliis. triginta tum coloniae populi Romani 7
erant; ex iis duodecim, cum omnium legationes Romae
essent, negaverunt consulibus esse, unde milites pecu-

The expatriation of the Fulvian soldiers, a large proportion of whom were Latins, is the immediate cause of twelve Latin Colonies through their deputies then at Rome refusing further assistance in the war.

niamque darent. eae fuere Ardea Nepete Sutrium Alba
Carseoli Cora Suessa Cercei Setia Cales Narnia Interamna.
8 nova re consules icti cum absterrere eos a tam detestabili
consilio vellent, castigando increpandoque plus quam
leniter agendo profecturos rati, eos ausos esse consulibus
9 dicere aiebant, quod consules ut in senatu pronuntiarent in
animum inducere non possent: non enim detractationem
eam munerum militiae sed apertam defectionem a populo
10 Romano esse. redirent itaque propere in colonias, et
tamquam integra re, locuti magis quam ausi tantum nefas,
cum suis consulerent; admonerent non Campanos neque
11 Tarentinos esse eos sed Romanos; inde oriundos, inde in
colonias atque in agrum bello captum stirpis augendae
causa missos; quae liberi parentibus deberent, ea illos
Romanis debere, si ulla pietas, si memoria antiquae patriae
12 esset. consulerent igitur de integro: nam tum quidem
quae temere agitassent, ea prodendi imperii Romani,
13 tradendae Hannibali victoriae esse. cum alternis haec
consules diu iactassent, nihil moti legati neque se, quod
domum renuntiarent, habere dixerunt, neque senatum suum,
quod novi consuleret, ubi nec miles, qui legeretur, nec
14 pecunia, quae daretur in stipendium, esset. cum obstinatos
eos viderent consules, rem ad senatum detulerunt, ubi
tantus pavor animis hominum est iniectus, ut magna pars
actum de imperio dicerent: idem alias colonias facturas,
idem socios; consensisse omnis ad prodendam Hannibali
10 urbem Romanam. Consules hortari et consolari senatum
et dicere alias colonias in fide atque officio
pristino fore: eas quoque ipsas, quae officio
decesserint, si legati circa eas colonias mit-
tantur, qui castigent, non qui precentur,
2 verecundiam imperii habituras esse. permis-

The deputies of the other eighteen colonies declare their readiness to furnish contingents as usual, and more

sum ab senatu iis cum esset, agerent facerentque, ut e re publica ducerent, pertemptatis prius
aliarum coloniarum animis citaverunt legatos
quaesiveruntque ab iis, ecquid milites ex formula

if required. They are publicly thanked. The twelve colonies are ignored.

paratos haberent. pro duodeviginta coloniis M. Sextilius 3
Fregellanus respondit et milites ex formula paratos esse, et
si pluribus opus esset, plures daturos, et, quidquid aliud 4
imperaret velletque populus Romanus, enixe facturos: ad
id sibi neque opes deesse et animum etiam superesse.
consules parum sibi videri praefati pro merito eorum sua 5
voce collaudari eos, nisi universi patres iis in curia gratias
egissent, sequi in senatum eos iusserunt. senatus quam 6
poterat honoratissimo decreto allocutus eos mandat consulibus, ut ad populum quoque eos producerent et inter
multa alia praeclara, quae ipsis maioribusque suis praestitis-
sent, recens etiam meritum eorum in rem publicam comme-
morarent. ne nunc quidem post tot saecula sileantur 7
fraudenturve laude sua: Signini fuere et Norbani Sati-
culanique et Fregellani et Lucerini et Venusini et Brundusini
et Hadriani et Firmani et Ariminenses, et ab altero mari 8
Pontiani et Paestani et Cosani, et mediterranei Beneventani
et Aesernini et Spoletini et Placentini et Cremonenses.
harum coloniarum subsidio tum imperium populi Romani 9
stetit, iisque gratiae in senatu et apud populum actae.
duodecim aliarum coloniarum, quae detractaverunt im- 10
perium, mentionem fieri patres vetuerunt, neque illos
dimitti neque retineri neque appellari a consulibus. ea
tacita castigatio maxime ex dignitate populi Romani visa
est.

Cetera expedientibus, quae ad bellum opus erant, con- 11
sulibus aurum vicensimarium, quod in sanctiore aerario ad ultimos casus servabatur,

The *aurum vicensimarium* a

fund reserved for extreme need is now drawn out and used.

12 promi placuit. prompta ad quattuor milia
pondo auri. inde quingena pondo data consulibus et M. Marcello et P. Sulpicio procon-
sulibus et L. Veturio praetori, qui Galliam provinciam erat
13 sortitus, additumque Fabio consuli centum pondo auri
praecipuum, quod in arcem Tarentinam portaretur; cetero
auro usi sunt ad vestimenta praesenti pecunia locanda
exercitui, qui in Hispania bellum secunda sua fama ducisque
11 gerebat. Prodigia quoque, priusquam ab urbe consules

Prodigies expiated.

2 proficiscerentur, procurari placuit. in Albano
monte tacta de caelo erant signum Iovis
arborque templo propinqua, et Ostiae lacus, et Capuae
murus Fortunaeque aedis, et Sinuessae murus portaque:
3 haec de caelo tacta. cruentam etiam fluxisse aquam
Albanam quidam auctores erant; et Romae intus in cella
aedis Fortis Fortunae de capite signum, quod in corona
4 erat, in manum sponte sua prolapsum; et Priverni satis
constabat bovem locutum, volturiumque frequenti foro in
tabernam devolasse, et Sinuessae natum ambiguo inter
5 marem ac feminam sexu infantem, quos androgynos vulgus,
ut pleraque, faciliore ad duplicanda verba Graeco sermone,
appellat, et lacte pluvisse, et cum elephanti capite puerum
6 natum. ea prodigia hostiis maioribus procurata, et supplicatio circa omnia pulvinaria et obsecratio in unum diem
indicta; et decretum, ut C. Hostilius praetor ludos Apollini,
sicut iis annis voti factique erant, voveret faceretque.
7 Per eos dies et censoribus creandis Q. Fulvius consul

Censors elected. Several eligible for the senate and the *equites* are 'passed over' for misconduct after Cannae.

comitia habuit. creati censores, ambo qui
nondum consules fuerant, M. Cornelius Ce-
8 thegus P. Sempronius Tuditanus. ii censores
ut agrum Campanum fruendum locarent, ex
auctoritate patrum latum ad plebem est,

[VII. 7—XI. B.C. 209. *Affairs in Rome. The disaffected Colonies.*]

Equites who served in that battle condemned to lose their public horse and to serve *privatis equis* for the full term (10 years) in Sicily.

plebesque scivit. senatus lectionem contentio 9
inter censores de principe legendo tenuit.
Semproni lectio erat; ceterum Cornelius morem
traditum a patribus sequendum aiebat, ut qui 10
primus censor ex iis, qui viverent, fuisset, eum
principem legerent: is T. Manlius Torquatus 11
erat; Sempronius, cui di sortem legendi dedissent, ei ius
liberum eosdem dedisse deos; se id suo arbitrio facturum
lecturumque Q. Fabium Maximum, quem tum principem
Romanae civitatis esse vel Hannibale iudice victurus esset.
cum diu certatum verbis esset, concedente collega lectus a 12
Sempronio princeps in senatu Q. Fabius Maximus consul.
inde alius lectus senatus octo praeteritis, inter quos M.
Caecilius Metellus erat, infamis auctor deserendae Italiae
post Cannensem cladem. in equestribus quoque notis 13
eadem servata causa; sed erant perpauci, quos ea infamia
attingeret. illis omnibus—et multi erant—adempti equi, 14
qui Cannensium legionum equites in Sicilia erant. addiderunt acerbitati etiam tempus, ne praeterita stipendia procederent iis, quae equo publico meruerant, sed dena stipendia
equis privatis facerent. magnum praeterea numerum eorum 15
conquisiverunt, qui equo merere deberent; atque ex iis, qui
principio eius belli septemdecim annos nati fuerant neque
militaverant, omnis aerarios fecerunt. locaverunt inde refi- 16
cienda, quae circa forum incendio consumpta erant, septem
tabernas, macellum, atrium regium.

[XII—XVI. B.C. 209. *Campaign in Italy. Capture of Tarentum.*]

Plan of the campaign.

Transactis omnibus, quae Romae agenda erant, consules 12
ad bellum profecti. prior Fulvius praegressus 2
Capuam; post paucos dies consecutus Fabius,

qui et collegam coram obtestatus et per litteras Marcellum,
ut quam acerrimo bello detinerent Hannibalem, dum ipse
3 Tarentum oppugnaret: ea urbe adempta hosti iam undique
pulso, nec ubi consisteret nec quod fidum respiceret
habenti, ne remorandi quidem causam in Italia fore.
4 Regium etiam nuntium mittit ad praefectum praesidii,
quod ab Laevino consule adversus Bruttios ibi locatum
5 erat, octo milia hominum, pars maxima ab Agathyrna, sicut
ante dictum est, ex Sicilia traducta, rapto vivere hominum
adsuetorum; additi erant Bruttiorum indidem perfugae, et
6 audacia et audendi omnia necessitatibus pares: hanc manum
ad Bruttium primum agrum depopulandum duci iussit, inde
ad Cauloneam urbem oppugnandam. imperata non impigre
solum sed etiam avide exsecuti direptis fugatisque cultoribus
7 agri summa vi urbem oppugnabant. Marcellus et consulis

Marcellus leaving Venusia follows Hannibal and forces him to give battle. The first engagement is indecisive; in the second Marcellus is defeated.

litteris excitus, et quia ita induxerat in animum
neminem ducem Romanum tam parem Hannibali quam se esse, ubi primum in agris pabuli
copia fuit, ex hibernis profectus ad Canusium
8 Hannibali occurrit. sollicitabat ad defectionem
Canusinos Poenus; ceterum ut appropinquare
Marcellum audivit, castra inde movit. aperta erat regio
sine ullis ad insidias latebris; itaque in loca saltuosa cedere
9 inde coepit. Marcellus vestigiis instabat castraque castris
conferebat et opere perfecto extemplo in aciem legiones
educebat. Hannibal turmatim per equites peditumque
iaculatores levia certamina serens casum universae pugnae
10 non necessarium ducebat. tractus est tamen ad id, quod
vitabat, certamen. nocte praegressum adsequitur locis
planis ac patentibus Marcellus; castra inde ponentem,
pugnando undique in munitores, operibus prohibet. ita
signa conlata pugnatumque totis copiis, et, cum iam nox

instaret, Marte aequo discessum est. castra exiguo distantia
spatio raptim ante noctem permunita.

Postero die luce prima Marcellus in aciem copias eduxit; 11
nec Hannibal detractavit certamen multis verbis adhortatus
milites, ut memores Trasumenni Cannarumque contunderent
ferociam hostis: urgere atque instare eum, non iter quietos 12
facere, non castra ponere pati, non respirare aut circum-
spicere; cotidie simul orientem solem et Romanam aciem
in campis videndam esse: si uno proelio haud incruentus 13
abeat, quietius deinde tranquilliusque eum bellaturum.
his irritati adhortationibus simulque taedio ferociae hostium
cotidie instantium lacessentiumque acriter proelium ineunt.
pugnatum amplius duabus horis est; cedere inde ab Ro- 14
manis dextra ala et extraordinarii coepere. quod ubi
Marcellus vidit, duodevicensimam legionem in primam
aciem inducit. dum alii trepide cedunt, alii segniter 15
subeunt, turbata tota acies est, dein prorsus fusa, et vincente
pudorem metu terga dabant. cecidere in pugna fugaque 16
ad duo milia et septingenti civium sociorumque; in iis
quattuor Romani centuriones, duo tribuni militum, M.
Licinius et M. Helvius. signa militaria quattuor de ala, 17
prima quae fugit, duo de legione, quae cedentibus sociis
successerat, amissa.

Marcellus, postquam in castra reditum est, contionem **13**
adeo saevam atque acerbam apud milites
habuit, ut proelio per diem totum infeliciter
tolerato tristior iis irati ducis oratio esset.
"dis immortalibus, ut in tali re, laudes 2
gratesque" inquit "ago, quod victor hostis
cum tanto pavore incidentibus vobis in vallum
portasque non ipsa castra est aggressus: de-
seruissetis profecto eodem terrore castra, quo

After a bitterly reproachful speech and after disgracing those who had shown special slackness in the fight Marcellus orders the soldiers to be ready to fight next day.

3 omisistis pugnam. qui pavor hic, qui terror, quae repente,
qui et cum quibus pugnaretis, oblivio animos cepit?
nempe idem sunt hi hostes, quos vincendo et victos
4 sequendo priorem aestatem absumpsistis, quibus dies noctesque fugientibus per hos dies institistis, quos levibus
proeliis fatigastis, quos hesterno die nec iter facere nec
5 castra ponere passi estis. omitto ea, quibus gloriari potestis;
cuius et ipsius pudere ac paenitere vos oportet, referam.
nempe aequis manibus hesterno die diremistis pugnam.
6 quid haec nox, quid hic dies attulit? vestrae iis copiae
imminutae sunt, an illorum auctae? non equidem mihi cum
exercitu meo loqui videor, nec cum Romanis militibus; cor-
7 pora tantum atque arma eadem sunt. an, si eosdem animos
habuissetis, terga vestra vidisset hostis? signa alicui manipulo aut cohorti ademisset? adhuc caesis legionibus Romanis gloriabatur; vos illi hodierno die primum fugati
8 exercitus dedistis decus." clamor inde ortus, ut veniam
eius diei daret; ubi vellet deinde, experiretur militum
suorum animos. "ego vero experiar" inquit, "milites, et
vos crastino die in aciem educam, ut victores potius quam
9 victi veniam impetretis quam petitis." cohortibus, quae
signa amiserant, hordeum dari iussit, centurionesque mani-
pulorum, quorum signa amissa fuerant, destrictis gladiis
discinctos destitui; et, ut postero die omnes, equites pedites,
10 armati adessent, edixit. ita contio dimissa fatentium iure
ac merito sese increpitos, neque illo die virum quemquam
in acie Romana fuisse praeter unum ducem, cui aut morte
satisfaciendum aut egregia victoria esset. postero die
11 armati ornatique ad edictum aderant. imperator eos con-
laudat pronuntiatque, a quibus orta pridie fuga esset,
cohortes, quaeque signa amisissent, se in primam aciem
12 inducturum; edicere iam sese omnibus pugnandum ac

vincendum esse et adnitendum singulis universisque, ne
prius hesternae fugae quam hodiernae victoriae fama Romam
perveniat. inde cibo corpora firmare iussi, ut, si longior 13
pugna esset, viribus sufficerent. ubi omnia dicta factaque
sunt, quibus excitarentur animi militum, in aciem procedunt.

Quod ubi Hannibali nuntiatum est, "cum eo nimirum" 14
inquit "hoste res est, qui nec bonam nec
malam ferre fortunam possit! seu vicit, ferociter instat victis; seu victus est, instaurat
cum victoribus certamen." signa inde canere 2
iussit et copias educit. pugnatum utrimque
aliquanto quam pridie acrius est, Poenis ad
obtinendum hesternum decus adnitentibus,
Romanis ad demendam ignominiam. sinistra ala ab Ro- 3
manis et cohortes, quae amiserant signa, in prima acie
pugnabant, et legio vicensima ab dextro cornu instructa.
L. Cornelius Lentulus et C. Claudius Nero legati cornibus 4
praeerant; Marcellus mediam aciem hortator testisque
praesens firmabat. ab Hannibale Hispani primam obtine- 5
bant frontem, et id roboris in omni exercitu erat. cum 6
anceps diu pugna esset, Hannibal elephantos in primam
aciem induci iussit, si quem inicere ea res tumultum ac
pavorem posset. et primo turbarunt signa ordinesque, et 7
partim occulcatis partim dissipatis terrore, qui circa erant,
nudaverant una parte aciem, latiusque fuga manasset, ni C. 8
Decimius Flavus tribunus militum signo arrepto primi
hastati manipulum eius signi sequi se iussisset. duxit ubi
maxime tumultum conglobatae beluae faciebant, pilaque in
eas conici iussit. haesere omnia tela haud difficili ex 9
propinquo in tanta corpora ictu et tum conferta turba. sed
ut non omnes vulnerati sunt, ita in quorum tergis infixa
stetere pila, ut est genus anceps, in fugam versi etiam

The next day in an obstinately contested battle Marcellus is victorious, but with so much loss, that he is quite unable to follow up his victory (cf. c. 20, § 10).

10 integros avertere. tum iam non unus manipulus, sed pro
se quisque miles, qui modo adsequi agmen fugientium
elephantorum poterat, pila conicere. eo magis ruere in
suos beluae tantoque maiorem stragem edere, quam inter
hostis ediderant, quanto acrius pavor consternatam agit,
11 quam insidentis magistri imperio regitur. in perturbatam
transcursu beluarum aciem signa inferunt Romani pedites
et haud magno certamine dissipatos trepidantesque avertunt.
12 tum in fugientes equitatum immittit Marcellus, nec ante
finis sequendi est factus, quam in castra paventes compulsi
13 sunt. nam super alia, quae terrorem trepidationemque
facerent, elephanti quoque duo in ipsa porta corruerant,
coactique erant milites per fossam vallumque ruere in castra.
ibi maxima hostium caedes facta: caesa ad octo milia
14 hominum, quinque elephanti. nec Romanis incruenta
victoria fuit: mille ferme et septingenti de duabus legionibus, et sociorum supra mille et trecentos occisi; vulnerati
15 permulti civium sociorumque. Hannibal nocte proxima
castra movit; cupientem insequi Marcellum prohibuit mul-
15 titudo sauciorum. speculatores, qui prosequerentur agmen,
missi postero die rettulerunt Bruttios Hannibalem petere.

The Hirpini, Lucani and Volcientes surrendering to Fulvius, are kindly treated. Similar indulgence promised to the Bruttii. Fabius advances to besiege Tarentum by land and sea.

2 Isdem ferme diebus et ad Q. Fulvium consulem Hirpini
et Lucani et Volcientes traditis praesidiis
Hannibalis, quae in urbibus habebant, dedi-
derunt sese, clementerque a consule cum
verborum tantum castigatione ob errorem
3 praeteritum accepti; et Bruttiis similis spes
veniae facta est, cum ab iis Vibius et Paccius
fratres, longe nobilissimi gentis eius, eandem,
quae data Lucanis erat, condicionem dedi-
4 tionis petentes venissent. Q. Fabius consul oppidum in
Sallentinis Manduriam vi cepit. ibi ad tria milia hominum

capta et ceterae praedae aliquantum. inde Tarentum profectus in ipsis faucibus portus posuit castra. naves, quas 5
Livius tutandis commeatibus habuerat, partim machinationibus onerat apparatuque moenium oppugnandorum,
partim tormentis et saxis omnique missilium telorum genere
instruit, onerarias quoque, non eas solum, quae remis
agerentur, ut alii machinas scalasque ad muros ferrent, 6
alii procul ex navibus vulnerarent moenium propugnatores.
hae naves ut ab aperto mari urbem aggrederentur instructae 7
parataeque sunt. et erat liberum mare classe Punica, cum
Philippus oppugnare Aetolos pararet, Corcyram tramissa.
in Bruttiis interim Cauloneae oppugnatores sub adventum 8
Hannibalis, ne opprimerentur, in tumulum a praesenti
impetu tutum, ad cetera inopem, concessere.

By good fortune he is able to induce Hannibal's Bruttian commander to betray the city, and admit the Romans.

Fabium Tarentum obsidentem leve dictu momentum ad 9
rem ingentem potiundam adiuvit. praesidium
Bruttiorum datum ab Hannibale Tarentini
habebant. eius praesidii praefectus deperibat
amore mulierculae, cuius frater in exercitu
Fabii consulis erat. is certior litteris sororis 10
factus de nova consuetudine advenae locupletis
atque inter populares tam honorati, spem nactus per sororem
quolibet impelli amantem posse, quid speraret ad consulem
detulit. quae cum haud vana cogitatio visa esset, pro 11
perfuga iussus Tarentum transire, ac per sororem praefecto
conciliatus, primo occulte temptando animum, dein satis
explorata levitate blanditiis muliebribus perpulit eum ad
proditionem custodiae loci, cui praepositus erat. ubi et 12
ratio agendae rei et tempus convenit, miles nocte per
intervalla stationum clam ex urbe emissus ea, quae acta
erant, quaeque ut agerentur convenerat, ad consulem refert.
Fabius vigilia prima dato signo iis, qui in arce erant, quique 13

custodiam portus habebant, ipse circumito portu ab regione
14 urbis in orientem versa occultus consedit. canere inde
tubae simul ab arce simul a portu et ab navibus, quae ab
aperto mari appulsae erant, clamorque undique cum ingenti
tumultu, unde minimum periculi erat, de industria ortus.
15 consul interim silentio continebat suos. igitur Democrates,
qui praefectus antea classis fuerat, forte illo loco praepositus, postquam quieta omnia circa se vidit, alias partes eo
16 tumultu personare, ut captae urbis interdum excitaretur
clamor, veritus, ne inter cunctationem suam consul aliquam
vim faceret ac signa inferret, praesidium ad arcem, unde
17 maxime terribilis accidebat sonus, traducit. Fabius cum et
ex temporis spatio et ex silentio ipso, quod, ubi paulo ante
strepebant excitantes vocantesque ad arma, inde nulla
accidebat vox, deductas custodias sensisset, ferri scalas ad
eam partem muri, qua Bruttiorum cohortem praesidium
18 agitare proditionis conciliator nuntiaverat, iubet. ea primum
captus est murus adiuvantibus recipientibusque Bruttiis, et
transcensum in urbem est; inde et proxuma refracta porta,
19 ut frequenti agmine signa inferrentur. tum clamore sublato
sub ortum ferme lucis nullo obvio armato in forum per-
veniunt, omnesque undique, qui ad arcem portumque
pugnabant, in se converterunt.

16 Proelium in aditu fori maiore impetu quam perseve-
rantia commissum est: non animo, non armis,
non arte belli, non vigore ac viribus corporis
2 par Romano Tarentinus erat. igitur pilis
tantum coniectis, prius paene, quam consererent manus, terga dederunt, dilapsique per
nota urbis itinera in suas amicorumque domos.
3 duo ex ducibus Nico et Democrates fortiter pugnantes
cecidere; Philemenus, qui proditionis ad Hannibalem

After feeble resistance, the city is captured and dismantled, many Carthaginians and Bruttians put to death and enormous booty taken.

auctor fuerat, cum citato equo ex proelio avectus esset,
vacuus paulo post equus errans per urbem cognitus, corpus 4
nusquam inventum est: creditum vulgo est in puteum
apertum ex equo praecipitasse. Carthalonem autem, prae- 5
fectum Punici praesidii, cum commemoratione paterni
hospitii positis armis venientem ad consulem miles obvius
obtruncat. alii alios passim sine discrimine armatos iner- 6
mesque caedunt, Carthaginienses Tarentinosque pariter.
Bruttii quoque multi passim interfecti, seu per errorem,
seu vetere in eos insito odio, seu ad proditionis famam, ut
vi potius atque armis captum Tarentum videretur, exstin-
guendam. tum ab caede ad diripiendam urbem discursum. 7
triginta milia servilium capitum dicuntur capta, ingens argenti
vis facti signatique, auri octoginta tria milia pondo, signa
ac tabulae, prope ut Syracusarum ornamenta aequaverint.
sed maiore animo generis eius praeda abstinuit Fabius quam 8
Marcellus; qui interroganti scriba, quid fieri signis vellet
ingentis magnitudinis—di sunt, suo quisque habitu in
modum pugnantium formati—, deos iratos Tarentinis relinqui iussit. murus inde, qui urbem ab arce dirimebat, 9
dirutus est ac disiectus.

Dum haec Tarenti aguntur, Hannibal, iis, qui Cauloneam
obsidebant, in deditionem acceptis, audita 10
oppugnatione Tarenti dies noctesque cursim
agmine acto, cum festinans ad opem ferendam
captam urbem audisset, "et Romani suum
Hannibalem" inquit "habent: eadem qua
ceperamus arte Tarentum amisimus." ne 11
tamen fugientis modo convertisse agmen videretur, quo constiterat loco, quinque milia
ferme ab urbe posuit castra. ibi paucos
moratus dies Metapontum sese recepit. inde 12

Meanwhile Hannibal having obliged the besiegers of Caulonea (cf. 15 § 7) to surrender and hastening to Tarentum hears of its capture. Retiring to Metapontum he seeks to draw Fabius into an ambuscade, but fails.

duos Metapontinos cum litteris principum eius civitatis ad
Fabium Tarentum mittit, fidem ab consule accepturos im-
punita iis priora fore, si Metapontum cum praesidio Punico
13 prodidissent. Fabius quae adferrent vera esse ratus diem,
qua accessurus esset Metapontum, constituit litterasque ad
14 principes dedit, quae ad Hannibalem delatae sunt. enimvero laetus successu fraudis, si ne Fabius quidem dolo
invictus fuisset, haud procul Metaponto insidias ponit.
15 Fabio auspicanti, priusquam egrederetur ab Tarento, aves
semel atque iterum non addixerunt; hostia quoque caesa
consulenti deos haruspex cavendum a fraude hostili et ab
16 insidiis praedixit. Metapontini, postquam ad constitutam
non venerat diem, remissi, ut cunctantem hortarentur, ac
repente comprehensi metu gravioris quaestionis detegunt
insidias.

[XVII—XX. 8. B.C. 209. *Scipio in Spain.*]

Desertions from the Carthaginian side to Scipio. He advances from Tarraco in order to engage with Hasdrubal alone.

17 Aestatis eius principio, qua haec agebantur, P. Scipio in
Hispania cum hiemem totam reconciliandis
barbarorum animis partim donis partim remis-
sione obsidum captivorumque absumpsisset,
Edesco ad eum clarus inter duces Hispanos
2 venit. erant coniunx liberique eius apud
Romanos; sed praeter eam causam etiam velut fortuita
inclinatio animorum, quae Hispaniam omnem averterat ad
3 Romanum a Punico imperio, traxit eum. eadem causa
Indibili Mandonioque fuit, haud dubie omnis Hispaniae
principibus, cum omni popularium manu relicto Hasdrubale
secedendi in imminentes castris eius tumulos, unde per
4 continentia iuga tutus receptus ad Romanos esset. Hasdrubal, cum hostium res tantis augescere incrementis cerneret,

suas imminui, ac fore ut, nisi audendo aliquid moveret, qua
coepissent, fluerent, dimicare quam primum statuit. Sci- 5
pio avidior etiam certaminis erat, cum a spe, quam successus
rerum augebat, tum quod, priusquam iungerentur hostium
exercitus, cum uno dimicare duce exercituque, quam simul
cum universis malebat. ceterum, etiamsi cum pluribus 6
pariter dimicandum foret, arte quadam copias auxerat.
nam cum videret nullum esse navium usum, quia vacua
omnis Hispaniae ora classibus Punicis erat, subductis
navibus Tarracone navales socios terrestribus copiis addidit.
et armorum adfatim erat ⟨et⟩ captorum Carthagine et quae 7
post captam eam fecerat tanto opificum numero incluso.
cum iis copiis Scipio veris principio ab Tarracone egressus 8
—iam enim et Laelius redierat ab Roma, sine quo nihil
maioris rei motum volebat—ducere ad hostem pergit. per 9
omnia pacata eunti, ut cuiusque populi fines
transiret, prosequentibus excipientibusque sociis, Indibilis et Mandonius cum suis copiis
occurrerunt. Indibilis pro utroque locutus, 10
haudquaquam ⟨ut⟩ barbarus stolide incauteve,

On his way he meets Indibilis and Mandonius, two deserting chieftains. Speech of Indibilis.

sed potius cum verecundia ⟨ac⟩ gravitate propiorque excu-
santi transitionem ut necessariam, quam glorianti eam velut
primam occasionem raptam: scire enim se transfugae nomen 11
exsecrabile veteribus sociis, novis suspectum esse; neque
eum se reprehendere morem hominum, si tamen anceps
odium causa, non nomen faciat. merita inde sua in duces 12
Carthaginiensis commemoravit, avaritiam contra eorum
superbiamque et omnis generis iniurias in se atque populares. itaque corpus dumtaxat suum ad id tempus apud 13
eos fuisse; animum iam pridem ibi esse, ubi ius ac fas
crederent coli. ad deos quoque confugere supplices, qui
nequeant hominum vim atque iniurias pati: se id Scipionem 14

orare, ut transitio sibi nec fraudi apud eum nec honori sit;
quales ex ea die experiundo cognorit, perinde operae eorum
15 pretium faceret. ita prorsus respondet facturum Romanus,
nec pro transfugis habiturum, qui non duxerint societatem
ratam, ubi nec divini quicquam nec humani sanctum esset.

Affecting scene at the restoration to them of their wives and children (cf. xxvi. 49).

16 productae deinde in conspectum iis coniuges
liberique lacrumantibus gaudio redduntur.
17 atque eo die in hospitium abducti; postero
die foedere accepta fides, dimissique ad copias
adducendas. isdem deinde castris tendebant,
donec ducibus iis ad hostem perventum est.

Scipio reaches Hasdrubal's camp near Baecula. The latter during the night posts his army in a strong position, which the Romans next day attack and force, winning a complete victory.

18 Proximus Carthaginiensium exercitus Hasdrubalis prope
2 urbem Baeculam erat. pro castris equitum
stationes habebant. in eas velites antesignani-
que et qui primi agminis erant, advenientes ex
itinere, priusquam castris locum caperent,
adeo contemptim impetum fecerunt, ut facile
appareret, quid utrique parti animorum esset.
3 in castra trepida fuga conpulsi equites sunt,
signaque Romana portis prope ipsis inlata.
4 atque illo quidem die irritatis tantum ad certamen animis
5 castra Romani posuerunt. nocte Hasdrubal in tumulum
copias recipit plano campo in summo patentem; fluvius ab
tergo, ante circaque velut ripa praeceps oram eius omnem
6 cingebat. suberat et altera inferior summissa fastigio plani-
ties; eam quoque altera crepido haud faciliori ascensu
7 ambibat. in hunc inferiorem campum postero die Hasdrubal, postquam stantem pro castris hostium aciem vidit,
equites Numidas leviumque armorum Baliares et Afros
8 demisit. Scipio, circumvectus ordines signaque, ostendebat
hostem, praedamnata spe aequo dimicandi campo captantem
tumulos, loci fiducia, non virtutis aut armorum stare in

conspectu; sed altiora moenia habuisse Carthaginem, quae
transcendisset miles Romanus; nec tumulos, nec arcem, ne 9
mare quidem armis obstitisse suis. ad id fore altitudines,
quas cepissent hostes, ut per praecipitia et praerupta sali-
entes fugerent; eam quoque se illis fugam clausurum.
cohortesque duas alteram tenere fauces vallis, per quam 10
deferretur amnis, iubet, alteram viam insidere, quae ab
urbe per tumuli obliqua in agros ferret. ipse expeditos,
qui pridie stationes hostium pepulerant, ad levem armaturam
infimo stantem supercilio ducit. per aspreta primum, nihil 11
aliud quam via impediti, iere. deinde, ut sub ictum
venerunt, telorum primo omnis generis vis ingens effusa in
eos est, ipsi contra saxa, quae locus strata passim, omnia 12
ferme missilia, praebet, ingerere, non milites solum sed etiam
turba calonum immixta armatis. ceterum quamquam ascen- 13
sus difficilis erat, et prope obruebantur telis saxisque,
adsuetudine tamen succedendi muros et pertinacia animi
subierunt primi. qui simul cepere aliquid aequi loci, ubi 14
firmo consisterent gradu, levem et concursatorem hostem
atque intervallo tutum, cum procul missilibus pugna eluditur,
instabilem eundem ad comminus conserendas manus, expu-
lerunt loco, et cum caede magna in aciem altiori super-
stantem tumulo impegere. inde Scipio iussis adversus 15
mediam evadere aciem victoribus ceteras copias cum Laelio
dividit, atque eum parte dextra tumuli circumire, donec
mollioris ascensus viam inveniret, iubet; ipse ab laeva
circumitu haud magno in transversos hostis incurrit. inde 16
primo turbata acies est, dum ad circumsonantem undique
clamorem flectere cornua et obvertere ordines volunt. hoc 17
tumultu et Laelius subiit, et, dum pedem referunt, ne ab
tergo vulnerarentur, laxata prima acies locusque ad evadendum et mediis datus est, qui per tam iniquum locum 18

stantibus integris ordinibus elephantisque ante signa locatis
19 numquam evasissent. cum ab omni parte caedes fieret,
Scipio, qui laevo cornu in dextrum incucurrerat, maxime in
20 nuda latera hostium pugnabat. et iam ne fugae quidem
patebat locus: nam et stationes utrimque Romanae dextra
laevaque insederant vias, et porta castrorum ducis principumque fuga clausa erat, addita trepidatione elephantorum,
quos territos aeque atque hostes timebant. caesa igitur ad
octo milia hominum.

19 Hasdrubal iam antequam dimicaret pecunia rapta elephantisque praemissis, quam plurumos poterat
de fuga excipiens praeter Tagum flumen ad

Scipio releases all the Spanish prisoners without ransom, sells the Africans. He refuses to be king of the Spaniards.

2 Pyrenaeum tendit. Scipio castris hostium
potitus, cum praeter libera capita omnem
praedam militibus concessisset, in recensendis
captivis decem milia peditum, duo milia equitum invenit.
ex iis Hispanos sine pretio omnes domum dimisit, Afros
3 vendere quaestorem iussit. circumfusa inde multitudo
Hispanorum et ante deditorum et pridie captorum regem
4 eum ingenti consensu appellavit. tum Scipio silentio per
praeconem facto sibi maximum nomen imperatoris esse
5 dixit, quo se milites sui appellassent; regium nomen, alibi
magnum, Romae intolerabile esse. regalem animum in
se esse; si id in hominis ingenio amplissimum ducerent,
6 tacite iudicarent, vocis usurpatione abstinerent. sensere
etiam barbari magnitudinem animi, cuius miraculo nominis alii mortales stuperent, id ex tam alto fastigio aspernantis.

7 Dona inde regulis principibusque Hispanorum divisa,
et ex magna copia captorum equorum trecentos, quos
8 vellet, eligere Indibilem iussit. cum Afros venderet iussu
imperatoris quaestor, puerum adultum inter eos forma

insigni cum audisset regii generis esse, ad Scipionem
misit. quem cum percunctaretur Scipio, quis 9
et cuias et cur id aetatis in castris fuisset,
Numidam esse se ait, Massivam populares
vocare; orbum a patre relictum, apud maternum avum Ga-
lam, regem Numidarum, educatum, cum avunculo Masinissa,
qui nuper cum equitatu subsidio Carthaginiensibus venisset,
in Hispaniam traiecisse. prohibitum propter aetatem a 10
Masinissa numquam ante proelium inisse; eo die, quo
pugnatum cum Romanis esset, inscio avunculo, clam armis
equoque sumpto in aciem exisse; ibi prolapso equo effusum 11
in praeceps captum ab Romanis esse. Scipio cum adser-
vari Numidam iussisset, quae pro tribunali agenda erant,
peragit; inde cum se in praetorium recepisset, vocatum
eum interrogat, velletne ad Masinissam reverti. cum effusis 12
gaudio lacrimis cupere vero diceret, tum puero anulum
aureum, tunicam lato clavo cum Hispano sagulo et aurea
fibula equumque ornatum donat, iussisque prosequi, quoad
vellet, equitibus dimisit.

The story of Massiva, nephew of Masinissa.

De bello inde consilium habitum. et auctoribus quibus- 20
dam, ut confestim Hasdrubalem conseque-
retur, anceps id ratus, ne Mago atque alter 2
Hasdrubal cum eo iungerent copias, praesidio
tantum ad insidendum Pyrenaeum misso ipse
reliquum aestatis recipiendis in fidem Hispaniae populis absumpsit. paucis post proelium 3
factum ad Baeculam diebus, cum Scipio re-
diens iam Tarraconem saltu Castulonensi
excessisset, Hasdrubal, Gisgonis filius et Mago imperatores
ex ulteriore Hispania ad Hasdrubalem venere, serum post
male gestam rem auxilium, consilio in cetera exsequenda
belli haud parum opportuni. ibi conferentibus, quid in 4

Scipio determines not to follow Hasdrubal (cf. c. 19 § 1) but sends a force 'to occupy the Pyrenees.' Conference of the Carthaginian generals and their plans.

[XVII—XX. 8. B.C. 209. *Scipio in Spain.*]

cuiusque provinciae regione animorum Hispanis esset, unus Hasdrubal Gisgonis ultimam Hispaniae oram, quae ad Oceanum et Gadis vergit, ignaram adhuc Romanorum
5 esse, eoque Carthaginiensibus satis fidam censebat; inter Hasdrubalem alterum et Magonem constabat beneficiis Scipionis occupatos omnium animos publice privatimque esse, nec transitionibus finem ante fore, quam omnes Hispani milites aut in ultima Hispaniae amoti aut traducti in
6 Galliam forent. itaque, etiam si senatus Carthaginiensium non censuisset, eundum tamen Hasdrubali fuisse in Italiam, ubi belli caput rerumque summa esset, simul ut Hispanos omnes procul ab nomine Scipionis ex Hispania abduceret:
7 exercitum eius cum transitionibus tum adverso proelio imminutum Hispanis repleri militibus, et Magonem Hasdrubali Gisgonis filio tradito exercitu ipsum cum grandi pecunia ad conducenda mercede auxilia in Baliaris traicere;
8 Hasdrubalem Gisgonis cum exercitu penitus in Lusitaniam abire nec cum Romano manus conserere; Masinissae ex omni equitatu, quod roboris esset, tria milia equitum expleri, eumque vagum per citeriorem Hispaniam sociis opem ferre, hostium oppida atque agros populari. his decretis, ad exsequenda quae statuerant duces digressi. haec eo anno in Hispania acta.

[XX. 9—XXI. B.C. 209. *Elections at Rome. Marcellus and his accusers.*]

Proposal to deprive Marcellus of his command. The people hearing his defence elect him consul.

9 Romae fama Scipionis in dies crescere, Fabio Tarentum captum astu magis quam virtute gloriae tamen
10 esse, Fulvi senescere fama, Marcellus etiam adverso rumore esse, superquam quod primo male pugnaverat, quia vagante per Italiam

[XX. 9—XXI. B.C. 209. *Elections at Rome. Marcellus and his accusers.*]

Other elections. Disquieting news from Arretium, and mission of Marcellus thither.

Hannibale media aestate Venusiam in tecta
milites abduxisset. inimicus erat ei C. Publicius Bibulus tribunus plebis. is iam a prima 11
pugna, quae adversa fuerat, adsiduis contionibus infamem invisumque plebei Claudium fecerat, et iam
de imperio abrogando eius agebat, cum tamen necessarii 12
Claudi obtinuerunt, ut relicto Venusiae legato Marcellus
Romam veniret ad purganda ea, quae inimici obicerent,
nec de imperio eius abrogando absente ipso ageretur.
forte sub idem tempus et Marcellus ad deprecandam 13
ignominiam et Q. Fulvius consul comitiorum causa Romam
venit. Actum de imperio Marcelli in circo Flaminio est **21**
ingenti concursu plebisque et omnium ordinum; accusa- 2
vitque tribunus plebis non Marcellum modo sed omnem
nobilitatem: fraude eorum et cunctatione fieri, ut Hannibal
decimum iam annum Italiam provinciam habeat, diutius ibi
quam Carthagine vixerit. habere fructum imperi prorogati 3
Marcello populum Romanum: bis caesum exercitum eius
aestiva Venusiae sub tectis agere. hanc tribuni orationem 4
ita obruit Marcellus commemoratione rerum suarum, ut
non rogatio solum de imperio eius abrogando antiquaretur,
sed postero die consulem eum ingenti consensu centuriae
omnes crearent. additur collega T. Quinctius Crispinus, 5
qui tum praetor erat. postero die praetores creati P.
Licinius Crassus Dives, pontifex maximus, P. Licinius
Varus, Sex. Iulius Caesar, Q. Claudius Flamen.

Comitiorum ipsorum diebus sollicita civitas de Etruriae 6
defectione fuit. principium eius rei ab Arretinis fieri C.
Calpurnius scripserat, qui eam provinciam pro praetore
obtinebat. itaque confestim eo missus Marcellus consul 7
designatus, qui rem inspiceret, ac, si digna videretur, exer-

[XX. 9—XXI. B.C. 209. *Elections at Rome. Marcellus and his accusers.*]

citu accito bellum ex Apulia in Etruriam transferret. eo
8 metu compressi Etrusci quieverunt. Tarentinorum legatis
pacem petentibus cum libertate ac legibus suis responsum
ab senatu est, ut redirent, cum Fabius consul Romam
9 venisset.—Ludi et Romani et plebei eo anno in singulos
dies instaurati. aediles curules fuere L. Cornelius Caudinus
et Ser. Sulpicius Galba, plebei C. Servilius et Q. Caecilius
10 Metellus. Servilium negabant iure aut tribunum plebis
fuisse aut aedilem esse, quod patrem eius, quem triumvirum
agrarium occisum a Boiis circa Mutinam esse opinio per
decem annos fuerat, vivere atque in hostium potestate esse
satis constabat.

[XXII—XXIII. B.C. 208. *Arrangements for Campaign. Prodigies.*]

Vigorous preparations for carrying on the war by land and sea. Twenty-one legions and four fleets to be employed.

22 Undecimo anno Punici belli consulatum inierunt M.
Marcellus quintum—ut numeretur consulatus,
quem vitio creatus non gessit—et T. Quinctius
2 Crispinus. utrisque consulibus Italia decreta
provincia est et duo consulum prioris anni
exercitus—tertius Venusiae tum erat, cui Marcellus
praefuerat—ita ut ex tribus eligerent
duo, quos vellent, tertius ei traderetur, cui Tarentum et
3 Sallentini provincia evenisset. ceterae provinciae ita divisae:
praetoribus P. Licinio Varo urbana, P. Licinio
Crasso, pontifici maximo, peregrina et quo senatus censuisset,
Sex. Iulio Caesari Sicilia, Q. Claudio Flamini Tarentum.
prorogatum in annum imperium est Q. Fulvio
Flacco, ut provinciam Capuam, quae T. Quincti praetoris
4 fuerat, cum una legione obtineret. prorogatum et C. Hos-

tilio Tubulo est, ut pro praetore in Etruriam ad duas
legiones succederet C. Calpurnio. prorogatum et L. Ve- 5
turio Philoni est, ut pro praetore Galliam eandem provinciam cum isdem duabus legionibus obtineret, quibus
praetor obtinuisset. quod in L. Veturio, idem in C. Aurun- 6
culeio decretum ab senatu latumque de prorogando imperio
ad populum est, qui praetor Sardiniam provinciam cum
duabus legionibus obtinuerat. additae ei ad praesidium
provinciae quinquaginta longae naves, quas P. Scipio ex
Hispania misisset. et P. Scipioni et M. Silano suae His- 7
paniae suique exercitus in annum decreti; Scipio ex octoginta navibus, quas aut secum ex Italia adductas aut captas
Carthagine habebat, quinquaginta in Sardiniam tramittere
iussus, quia fama erat magnum navalem apparatum eo anno 8
Carthagine esse, ducentis navibus omnem oram Italiae
Siciliaeque ac Sardiniae impleturos. et in Sicilia ita divisa 9
res est: Sex. Caesari exercitus Cannensis datus est; M.
Valerius Laevinus—ei quoque enim prorogatum imperium
est—classem, quae ad Siciliam erat, navium septuaginta
obtineret; adderet eo triginta naves, quae ad Tarentum
priore anno fuerant; cum ea centum navium classe, si
videretur ei, praedatum in Africam traiceret. et P. Sulpicio, 10
ut eadem classe Macedoniam Graeciamque provinciam
haberet, prorogatum in annum imperium est. de duabus,
quae ad urbem Romam fuerant, legionibus nihil mutatum.
supplementum, quo opus esset, ut scriberent consulibus 11
permissum. una et viginti legionibus eo anno defensum
imperium Romanum est. et P. Licinio Varo praetori 12
urbano negotium datum, ut naves longas triginta veteres
reficeret, quae Ostiae erant, et viginti novas naves sociis
navalibus compleret, ut quinquaginta navium classe oram

13 maris vicinam urbi Romanae tueri posset. C. Calpurnius
vetitus ab Arretio movere exercitum, nisi cum successor
venisset; idem et Tubulo imperatum, ut inde praecipue
caveret, ne qua nova consilia caperentur.

23 Praetores in provincias profecti; consules religio tenebat, quod prodigiis aliquot nuntiatis non facile
2 litabant. et ex Campania nuntiata erant,
Capuae duas aedes, Fortunae et Martis, et
sepulcra aliquot de caelo tacta, Cumis—adeo
minimis etiam rebus prava religio inserit deos
3 —mures in aede Iovis aurum rosisse, Casini
examen apium ingens in foro consedisse, et
Ostiae murum portamque de caelo tactam,
Caere vulturium volasse in aedem Iovis, Vul-
4 siniis sanguine lacum manasse. horum prodigiorum causa
diem unum supplicatio fuit. per dies aliquot hostiae maiores sine litatione caesae, diuque non impetrata pax deum.
in capita consulum re publica incolumi exitiabilis prodigiorum eventus vertit.

The consuls are detained in Rome to expiate reported prodigies. In consequence of an epidemic an act is passed ordering the perpetual celebration of the *ludi Apollinares*, as a regular yearly festival.

5 Ludi Apollinares Q. Fulvio Ap. Claudio consulibus a
P. Cornelio Sulla praetore urbano primum facti erant; inde
omnes deinceps praetores urbani fecerant; sed in unum
6 annum vovebant dieque incerta faciebant. eo anno pesti-
lentia gravis incidit in urbem agrosque, quae tamen magis
7 in longos morbos quam in perniciabiles evasit. eius pesti-
lentiae causa et supplicatum per compita tota urbe est, et
P. Licinius Varus praetor urbanus legem ferre ad populum
iussus, ut ii ludi in perpetuum in statam diem voverentur.
ipse primus ita vovit, fecitque ante diem tertium nonas
Quintiles. is dies deinde sollemnis servatus.

[XXIV—XXV. 5. B.C. 208. *Arretium and Tarentum.*]

24 De Arretinis et fama in dies gravior et cura crescere patribus. itaque C. Hostilio scriptum est, ne differret obsides ab Arretinis accipere, et, cui traderet Romam deducendos, C. Terentius Varro cum imperio missus. qui ut venit, ex- 2
templo Hostilius legionem unam, quae ante urbem castra habebat, signa in urbem ferre iussit, praesidiaque locis idoneis disposuit; tum in forum citatis senatoribus obsides imperavit. cum 3
senatus biduum ad considerandum [tempus] peteret, aut ipsos extemplo dare aut se postero die senatorum omnis liberos sumpturum edixit. inde portas custodire iussit tribunos militum praefectosque socium et centuriones, ne quis nocte urbe exiret. id segnius neglegentiusque factum: septem 4
principes senatus, priusquam custodiae in portis locarentur, ante noctem cum liberis evaserunt. postero die luce prima, 5
cum senatus in forum citari coeptus esset, desiderati, bonaque eorum venierunt. a ceteris senatoribus centum viginti obsides, liberi ipsorum, accepti traditique C. Terentio Romam deducendi. is omnia suspectiora, quam ante fuerant, in senatu fecit. itaque tamquam imminente Etrusco tu- 6
multu legionem unam, alteram ex urbanis, Arretium ducere iussus ipse C. Terentius, eamque habere in praesidio urbis; C. Hostilium cum cetero exercitu placuit totam provinciam 7
peragrare et cavere, ne qua occasio novare cupientibus res daretur. C. Terentius ut Arretium cum legione venit, 8
claves portarum cum magistratus poposcisset, negantibus iis comparere, fraude amotas magis ratus quam neglegentia intercidisse, ipse alias clavis omnibus portis imposuit, cavitque cum cura, ut omnia in potestate sua essent; Hostilium 9
intentius monuit, ut in eo spem non moturos quicquam Etruscos poneret, si, ne quid movere possent praecavisset.

The Arretines (cf. c. 21 § 6) are required to give hostages. Two legions are sent into Etruria, Arretium secured, and precautions taken against a general rising.

[XXIV—XXV. 5. B.C. 208. *Arretium and Tarentum.*]

Debate in the Senate on the treatment of Tarentum, and of M. Livius, who lost it. Saying of M. Fabius.

25 De Tarentinis inde magna contentione in senatu actum
coram Fabio, defendente ipso quos ceperat
armis, aliis infensis et plerisque aequantibus
2 eos Campanorum noxae poenaeque. senatus
consultum in sententiam M'. Acili factum est,
ut oppidum praesidio custodiretur, Tarentini-
que omnes intra moenia continerentur, res integra postea
3 referretur, cum tranquillior status Italiae esset. et de
M. Livio praefecto arcis Tarentinae haud minore certamine
actum est, aliis senatus consulto notantibus praefectum,
quod eius socordia Tarentum proditum hosti esset, aliis
4 praemia decernentibus, quod per quinquennium arcem
tutatus esset, maximeque unius eius opera receptum Ta-
5 rentum foret, mediis ad censores, non ad senatum notionem
de eo pertinere dicentibus. cuius sententiae et Fabius fuit;
adiecit tamen fateri se opera Livi Tarentum receptum, quod
amici eius vulgo in senatu iactassent: neque enim recipiun-
dum fuisse, nisi amissum foret.

[XXV. 6—XXVII. B.C. 208. *Death of Marcellus.*]

Religious difficulty of Marcellus about his temple at Clastidium.

6 Consulum alter T. Quinctius Crispinus ad exercitum,
quem Q. Fulvius Flaccus habuerat, cum sup-
7 plemento in Lucanos est profectus. Marcellum aliae atque aliae obiectae animo religiones
tenebant, in quibus, quod, cum bello Gallico ad Clastidium
aedem Honori et Virtuti vovisset, dedicatio eius a ponti-
8 ficibus impediebatur, quod negabant unam cellam duobus
diis recte dedicari, quia, si de caelo tacta aut prodigii
aliquid in ea factum esset, difficilis procuratio foret, quod
9 utri deo res divina fieret, sciri non posset: neque enim

duobus nisi certis deis rite una hostia fieri. ita addita
Virtutis aedes approperato opere; neque tamen ab ipso
aedes eae dedicatae sunt. tum demum ad exercitum, quem 10
priore anno Venusiae reliquerat, cum supplemento profi-
ciscitur.

Locros in Bruttiis Crispinus oppugnare conatus, quia 11
magnam famam attulisse Fabio Tarentum
rebatur, omne genus tormentorum machina-
rumque ex Sicilia arcessierat; et naves indidem accitae erant, quae vergentem ad mare
partem urbis oppugnarent. ea omissa oppug- 12
natio est, quia Lacinium Hannibal admoverat copias, et
collegam eduxisse iam a Venusia exercitum fama erat,
cui coniungi volebat. itaque in Apuliam ex Bruttiis re- 13
ditum, et inter Venusiam Bantiamque minus trium milium
passuum intervallo consules binis castris consederunt. in 14
eandem regionem et Hannibal redit averso ab Locris bello.
ibi consules ambo ingenio feroces prope cotidie in aciem
exire haud dubia spe, si duobus exercitibus consularibus
iunctis commisisset sese hostis, debellari posse.

Crispinus commences the siege of Locri but raises it on the approach of Hannibal and joins Marcellus in Apulia.

Hannibal quia cum Marcello bis priore anno congressus **26**
vicerat victusque erat, ut, cum eodem si dimicandum foret, nec spem nec metum ex vano
habebat, ita duobus consulibus haud quaquam
sese parem futurum credebat. itaque totus in 2
suas artes versus insidiis locum quaerebat.
levia tamen proelia inter bina castra vario 3
eventu fiebant; quibus cum extrahi aestatem
posse consules crederent, nihilo minus oppugnari Locros
posse rati, L. Cincio, ut ex Sicilia Locros cum classe
traiceret, scribunt, et ut ab terra quoque oppugnari moenia 4
possent, ab Tarento partem exercitus, qui in praesidio erat,

Hannibal cuts off a detachment of Romans marching from Tarentum to Locri, to recommence the siege in conjunction with the fleet from Sicily.

5 duci eo iusserunt. ea ita futura per quosdam Thurinos
comperta Hannibali cum essent, mittit ad insidendam ab
Tarento viam. ibi sub tumulo Peteliae tria milia equitum
6 duo peditum in occulto locata; in quae inexplorato euntes
Romani cum incidissent, ad duo milia armatorum caesa,
mille et quingenti ferme vivi capti, alii dissipati fuga per
agros saltusque Tarentum rediere.

7 Tumulus erat silvestris inter Punica et Romana castra,
ab neutris primo occupatus, quia Romani,
qualis pars eius, quae vergeret ad hostium
castra, esset, ignorabant, Hannibal insidiis
8 quam castris aptiorem eum crediderat. itaque nocte ad id missas aliquot Numidarum
turmas medio in saltu condiderat, quorum
interdiu nemo ab statione movebatur, ne aut
9 arma aut ipsi procul conspicerentur. fremebant vulgo in
castris Romanis occupandum eum tumulum esse et castello
firmandum, ne, si occupatus ab Hannibale foret, velut in
10 cervicibus haberent hostem. movit ea res Marcellum, et
collegae "quin imus" inquit "ipsi cum equitibus paucis
exploratum? subiecta res oculis nostris certius dabit con-
11 silium." adsentienti Crispino cum equitibus ducentis viginti, ex quibus quadraginta Fregellani, ceteri Etrusci erant,
12 proficiscuntur; secuti tribuni militum M. Marcellus consulis
filius et A. Manlius, simul et duo praefecti socium L.
13 Arrenius et M'. Aulius. immolasse eo die quidam prodi-
dere memoriae consulem Marcellum, et prima hostia caesa
iocur sine capite inventum, in secunda omnia comparuisse,
14 quae adsolent, auctum etiam visum in capite; nec id sane
haruspici placuisse, quod secundum trunca et turpia exta
27 nimis laeta apparuissent. Ceterum consulem Marcellum
tanta cupiditas tenebat dimicandi cum Hannibale, ut num-

The Roman consuls go out to reconnoitre a wooded hill between the two camps, on which Hannibal has placed Numidians in ambush.

The reconnoitring party is cut off by the ambush. Marcellus is killed, Crispinus severely wounded.

quam satis castra castris collata crederet. tum 2
quoque vallo egrediens signum dedit, ut ad
locum miles esset paratus, ut, si collis, in quem
speculatum irent, placuisset, vasa colligerent
ac sequerentur. exiguum campi ante castra 3
erat; inde in collem aperta undique et conspecta ferebat
via. Numidis speculator, nequaquam in spem tantae rei
positus, sed si quos vagos pabuli aut lignorum causa longius
a castris progressos possent excipere, signum dat, ut pariter
ab suis quisque latebris exorerentur. non ante apparuere, 4
quibus obviis ab iugo ipso consurgendum erat, quam cir-
cumiere, qui ab tergo intercluderent viam. tum undique
omnes exorti et clamore sublato impetum fecere. cum in 5
ea valle consules essent, ut neque evadere possent in iugum
occupatum ab hoste nec receptum ab tergo circumventi
haberent, extrahi tamen diutius certamen potuisset, ni
coepta ab Etruscis fuga pavorem ceteris iniecisset. non 6
tamen omisere pugnam deserti ab Etruscis Fregellani,
donec integri consules hortando ipsique ex parte pugnando
rem sustinebant; sed postquam vulneratos ambo consules, 7
Marcellum etiam transfixum lancea prolabentem ex equo
moribundum videre, tum et ipsi—perpauci autem supere-
rant—cum Crispino consule duobus iaculis icto et Marcello
adulescente saucio et ipso effugerunt. interfectus A. Man- 8
lius tribunus militum, et ex duobus praefectis socium
M'. Aulius occisus, ⟨L.⟩ Arrenius captus; et lictores consulum quinque vivi in hostium potestatem venerunt, ceteri 9
aut interfecti aut cum consule effugerunt; equitum tres et
quadraginta aut in proelio aut in fuga ceciderunt, duodevi-
ginti vivi capti. tumultuatum in castris fuerat, ut consulibus 10
irent subsidio, cum consulem et filium alterius consulis
saucios exiguasque infelicis expeditionis reliquias ad castra

[XXV. 6—XXVII. B.C. 208. *Death of Marcellus.*]

11 venientes cernunt. mors Marcelli cum alioqui miserabilis fuit, tum quod nec pro aetate—iam enim maior sexaginta annis erat—neque pro veteris prudentia ducis tam improvide se collegamque et prope totam rem publicam in praeceps dederat.

12 Multos circa unam rem ambitus fecerim, si, quae de
13 Marcelli morte variant auctores, omnia exsequi velim. ut omittam alios, Coelius triplicem gestae rei memoriam edit: unam traditam fama, alteram scriptam laudatione fili, qui rei gestae interfuerit, tertiam, quam ipse pro inquisita ac
14 sibi comperta adfert. ceterum ita fama variat, ut tamen plerique loci speculandi causa castris egressum, omnes insidiis circumventum tradant.

[XXVIII—XXIX. 8. B.C. 208. *Hannibal outwitted at Salapia.*]

Hannibal getting possession of Marcellus' signets sends a letter in his name to the Salapitani to be in readiness to receive him. They forewarned by Crispinus defeat his scheme.

28 Hannibal magnum terrorem hostibus morte consulis unius vulnere alterius iniectum esse ratus, ne cui deesset occasioni, castra in tumulum, in quo pugnatum erat, extemplo transfert. ibi
2 inventum Marcelli corpus sepelit. Crispinus, et morte collegae et suo vulnere territus, silentio insequentis noctis profectus, quos proxumos nanctus est montes, in iis loco alto et
3 tuto undique castra posuit. ibi duo duces sagaciter moti sunt, alter ad inferendam, alter ad cavendam
4 fraudem. anulis Marcelli simul cum corpore Hannibal potitus erat. eius signi errore ne cui dolus necteretur a Poeno metuens, Crispinus circa civitates proximas miserat nuntios, occisum collegam esse anulisque eius hostem potitum; ne quibus litteris crederent nomine Marcelli

compositis. paulo ante hic nuntius consulis Salapiam vene- 5
rat, quam litterae ab Hannibale allatae sunt Marcelli nomine
compositae se nocte, quae diem illum secutura esset, Salapiam venturum: parati milites essent, qui in praesidio
erant, si quo opera eorum opus esset. sensere Salapitani 6
fraudem, et ab ira non defectionis modo sed etiam equitum
interfectorum rati occasionem supplicii peti, remisso retro 7
nuntio—perfuga autem Romanus erat—, ut sine arbitro
milites quae vellent agerent, oppidanos per muros urbisque
opportuna loca in stationibus disponunt, custodias vigilias- 8
que in eam noctem intentius instruunt, circa portam, qua
venturum hostem rebantur, quod roboris in praesidio erat
opponunt. Hannibal quarta vigilia ferme ad urbem acces- 9
sit. primi agminis erant perfugae Romanorum et arma
Romana habebant. ii, ubi ad portam est ventum, Latine
omnes loquentes excitant vigiles aperirique portam iubent:
consulem adesse. vigiles velut ad vocem eorum excitati 10
tumultuari, trepidare, moliri portam. cataracta deiecta
clausa erat; eam partim vectibus levant, partim funibus
subducunt in tantum altitudinis, ut subire recti possent.
vixdum satis patebat iter, cum perfugae certatim ruunt 11
per portam; et cum sescenti ferme intrassent, remisso
fune quo suspensa erat, cataracta magno sonitu cecidit.
Salapitani alii perfugas neglegenter ex itinere suspensa 12
umeris, ut inter pacatos, gerentes arma invadunt, alii e
turri eius portae murisque saxis sudibus pilis absterrent
hostem. ita inde Hannibal suamet ipse fraude captus 13
abiit, profectusque ad Locrorum solvendam

Hannibal raises the siege of Locri.

obsidionem, quam ⟨L.⟩ Cincius summa vi, operibus tormentorumque omni genere ex Sicilia advecto op-
pugnabat. Magoni iam haud ferme fidenti retenturum de- 14
fensurumque se urbem prima spes morte nuntiata Marcelli

15 adfulsit. secutus inde nuntius Hannibalem Numidarum
equitatu praemisso ipsum, quantum accelerare posset, cum
16 peditum agmine sequi. itaque ubi primum Numidas edito
e speculis signo adventare sensit, et ipse patefacta repente
porta ferox in hostes erumpit. et primo magis quia improviso id fecerat, quam quod par viribus esset, anceps certa-
17 men erat; deinde, ut supervenere Numidae, tantus pavor
Romanis est iniectus, ut passim ad mare ac naves fugerent
relictis operibus machinisque, quibus muros quatiebant.
ita adventu Hannibalis soluta Locrorum obsidio est.

Crispinus sends news of the disaster in Apulia to Rome.

29 Crispinus postquam in Bruttios profectum Hannibalem sensit, exercitum, cui collega praefuerat, M. Marcellum tribunum militum Venu-
2 siam abducere iussit; ipse cum legionibus
suis Capuam profectus, vix lecticae agitationem prae gravitate vulnerum patiens, Romam litteras de morte col
3 legae scripsit, quantoque ipse in discrimine esset: se comitiorum causa non posse Romam venire, quia nec viae
laborem passurus videretur et de Tarento sollicitus esset,
ne ex Bruttiis Hannibal eo converteret agmen; legatos
opus esse ad se mitti, viros prudentes, cum quibus, quae
4 vellet, de re publica loqueretur. hae litterae recitatae
magnum et luctum morte alterius consulis et metum de
altero fecerunt. itaque et Q. Fabium filium ad exercitum
Venusiam miserunt, et ad consulem tres legati missi, Sex.
Iulius Caesar L. Licinius Pollio L. Cincius Alimentus, cum
5 paucis ante diebus ex Sicilia redisset. hi nuntiare consuli
iussi, ut, si ad comitia ipse venire Romam non posset,
dictatorem in agro Romano diceret comitiorum causa;
6 si consul Tarentum profectus esset, Q. Claudium praetorem placere in eam regionem inde abducere legiones,
in qua plurimas sociorum urbes tueri posset.

[XXVIII—XXIX. 8. B.C. 208. *Hannibal outwitted at Salapia.*]

Eadem aestate M. Valerius cum classe centum navium 7
ex Sicilia in Africam tramisit et ad Clupeam
urbem escensione facta agrum late nullo ferme
obvio armato vastavit. inde ad naves raptim
praedatores recepti, quia repente fama accidit
classem Punicam adventare. octoginta erant et tres naves.
cum his haud procul Clupea prospere pugnat Romanus. 8
decem et octo navibus captis, fugatis aliis, cum magna
terrestri navalique praeda Lilybaeum rediit.

M. Valerius makes a successful descent on the coast of Africa.

[XXIX. 9—XXXIII. 5. B.C. 208. *Events in Greece.*]

Eadem aestate et Philippus implorantibus Achaeis auxi- 9
lium tulit, quos et Machanidas tyrannus Lace-
daemoniorum finitimo bello urebat, et Aetoli
navibus per fretum, quod Naupactum et Patras
interfluit—Rhion incolae vocant—, exercitu
traiecto depopulati erant. Attalum quoque 10
regem Asiae, quia Aetoli summum gentis
suae magistratum ad eum proximo concilio
detulerant, fama erat in Europam traiecturum.

Conflicts between Philip V. of Macedonia invited by the Achaeans and the Aetolians. Fruitless attempts at negotiation. Interference of Attalus and the Romans.

Ob haec Philippo in Graeciam descendenti ad Lamiam 30
urbem Aetoli duce Pyrrhia, qui praetor in eum annum
cum absente Attalo creatus erat, occurrerunt. habebant 2
et ab Attalo auxilia secum et mille ferme ex Romana
classe a P. Sulpicio missos. adversus hunc ducem atque
has copias Philippus bis prospero eventu pugnavit; mille
admodum hostium utraque pugna occidit. inde cum Aetoli 3
metu compulsi Lamiae urbis moenibus tenerent sese, Philippus ad Phalara exercitum reduxit. in Maliaco sinu is locus
est, quondam frequenter habitatus propter egregium portum

tutasque circa stationes et aliam opportunitatem maritumam
4 terrestremque. eo legati ab rege Aegypti Ptolomaeo Rho-
diisque et Atheniensibus et Chiis venerunt ad dirimendum
inter Philippum atque Aetolos bellum. adhibitus ab Aetolis
et ex finitimis pacificator Amynander rex Athamanum.
5 omnium autem non tanta pro Aetolis cura erat, ferociori
quam pro ingeniis Graecorum gente, quam ne Philippus
regnumque eius grave libertati futurum rebus Graeciae
6 immisceretur. de pace dilata consultatio est in concilium
Achaeorum, concilioque ei et locus et dies certa indicta;
7 interim triginta dierum indutiae impetratae. profectus inde
rex per Thessaliam Boeotiamque Chalcidem Euboeae venit,
ut Attalum, quem classe Euboeam petiturum audierat,
8 portibus et litorum appulsu arceret. inde praesidio relicto
adversus Attalum, si forte interim traiecisset, profectus ipse
9 cum paucis equitum levisque armaturae Argos venit. ibi
curatione Heraeorum Nemeorumque suffragiis populi ad
eum delata, quia se Macedonum reges ex ea civitate oriundos
ferunt, Heraeis peractis ab ipso ludicro extemplo Aegium
profectus est ad indictum multo ante sociorum concilium.
10 Ibi de Aetolico finiendo bello actum, ne causa aut
11 Romanis aut Attalo intrandi Graeciam esset. sed ea omnia
vixdum indutiarum tempore circumacto Aetoli turbavere,
postquam et Attalum Aeginam venisse et Romanam classem
12 stare ad Naupactum audivere. vocati enim in concilium
Achaeorum, in quo et eae legationes erant, quae ad Phalara
egerant de pace, primum questi sunt quaedam parva contra
13 fidem conventionis tempore indutiarum facta; postremo
negarunt dirimi bellum posse, nisi Messeniis Achaei Pylum
redderent, Romanis restitueretur Atintania, Scerdilaedo et
14 Pleurato Ardiaei. enimvero indignum ratus Philippus victos
victori sibi ultro condiciones ferre, ne antea quidem se aut

de pace audisse aut indutias pepigisse dixit spem ullam
habentem quieturos Aetolos, sed uti omnes socios testes
haberet se pacis, illos belli causam quaesisse. ita infecta 15
pace concilium dimisit quattuor milibus armatorum relictis
ad praesidium Achaeorum et quinque longis navibus acceptis,
quas si adiecisset missae nuper ad se classi Carthagini- 16
ensium et ex Bithynia ab rege Prusia venientibus navibus,
statuerat navali proelio lacessere Romanos iam diu in
regione ea potentes maris. ipse ab eo concilio Argos 17
regressus; iam enim Nemeorum adpetebat tempus, quae
celebrari volebat praesentia sua.

Occupato rege apparatu ludorum et per dies festos **31**
licentius quam inter belli tempora remittente
animum P. Sulpicius ab Naupacto profectus
classem appulit inter Sicyonem et Corinthum,
agrumque nobilissimae fertilitatis effuse vastavit. fama eius rei Philippum ab ludis excivit; 2
raptimque cum equitatu profectus iussis subse-
qui peditibus, palatos passim per agros graves-
que praeda, ut qui nihil tale metuerent, adortus Romanos
compulit ad naves. classis Romana haudquaquam laeta 3
praeda Naupactum redit. Philippo ludorum quoque, qui
reliqui erant, celebritatem quantaecumque, de Romanis
tamen, victoriae partae fama auxerat, laetitiaque ingenti 4
celebrati festi dies, eo magis etiam, quod populariter
dempto capitis insigni purpuraque atque alio regio habitu
aequaverat ceteris se in speciem, quo nihil gratius est
civitatibus liberis; praebuissetque haud dubiam eo facto 5
spem libertatis, nisi omnia intoleranda libidine foeda ac
deformia effecisset. vagabatur enim cum uno aut altero
comite per maritas domos dies noctesque, et summittendo 6
se in privatum fastigium quo minus conspectus, eo solutior

A Roman force making descent on the Peloponnesian coast is severely handled by Philip. The Nemean games. Philip's licentious conduct.

erat, et libertatem, cum aliis vanam ostendisset, totam in
7 suam licentiam verterat. neque enim omnia emebat aut
eblandiebatur, sed vim etiam flagitiis adhibebat, periculosumque et viris et parentibus erat moram incommoda
8 severitate libidini regiae fecisse. uni etiam principi Achaeorum Arato adempta uxor nomine Polycratia ac spe regiarum nuptiarum in Macedoniam asportata fuerat.

Attack on Elis by Philip and the Achaeans repulsed by the Eleans assisted by the Romans. Philip recalled to Macedonia.

9 Per haec flagitia sollemni Nemeorum peracto paucisque
additis diebus Dymas est profectus ad praesidium Aetolorum, quod ab Eleis adcitum
10 acceptumque in urbem erat, eiciendum. Cycliadas—penes eum summa imperii erat—Achaeique ad Dymas regi occurrere, et Eliorum accensi odio, quod a ceteris Achaeis dissentirent, et infensi Aetolis, quos Romanum quoque adversus
11 se movisse bellum credebant. profecti ab Dymis coniuncto exercitu transeunt Larisum amnem, qui Elium agrum ab
32 Dymaeo dirimit. Primum diem, quo fines hostium ingressi sunt, populando absumpserunt. postero die acie instructa ad urbem accesserunt praemissis equitibus, qui obequitando portis promptum ad excursiones genus lacesserent Aeto-
2 lorum. ignorabant Sulpicium cum quindecim navibus ab Naupacto Cyllenen traiecisse et expositis in terram quattuor milibus armatorum silentio noctis, ne conspici agmen posset,
3 intrasse Elim. itaque improvisa res ingentem iniecit terrorem, postquam inter Aetolos Eliosque Romana signa
4 atque arma cognovere. et primo recipere suos voluerat rex; dein contracto iam inter Aetolos et Tralles—Illyriorum id est genus—certamine cum urgeri videret suos, et ipse rex
5 cum equitatu in cohortem Romanam incurrit. ibi equus pilo traiectus cum prolapsum super caput regem effudisset, atrox pugna utrimque accensa est et ab Romanis impetu in

regem facto et protegentibus regiis. insignis et ipsius pugna 6
fuit, cum pedes inter equites coactus esset proelium inire.
dein, cum iam impar certamen esset, caderentque circa
eum multi et vulnerarentur, raptus ab suis atque alteri equo
iniectus fugit. eo die castra quinque milia passuum ab 7
urbe Eliorum posuit. postero die omnes copias ad propin-
quum Eliorum castellum—Pyrgum vocant—eduxit, quo
agrestium multitudinem cum pecoribus metu populationum
compulsam audierat. eam inconditam inermemque multi- 8
tudinem primo statim terrore adveniens cepit; compensa-
veratque ea praeda quod ignominiae ad Elim acceptum
fuerat. dividenti praedam captivosque—fuere autem quat- 9
tuor milia hominum, pecorumque omnis generis ad viginti
milia—nuntius ex Macedonia venit Eropum quendam
corrupto arcis praesidiique praefecto Lychnidum cepisse,
tenere et Dassaretiorum quosdam vicos, et Dardanos etiam
concire. omisso igitur Achaico atque Aetolico bello, relictis 10
tamen duobus milibus et quingentis omnis generis armatorum cum Menippo et Polyphanta ducibus ad praesidium
sociorum, profectus ab Dymis per Achaiam Boeotiamque 11
et Euboeam decumis castris Demetriadem in Thessaliam
pervenit.

Ibi alii maiorem adferentes tumultum nuntii occurrunt: 33
Dardanos in Macedoniam effusos Orestidem iam tenere ac
descendisse in Argestaeum campum, famamque inter bar-
baros celebrem esse Philippum occisum. expeditione ea, qua 2
cum populatoribus agri ad Sicyonem pugnavit, in arborem
illatus impetu equi ad eminentem ramum cornu alterum
galeae praefregit; id inventum ab Aetolo quodam perlatum- 3
que in Aetoliam ad Scerdilaedum, cui notum erat insigne
galeae, famam interfecti regis vulgavit. post profectionem 4
ex Achaia regis Sulpicius Aeginam classe profectus cum

[XXIX. 9—XXXIII. 5. B.C. 208. *Events in Greece.*]

5 Attalo sese coniunxit. Achaei cum Aetolis Eleisque haud procul Messene prosperam pugnam fecerunt. Attalus rex et P. Sulpicius Aeginae hibernarunt.

[XXXIII. 6—XXXV. B.C. 208. *Elections in Rome.*]

Appointment of a dictator and death of Crispinus.

6 Exitu huius anni T. Quinctius consul dictatore comitiorum ludorumque faciendorum causa dicto T. Manlio Torquato ex vulnere moritur; alii Tarenti, alii in Campania mortuum tradunt.
7 ita, quod nullo ante bello acciderat, duo consules sine memorando proelio interfecti velut orbam rem publicam reliquerant. dictator Manlius magistrum equitum C. Ser-
8 vilium—tum aedilis curulis erat—dixit. senatus quo die primum est habitus, ludos magnos facere dictatorem iussit, quos M. Aemilius praetor urbanus C. Flaminio Cn. Servilio consulibus fecerat et in quinquennium voverat. tum dicta-
9 tor et fecit ludos et in insequens lustrum vovit. ceterum cum duo consulares exercitus tam prope hostem sine ducibus essent, omnibus aliis omissis una praecipua cura patres populumque incessit consules primo quoque tempore creandi, et ut eos crearent potissimum, quorum virtus satis
10 tuta a fraude Punica esset: cum toto eo bello damnosa praepropera ac fervida ingenia imperatorum fuisse, tum eo ipso anno consules nimia cupiditate conserendi cum hoste
11 manum in necopinatam fraudem lapsos esse; ceterum deos immortalis, miseritos nominis Romani, pepercisse innoxiis exercitibus, temeritatem consulum ipsorum capitibus damnasse.

Choice of consuls, C. Claudius

34 Cum circumspicerent patres, quosnam consules facerent, longe ante alios eminebat C. Claudius Nero;
2 ei collega quaerebatur. et virum quidem eum

Nero and M. Livius. Previous history of the latter and his reluctance to accept the office.

egregium ducebant, sed promptiorem acriorem-
que, quam tempora belli postularent aut hostis
Hannibal; temperandum acre ingenium eius 3
moderato et prudenti viro adiuncto collega
censebant. M. Livius erat, multis ante annis ex consulatu 4
populi iudicio damnatus, quam ignominiam adeo aegre
tulerat, ut rus migraret et per multos annos et urbe et omni
coetu caruerit hominum. octavo ferme post damnationem 5
anno M. Claudius Marcellus et M. Valerius Laevinus
consules reduxerant eum in urbem; sed erat veste obsoleta
capilloque et barba promissa, prae se ferens in vultu habitu-
que insignem memoriam ignominiae acceptae. L. Veturius 6
et P. Licinius censores eum tonderi et squalorem deponere
et in senatum venire fungique aliis publicis muneribus
coegerunt. sed tum quoque aut verbo adsentiebatur aut 7
pedibus in sententiam ibat, donec cognati hominis eum
causa M. Livi Macati, cum fama eius ageretur, stantem
coegit in senatu sententiam dicere. tunc ex tanto intervallo 8
auditus convertit ora hominum in se, causamque sermonibus
praebuit, indigno iniuriam a populo factam, magnoque id
damno fuisse, quod tam gravi bello nec opera nec consilio
talis viri usa res publica esset: C. Neroni neque Q. Fabium 9
neque M. Valerium Laevinum dari collegam posse, quia
duos patricios creari non liceret; eandem causam in T. 10
Manlio esse, praeterquam quod recusasset delatum consulatum recusaturusque esset. egregium par consulum fore, si 11
M. Livium C. Claudio collegam adiunxissent. nec populus
mentionem eius rei ortam a patribus est aspernatus. unus 12
eam rem in civitate is, cui deferebatur honos, abnuebat,
levitatem civitatis accusans: sordidati rei non miseritos
candidam togam invito offerre; eodem honores poenasque
congeri. si virum bonum ducerent, quid ita pro malo ac 13

noxio damnassent? si noxium comperissent, quid ita male
14 credito priore consulatu alterum crederent? haec taliaque arguentem et querentem castigabant patres, et M. Furium memorantes revocatum de exilio patriam pulsam sede sua restituisse, ut parentium saevitiam sic patriae patiendo ac
15 ferendo leniendam esse, adnisi omnes cum ⟨C.⟩ Claudio M. Livium consulem fecerunt.

Mission of L. Manlius to Greece. Division of provinces between the two consuls.

35 Post diem tertium eius diei praetorum comitia habita. praetores creati L. Porcius Licinus C. Mamilius C. et A. Hostilii Catones. comitiis perfectis ludisque factis dictator et magister
2 equitum magistratu abierunt. C. Terentius Varro in Etruriam pro praetore missus, ut ex ea provincia C. Hostilius Tarentum ad eum exercitum iret, quem T.
3 Quinctius consul habuerat; et L. Manlius trans mare legatus iret viseretque, quae res ibi gererentur; simul, quod Olympiae ludicrum ea aestate futurum erat, quod maximo coetu Graeciae celebraretur, ut, si tuto per hostem posset,
4 adiret id concilium, ut, qui Siculi bello ibi profugi aut Tarentini cives relegati ab Hannibale essent, domos redirent scirentque sua omnia iis, quae ante bellum habuissent, reddere populum Romanum.

5 Quia periculosissimus annus imminere videbatur, neque consules in re publica erant, in consules designatos omnes versi, quam primum eos sortiri provincias et praesciscere, quam quisque eorum provinciam, quem hostem haberet,
6 volebant. de reconciliatione etiam gratiae eorum in senatu
7 actum est principio facto a Q. Fabio Maximo. inimicitiae autem nobiles inter eos erant et acerbiores eas indignioresque Livio sua calamitas fecerat, quod spretum se in ea
8 fortuna credebat. itaque is magis implacabilis erat et nihil opus esse reconciliatione aiebat; acrius et intentius omnia

gesturos timentes, ne crescendi ex se inimico collegae
potestas fieret. vicit tamen auctoritas senatus, ut positis 9
simultatibus communi animo consilioque administrarent
rem publicam. provinciae iis non permixtae regionibus, 10
sicut superioribus annis, sed diversae extremis Italiae finibus,
alteri adversus Hannibalem Bruttii et Lucani, alteri Gallia
adversus Hasdrubalem, quem iam Alpibus appropinquare
fama erat, decreta. exercitum e duobus, qui in Gallia 11
quique in Etruria esset, addito urbano, eligeret, quem
mallet, qui Galliam esset sortitus; cui Bruttii provincia 12
evenisset, novis legionibus urbanis scriptis, utrius mallet
consulum prioris anni exercitum sumeret; relictum a con- 13
sule exercitum Q. Fulvius proconsul acciperet, eique in
annum imperium esset. et C. Hostilio, cui pro Etruria 14
Tarentum mutaverant provinciam, pro Tarento Capuam
mutaverunt; legio una data est, cui Fulvius proximo anno
praefuerat.

[XXXVI—LI. B.C. 207. *Arrival of Hasdrubal. The Metaurus.*]

News received that Hasdrubal is in Gaul. Religious celebrations at Rome. Allotment of commands.

De Hasdrubalis adventu in Italiam cura in dies cresce- **36**
bat. Massiliensium primum legati nuntiave-
rant eum in Galliam transgressum, erectosque
adventu eius, quia magnum pondus auri 2
attulisse diceretur ad mercede auxilia conducenda, Gallorum animos. missi deinde cum 3
iis legati ab Roma Sex. Antistius et M. Raecius ad rem
inspiciendam rettulerant misisse se cum Massiliensibus
ducibus, qui per hospites eorum, principes Gallorum, omnia
explorata referrent; pro comperto habere, Hasdrubalem 4
ingenti iam coacto exercitu proximo vere Alpes traiecturum,

nec tum eum quicquam aliud morari, nisi quod clausae
hieme essent.

5 In locum M. Marcelli P. Aelius Paetus augur creatus
inauguratusque; et Cn. Cornelius Dolabella rex sacrorum
inauguratus est in locum M. Marcii, qui biennio ante
6 mortuus erat. hoc eodem anno et lustrum conditum est
a censoribus P. Sempronio Tuditano et M. Cornelio
7 Cethego. censa civium capita centum triginta septem milia
centum octo, minor aliquanto numerus, quam qui ante
8 bellum fuerat. eo anno primum, ex quo Hannibal in Italiam
venisset, comitium tectum esse memoriae proditum est,
et ludos Romanos semel instauratos ab aedilibus curulibus
9 Q. Metello et C. Servilio. et plebeis ludis biduum instauratum ab C. Mamilio et M. Caecilio Metello aedilibus
plebis; et tria signa ad Cereris iidem dederunt; et Iovis
epulum fuit ludorum causa.

10 Consulatum inde ineunt C. Claudius Nero et M. Livius
iterum. qui quia iam designati provincias sortiti erant,
11 praetores sortiri iusserunt. C. Hostilio iurisdictio urbana
evenit; addita et peregrina, ut tres in provincias exire
possent; A. Hostilio Sardinia, C. Mamilio Sicilia, L. Porcio
12 Gallia evenit. summa legionum trium et viginti ita per
provincias divisa: ut binae consulum essent, quattuor
Hispania haberet, binas tres praetores, in Sicilia et Sardinia
13 et Gallia, duas C. Terentius in Etruria, duas Q. Fulvius
in Bruttiis, duas Q. Claudius circa Tarentum et Sallentinos,
unam C. Hostilius Tubulus Capuae; duae urbanae ut
14 scriberentur. primis quattuor legionibus populus tribunos
creavit, in ceteras consules miserunt.

37 Priusquam consules proficiscerentur, novendiale sacrum
2 fuit, quia Veis de caelo lapidaverat. sub unius prodigii,
ut fit, mentionem alia quoque nuntiata: Minturnis aedem

Iovis et lucum Maricae, item Atellae murum et portam de caelo tactam. Minturnenses, terribilius 3 quod esset, adiciebant sanguinis rivum in porta fluxisse, et Capuae lupus nocte portam ingressus vigilem laniaverat. haec procurata hostiis maiori- 4 bus prodigia, et supplicatio diem unum fuit ex decreto pontificum. inde iterum novendiale instauratum, quod in Armilustro lapidibus visum pluere. liberatas religione 5 mentes turbavit rursus nuntiatum Frusinone natum esse infantem quadrimo parem, nec magnitudine tam mirandum, quam quod is quoque, ut Sinuessae biennio ante, incertus, mas an femina esset, natus erat. id vero haruspices ex 6 Etruria acciti foedum ac turpe prodigium dicere, extorrem agro Romano, procul terrae contactu, alto mergendum. vivum in arcam condidere, provectumque in mare proiecerunt. decrevere item pontifices, ut virgines ter novenae 7 per urbem euntes carmen canerent. id cum in Iovis Statoris aede discerent conditum ab Livio poeta carmen, tacta de caelo aedes in Aventino Iunonis Reginae; pro- 8 digiumque id ad matronas pertinere haruspices cum respondissent donoque divam placandam esse, aedilium 9 curulium edicto in Capitolium convocatae, quibus in urbe Romana intraque decimum lapidem ab urbe domicilia essent, ipsae inter se quinque et viginti delegerunt, ad quas ex dotibus stipem conferrent. inde donum pelvis aurea 10 facta lataque in Aventinum, pureque et caste a matronis sacrificatum. confestim ad aliud sacrificium eidem divae 11 ab decemviris edicta dies, cuius ordo talis fuit: ab aede Apollinis boves feminae albae duae porta Carmentali in urbem ductae; post eas duo signa cupressea Iunonis 12 Reginae portabantur; tum septem et viginti virgines, longam indutae vestem, carmen in Iunonem Reginam 13

Prodigies, and ceremonies of atonement.

canentes ibant, illa tempestate forsitan laudabile rudibus
ingeniis, nunc abhorrens et inconditum, si referatur; virgi-
num ordinem sequebantur decemviri coronati laurea prae-
14 textatique. a porta Iugario vico in forum venere. in foro
pompa constitit, et per manus reste data virgines sonum
15 vocis pulsu pedum modulantes incesserunt. inde vico
Tusco Velabroque per Bovarium forum in clivum Publi-
cium atque aedem Iunonis Reginae perrectum. ibi duae
hostiae ab decemviris immolatae et simulacra cupressea in
aedem illata.

Military arrangements. Strictness of the levy. *Volones* enrolled.

38 Deis rite placatis dilectum consules habebant acrius
intentiusque, quam prioribus annis quisquam
2 meminerat habitum: nam et belli terror dupli-
catus novi hostis in Italiam adventu, et minus
3 iuventutis erat, unde scriberent milites. itaque
colonos etiam maritimos, qui sacrosanctam vacationem
dicebantur habere, dare milites cogebant. quibus recu-
santibus edixere in diem certam, ut, quo quisque iure
4 vacationem haberet, ad senatum deferret. ea die ad
senatum hi populi venerunt: Ostiensis Alsiensis Antias
Anxurnas Minturnensis Sinuessanus et ab supero mari
5 Senensis. cum vacationes suas quisque populus recitaret,
nullius, cum in Italia hostis esset, praeter Antiatem Ostiensemque vacatio observata est, et earum coloniarum iuniores
iure iurando adacti, supra dies triginta non pernoctaturos se
esse extra moenia coloniae suae, donec hostis in Italia
6 esset. cum omnes censerent primo quoque tempore consulibus eundum ad bellum—nam et Hasdrubali occurrendum
esse descendenti ab Alpibus, ne Gallos Cisalpinos neve
7 Etruriam erectam in spem rerum novarum sollicitaret, et
Hannibalem suo proprio occupandum bello, ne emergere ex
Bruttiis atque obviam ire fratri posset—, Livius cunctabatur,

parum fidens suarum provinciarum exercitibus: collegam 8
ex duobus consularibus egregiis exercitibus et tertio, cui Q.
Claudius Tarenti praeesset, electionem habere; intuleratque
mentionem de volonibus revocandis ad signa. senatus libe- 9
ram potestatem consulibus fecit et supplendi, unde vellent,
et eligendi de omnibus exercitibus, quos vellent permutandi-
que ⟨et⟩ ex provinciis, quo e re publica censerent esse,
traducendi. ea omnia cum summa concordia consulum 10
acta. volones in undevicensimam et vicensimam legiones
scripti. magni roboris auxilia ex Hispania quoque a P. 11
Scipione M. Livio missa quidam ad id bellum auctores
sunt, octo milia Hispanorum Gallorumque et duo milia de
legione militum, equitum mille, mixtos Numidas Hispanos-
que, M. Lucretium has copias navibus advexisse; et 12
sagittariorum funditorumque ad tria milia ex Sicilia C.
Mamilium misisse.

News arrives that Hasdrubal is crossing the Alps. Causes that facilitated his passage.

Auxerunt Romae tumultum litterae ex Gallia allatae ab **39**
L. Porcio praetore: Hasdrubalem movisse ex 2
hibernis et iam Alpes transire; octo milia
Ligurum conscripta armataque coniunctura se
transgresso in Italiam esse, nisi mitteretur in
Ligures, qui eos bello occuparet; se cum
invalido exercitu, quoad tutum putaret, progressurum. hae 3
litterae consules raptim confecto dilectu maturius, quam
constituerant, exire in provincias coegerunt ea mente, ut
uterque hostem in sua provincia contineret neque coniungi
aut conferre in unum vires pateretur. plurimum in eam 4
rem adiuvit opinio Hannibalis, quod, etsi ea aestate transi-
turum in Italiam fratrem crediderat, recordando, quae ipse
in transitu nunc Rhodani nunc Alpium cum hominibus
locisque pugnando per quinque menses exhausisset, haud- 5
quaquam tam facilem maturumque transitum exspectabat;

6 ea tardius movendi ex hibernis causa fuit. ceterum Hasdrubali et sua et aliorum spe omnia celeriora atque
expeditiora fuere. non enim receperunt modo Arverni eum
deincepsque aliae Gallicae atque Alpinae gentes, sed etiam
7 secutae sunt ad bellum. et cum per munita pleraque
transitu fratris, quae antea invia fuerant, ducebat, tum etiam
duodecim annorum adsuetudine perviis Alpibus factis inter
8 mitiora iam transibat hominum ingenia. invisitati namque
antea alienigenis, nec videre ipsi advenam in sua terra
adsueti, omni generi humano insociabiles erant. et primo
ignari, quo Poenus pergeret, suas rupes suaque castella et
9 pecorum hominumque praedam peti crediderant; fama
deinde Punici belli, quo duodecimum annum Italia urebatur,
satis edocuerat viam tantum Alpes esse, duas praevalidas
urbes, magno inter se maris terrarumque spatio discretas,
10 de imperio et opibus certare. hae causae aperuerant Alpes
11 Hasdrubali. ceterum quod celeritate itineris profectum
erat, id mora ad Placentiam, dum frustra obsidet magis
12 quam oppugnat, corrupit. crediderat campestris oppidi
facilem expugnationem esse, et nobilitas coloniae induxerat
eum, magnum se excidio eius urbis terrorem ceteris ratum
13 iniecturum. non ipse se solum ea oppugnatione impediit,
sed Hannibalem post famam transitus eius tanto spe sua
14 celeriorem iam moventem ex hibernis continuerat, quippe
reputantem, non solum quam lenta urbium oppugnatio
esset, sed etiam quam ipse frustra eandem illam coloniam
ab Trebia victor regressus temptasset.

40 Consules diversis itineribus profecti ab urbe velut in
duo pariter bella distenderant curas hominum,
2 simul recordantium, quas primus adventus
Hannibalis intulisset Italiae clades, simul cum illa angeret
cura; quos tam propitios urbi atque imperio fore deos, ut

Anxious forebodings at Rome.

eodem tempore utrubique res publica prospere gereretur?
adhuc adversa secundis pensando rem ad id tempus 3
extractam esse: cum in Italia ad Trasumennum et Cannas
praecipitasset Romana res, prospera bella in Hispania
prolapsam eam erexisse; postea, cum in Hispania alia 4
super aliam clades duobus egregiis ducibus amissis duos
exercitus ex parte delesset, multa secunda in Italia Sicilia-
que gesta quassatam rem publicam excepisse; et ipsum 5
intervallum loci, quod in ultimis terrarum oris alterum
bellum gereretur, spatium dedisse ad respirandum: nunc 6
duo bella in Italiam accepta, duo celeberrimi nominis duces
circumstare urbem Romanam, et unum in locum totam
periculi molem, omne onus incubuisse. qui eorum prior
vicisset, intra paucos dies castra cum altero iuncturum.
terrebat et proximus annus lugubris duorum consulum 7
funeribus. his anxii curis homines digredientes in provincias consules prosecuti sunt. memoriae proditum est 8
plenum adhuc irae in cives M. Livium ad bellum pro-
ficiscentem monenti Q. Fabio, ne, priusquam genus hostium
cognosset, temere manum consereret, respondisse, ubi
primum hostium agmen conspexisset, pugnaturum. cum 9
quaereretur, quae causa festinandi esset, "aut ex hoste
egregiam gloriam" inquit "aut ex civibus victis gaudium
meritum certe, etsi non honestum, capiam."

Successful attack on Hannibal by C. Hostilius Tubulus. Hannibal retires into Bruttium.

Priusquam Claudius consul in provinciam perveniret, 10
per extremum finem agri Larinatis ducentem
in Sallentinos exercitum Hannibalem expeditis
cohortibus adortus C. Hostilius Tubulus in-
composito agmini terribilem tumultum intulit;
ad quattuor milia hominum occidit, novem signa militaria 11
cepit. moverat ex hibernis ad famam hostis Q. Claudius,
qui per urbes agri Sallentini castra disposita habebat. itaque 12

ne cum duobus exercitibus simul confligeret, Hannibal
nocte castra ex agro Tarentino movit atque in Bruttios
13 concessit. Claudius in Sallentinos agmen convertit; Hostilius Capuam petens obvius ad Venusiam fuit consuli
14 Claudio. ibi ex utroque exercitu electa peditum quadraginta milia, duo milia et quingenti equites, quibus consul
adversus Hannibalem rem gereret: reliquas copias Hostilius
Capuam ducere iussus, ut Q. Fulvio proconsuli traderet.

Hannibal moves to Grumentum in Lucania, and is there defeated by Nero.

41 Hannibal undique contracto exercitu, quem in hibernis
aut in praesidiis agri Bruttii habuerat, in
Lucanos ad Grumentum venit spe recipiendi
oppida, quae per metum ad Romanos defecis-
2 sent. eodem a Venusia consul Romanus
exploratis itineribus contendit, et mille fere
3 et quingentos passus castra ab hoste locat. Grumenti
moenibus prope iniunctum videbatur Poenorum vallum;
4 quingenti passus intererant. castra Punica ac Romana
interiacebat campus; colles imminebant nudi sinistro lateri
Carthaginiensium, dextro Romanorum, neutris suspecti,
quod nihil silvae neque ad insidias latebrarum habebant.
5 in medio campo ab stationibus procursantes certamina haud
satis digna dictu serebant. id modo Romanum quaerere
apparebat, ne abire hostem pateretur: Hannibal inde
6 evadere cupiens totis viribus in aciem descendebat. tum
consul ingenio hostis usus, quo minus in tam apertis
collibus timeri insidiae poterant, quinque cohortes additis
quinque manipulis nocte iugum superare et in aversis
7 vallibus considere iubet. tempus exsurgendi ex insidiis et
aggrediendi hostem Ti. Claudium Asellum tribunum militum et P. Claudium praefectum socium edocet, quos cum
8 iis mittebat; ipse luce prima copias omnis peditum equitumque in aciem eduxit. paulo post et ab Hannibale

signum pugnae propositum est, clamorque in castris ad
arma discurrentium est sublatus. inde eques pedesque
certatim portis ruere ac palati per campum properare ad
hostes. quos ubi effusos consul videt, tribuno militum 9
tertiae legionis C. Aurunculeio imperat, ut equites legionis
quanto maximo impetu possit in hostem emittat: ita 10
pecorum modo incompositos toto passim campo se fudisse,
ut sterni obterique, priusquam instruantur, possint. Nondum **42**
Hannibal e castris exierat, cum pugnantium clamorem audivit. itaque excitus tumultu raptim ad hostem copias agit.
iam primos occupaverat equestris terror; peditum etiam 2
prima legio et dextra ala proelium inibat; incompositi
hostes, ut quemque aut pediti aut equiti casus obtulit, ita
conserunt manus. crescit pugna subsidiis et procurrentium 3
ad certamen numero augetur; pugnantesque, quod nisi in
vetere exercitu et duci veteri haud facile est, inter tumultum 4
ac terrorem instruxisset Hannibal, ni cohortium ac mani-
pulorum decurrentium per colles clamor ab tergo auditus
metum, ne intercluderentur a castris, iniecisset. inde pavor 5
incussus et fuga passim fieri coepta est. minorque caedes
fuit, quia propinquitas castrorum breviorem fugam perculsis
fecit. equites enim tergo inhaerebant; in transversa latera 6
invaserant cohortes secundis collibus via nuda ac facili
decurrentes. tamen supra octo milia hominum occisa, 7
supra septingentos capti, signa militaria novem adempta;
elephanti etiam, quorum nullus usus in repentina ac tumultuaria pugna fuerat, quattuor occisi, duo capti. circa 8
quingentos Romanorum sociorumque victores ceciderunt.
postero die Poenus quievit; Romanus in aciem copiis
eductis postquam neminem signa contra efferre vidit, spolia
legi caesorum hostium et suorum corpora collata in unum
sepeliri iussit. inde insequentibus continuis diebus aliquot 9

Hannibal retires into Apulia. Near Venusia he suffers more loss, thence moves to Metapontum, thence to Canusium, closely followed by Nero.

10 ita instituit portis, ut prope inferre signa videretur, donec
Hannibal tertia vigilia crebris ignibus tabernaculisque, quae pars castrorum ad hostes
vergebat, et Numidis paucis, qui in vallo
portisque se ostenderent, relictis profectus
11 Apuliam petere intendit. ubi illuxit, successit vallo Romana acies, et Numidae ex
composito paulisper in portis se valloque ostentavere
frustratique aliquamdiu hostes citatis equis agmen suorum
12 adsequuntur. consul ubi silentium in castris et ne paucos
quidem, qui prima luce obambulaverant, parte ulla cernebat,
duobus equitibus speculatum in castra praemissis postquam
satis tuta omnia esse exploratum est, inferri signa iussit;
13 tantumque ibi moratus, dum milites ad praedam discurrunt,
receptui deinde cecinit multoque ante noctem copias re-
14 duxit. postero die luce prima profectus, magnis itineribus
famam et vestigia agminis sequens haud procul Venusia
15 hostem adsequitur. ibi quoque tumultuaria pugna fuit;
supra duo milia Poenorum caesa. inde nocturnis monta-
nisque itineribus Poenus, ne locum pugnandi daret, Meta-
16 pontum petiit. Hanno inde—is enim praesidio eius loci
praefuerat—in Bruttios cum paucis ad exercitum novum
comparandum missus; Hannibal copiis eius ad suas additis
Venusiam retro quibus venerat itineribus repetit, atque
17 inde Canusium procedit. numquam Nero vestigiis hostis
abstiterat et Q. Fulvium, cum Metapontum ipse profi-
cisceretur, in Lucanos, ne regio ea sine praesidio esset,
arcessierat.

A despatch from Hasdrubal to Hannibal being intercept-

43 Inter haec ab Hasdrubale, postquam a Placentiae obsidione abscessit, quattuor Galli equites, duo Numidae cum litteris ad Hannibalem missi cum per medios hostes totam ferme

ed, Nero determines at once to take the best of his troops and join Livius. His despatch to the Senate.

longitudinem Italiae emensi essent, dum 2
Metapontum cedentem Hannibalem sequuntur, incertis itineribus Tarentum delati a vagis per agros pabulatoribus Romanis ad Q. Claudium propraetorem deducuntur. eum 3
primo incertis implicantes responsis, ut metus tormentorum admotus fateri vera coegit, edocuerunt litteras se ab Hasdrubale ad Hannibalem ferre. cum iis litteris sicut erant 4
signatis L. Verginio tribuno militum ducendi ad Claudium
consulem traduntur; duae simul turmae Samnitium praesidii 5
causa missae. qui ubi ad consulem pervenerunt, litteraeque lectae per interpretem sunt, et ex captivis percunctatio
facta, tum Claudius non id tempus esse rei publicae ratus, 6
quo consiliis ordinariis provinciae suae quisque finibus per exercitus suos cum hoste destinato ab senatu bellum
gereret; audendum ac novandum aliquid improvisum, in- 7
opinatum, quod coeptum non minorem apud cives quam hostes terrorem faceret, perpetratum in magnam laetitiam
ex magno metu verteret, litteris Hasdrubalis Romam ad 8
senatum missis simul et ipse patres conscriptos, quid pararet, edocet, ⟨et⟩ ut, cum in Umbria se occursurum Hasdrubal fratri scribat, legionem a Capua Romam arces-
sant, dilectum Romae habeant, exercitum urbanum ad 9
Narniam hosti opponant. haec senatu scripta. praemissi 10
item per agrum Larinatem Marrucinum Frentanum Praetutianum, qua exercitum ducturus erat, ut omnes ex agris urbibusque commeatus paratos militi ad vescendum in viam deferrent, equos iumentaque alia producerent, ut vehiculorum fessis
copia esset. ipse de toto exercitu civium sociorumque quod 11
roboris erat delegit, sex milia peditum, mille equites; pronuntiat occupare se in Lucanis proximam urbem Puni-

Messengers are sent to the peoples along the line of his intended route.

cumque in ea praesidium velle: ut ad iter parati omnes
12 essent. profectus nocte flexit in Picenum.

Et consul quidem quantis maximis itineribus poterat ad
collegam ducebat relicto Q. Catio legato, qui castris praeesset.

44 What Rome thought of his action (cf. c. 50, §§ 1—5).

Romae haud minus terroris ac tumultus
erat, quam fuerat biennio ante, cum castra
Punica obiecta Romanis moenibus portisque
fuerant. neque satis constabat animis, tam audax iter
2 consulis laudarent vituperarentne; apparebat, quo nihil
iniquius est, ex eventu famam habiturum: castra prope
Hannibalem hostem relicta sine duce, cum exercitu, cui
detractum foret omne quod roboris, quod floris fuerit, et
consulem in Lucanos ostendisse iter, cum Picenum et
3 Galliam peteret, castra relinquentem nulla alia re tutiora
quam errore hostis, qui ducem inde atque exercitus partem
4 abisse ignoraret. quid futurum, si id palam fiat, et aut
insequi Neronem cum sex milibus armatorum profectum
Hannibal toto exercitu velit aut castra invadere praedae
5 relicta sine viribus, sine imperio, sine auspicio? veteres eius
belli clades, duo consules proximo anno interfecti terrebant: et ea omnia accidisse, cum unus imperator, unus
exercitus hostium in Italia esset; nunc duo bella Punica
facta, duos ingentes exercitus, duos prope Hannibales in
6 Italia esse. quippe et Hasdrubalem patre eodem Hamilcare genitum, aeque impigrum ducem, per tot annos in
Hispania Romano exercitatum bello, gemina victoria insignem duobus exercitibus cum clarissimis ducibus deletis.
7 nam itineris quidem celeritate ex Hispania et concitatis ad
arma Gallicis gentibus multo magis quam Hannibalem
8 ipsum gloriari posse: quippe in iis locis hunc coegisse
exercitum, quibus ille maiorem partem militum fame ac
frigore, quae miserrima mortis genera sint, amisisset.

adiciebant etiam periti rerum Hispaniae, haud cum ignoto 9
eum duce C. Nerone congressurum, sed quem in saltu
impedito deprensus forte haud secus quam puerum conscri-
bendis fallacibus condicionibus pacis frustratus elusisset.
omnia maiora etiam vero praesidia hostium, minora sua, 10
metu interprete semper in deteriora inclinato, ducebant.

At a safe distance from the enemy Nero reveals his plan to the soldiers. Their devotion. Enthusiastic reception of the army everywhere.

Nero postquam iam tantum intervalli ab hoste fecerat, **45**
ut detegi consilium satis tutum esset, paucis
milites alloquitur. negat ullius consilium im- 2
peratoris in speciem audacius, re ipsa tutius
fuisse quam suum. ad certam eos se victo- 3
riam ducere: quippe ad quod bellum collega
non ante, quam ad satietatem ipsius peditum
atque equitum datae ab senatu copiae fuissent, maiores
instructioresque, quam si adversus ipsum Hannibalem iret,
profectus sit, eo ipsi si quantumcumque virium momentum addiderint, rem omnem inclinaturos. auditum 4
modo in acie—nam ne ante audiatur, daturum operam
—alterum consulem et alterum exercitum advenisse haud
dubiam victoriam facturum. famam bellum conficere, et 5
parva momenta in spem metumque impellere animos;
gloriae quidem ex re bene gesta partae fructum prope
omnem ipsos laturos; semper quod postremum adiectum 6
sit, id rem totam videri traxisse. cernere ipsos, quo concursu, qua admiratione, quo favore hominum iter suum
celebretur. et hercule per instructa omnia ordinibus viro- 7
rum mulierumque undique ex agris effusorum inter vota
ac preces et laudes ibant: illos praesidia rei publicae,
vindices urbis Romanae imperiique appellabant; in illorum
armis dextrisque suam liberorumque suorum salutem ac
libertatem repositam esse. deos omnes deasque preca- 8
bantur, ut illis faustum iter, felix pugna, matura ex hostibus

victoria esset, damnarenturque ipsi votorum, quae pro iis
9 suscepissent, ut, quem ad modum nunc solliciti prosequerentur eos, ita paucos post dies laeti ovantibus victoria
10 obviam irent. invitare inde pro se quisque et offerre et
fatigare precibus, ut quae ipsis iumentisque usui essent, ab
se potissimum sumerent; benigne omnia cumulata dare.
11 modestia certare milites, ne quid ultra usum necessarium
sumerent; nihil morari, nec ⟨abscedere⟩ ab signis nec subsistere cibum capientes; diem ac noctem ire; vix quod
satis ad naturale desiderium corporum esset, quieti dare.
12 et ad collegam praemissi erant, qui nuntiarent adventum
percunctarenturque, clam an palam, interdiu an noctu
venire sese vellet, isdem an aliis considere castris. nocte
clam ingredi melius visum est.

46 Tessera per castra ab Livio consule data erat, ut tribunus

Arrangements of Livius for receiving Nero's force. Junction of the two armies. Nero urges immediate battle.

tribunum, centurio centurionem, eques equi-
2 tem, pedes peditem acciperet: neque enim
dilatari castra opus esse, ne hostis adventum
alterius consulis sentiret; et coartatio plurium
in angusto tendentium facilior futura erat, quod
Claudianus exercitus nihil ferme praeter arma secum in
3 expeditionem tulerat. ceterum in ipso itinere auctum
voluntariis agmen erat, offerentibus ultro sese et veteribus
militibus perfunctis iam militia et iuvenibus, quos certatim
nomina dantes, si quorum corporis species roburque virium
4 aptum militiae videbatur, conscripserat. ad Senam castra
alterius consulis erant, et quingentos ferme inde passus
Hasdrubal aberat. itaque cum iam appropinquaret, tectus
montibus substitit Nero, ne ante noctem castra ingrederetur.
5 silentio ingressi, ab sui quisque ordinis hominibus in tentoria
abducti, cum summa omnium laetitia hospitaliter excipiuntur. postero die consilium habitum, cui et L. Porcius

Licinus praetor adfuit. castra iuncta consulum castris 6
habebat, et ante adventum eorum per loca alta ducendo
exercitum, cum modo insideret angustos saltus, ut transitum
clauderet, modo ab latere aut ab tergo carperet agmen,
ludificatus hostem omnibus artibus belli fuerat; is tum in
consilio aderat. multorum eo inclinabant sententiae, ut, 7
dum fessum via ac vigiliis reficeret militem Nero, simul et
ad noscendum hostem paucos sibi sumeret dies, tempus
pugnae differretur; Nero non suadere modo, sed summa 8
ope orare institit, ne consilium suum, quod tutum celeritas
fecisset, temerarium morando facerent; errore, qui non 9
diuturnus futurus esset, velut torpentem Hannibalem nec
castra sua sine duce relicta aggredi, nec ad sequendum se
iter intendisse. antequam se moveat, deleri exercitum
Hasdrubalis posse redirique in Apuliam. qui prolatando 10
spatium hosti det, eum et illa castra prodere Hannibali et
aperire in Galliam iter, ut per otium, ubi velit, Hasdrubali
coniungatur. extemplo signum dandum et exeundum in 11
aciem abutendumque errore hostium absentium praesen-
tiumque, dum neque illi sciant cum paucioribus nec hi cum
pluribus et validioribus rem esse. consilio dimisso signum 12
pugnae proponitur, confestimque in aciem procedunt.

Hasdrubal becoming aware of the arrival of Nero refuses battle and retreats towards the Metaurus.

Iam hostes ante castra instructi stabant. moram pugnae 47
attulit, quod Hasdrubal, provectus ante signa
cum paucis equitibus, scuta vetera hostium
notavit, quae ante non viderat, et strigosiores
equos; multitudo quoque maior solita visa est.
suspicatus enim id, quod erat, receptui propere 2
cecinit ac misit ad flumen, unde aquabantur, ubi et excipi
aliqui possent et notari oculis, si qui forte adustioris coloris
ut ex recenti via essent; simul circumvehi procul castra 3
iubet specularique, num auctum aliqua parte sit vallum, et

4 ut attendant, semel bisne signum canat in castris. ea cum
ordine omnia relata essent, castra nihil aucta errorem faciebant: bina erant, sicut ante adventum consulis alterius
fuerant, una M. Livi, altera L. Porci, neutris quicquam,
5 quo latius tenderetur, ad munimenta adiectum. illud
veterem ducem adsuetumque Romano hosti movit, quod
semel in praetoriis castris signum, bis in consularibus
referebant cecinisse. duos profecto consules esse, et quo-
nam modo alter ab Hannibale abscessisset, cura angebat.
6 minime id, quod erat, suspicari poterat, tantae rei frustratione Hannibalem elusum, ut, ubi dux, ubi exercitus esset,
7 cum quo castra collata habuerit ignoraret; profecto haud
mediocri clade absterritum insequi non ausum; magno
opere vereri, ne perditis rebus serum ipse auxilium venisset
Romanisque eadem iam fortuna in Italia quae in Hispania
8 esset. interdum litteras suas ad eum non pervenisse credere, interceptisque iis consulem ad sese opprimendum
accelerasse. his anxius curis extinctis ignibus vigilia prima
9 dato signo, ut taciti vasa colligerent, signa ferri iussit. in
trepidatione et nocturno tumultu duces parum intente ad-
servati, alter in destinatis iam ante animo latebris subsedit,
alter per vada nota Metaurum flumen tranavit. ita desertum
ab ducibus agmen primo per agros palatur, fessique aliquot
somno ac vigiliis sternunt corpora passim atque infre-
10 quentia relinquunt signa. Hasdrubal, dum lux viam osten-
deret, ripa fluminis signa ferri iubet; et per tortuosi amnis
sinus flexusque cum errorem volvens haud multum proces-
sisset, ubi prima lux transitum opportunum ostendisset,
11 transiturus erat. sed cum, quantum a mari abscedebat,
tanto altioribus coercentibus amnem ripis non inveniret
vada, diem terendo spatium dedit ad insequendum sese
hosti.

[XXXVI—LI. B.C. 207. *Arrival of Hasdrubal. The Metaurus.*]

The consuls follow and overtake him. The battle of the Metaurus.

Nero primum cum omni equitatu advenit, Porcius 48
deinde adsecutus cum levi armatura. qui cum 2
fessum agmen carperent ab omni parte incur-
sarentque, et iam omisso itinere, quod fugae
simile erat, castra metari Poenus in tumulo super fluminis
ripam vellet, advenit Livius peditum omnibus copiis non 3
itineris modo, sed ad conserendum extemplo proelium
instructis armatisque. sed ubi omnes copias coniunxerunt, 4
derectaque acies est, Claudius dextro in cornu, Livius ab
sinistro pugnam instruit, media acies praetori tuenda data.
Hasdrubal omissa munitione castrorum postquam pugnan- 5
dum vidit, in prima acie ante signa elephantos locat, circa
eos laevo in cornu adversus Claudium Gallos opponit, haud
tantum iis fidens, quantum ab hoste timeri eos credebat;
ipse dextrum cornu adversus M. Livium sibi atque Hispanis 6
—et ibi maxime in vetere milite spem habebat—sumpsit;
Ligures in medio post elephantos positi. sed longior quam 7
latior acies erat; Gallos prominens collis tegebat. ea frons, 8
quam Hispani tenebant, cum sinistro Romanorum cornu
concurrit; dextra omnis acies extra proelium eminens
cessabat; collis oppositus arcebat, ne aut a fronte aut ab
latere aggrederentur. inter Livium Hasdrubalemque ingens 9
contractum certamen erat, atroxque caedes utrimque edebatur. ibi duces ambo, ibi pars maior peditum equitumque
Romanorum, ibi Hispani, vetus miles peritusque Romanae 10
pugnae, et Ligures, durum in armis genus. eodem versi
elephanti, qui primo impetu turbaverant antesignanos et
iam signa moverant loco; deinde crescente certamine et 11
clamore impotentius iam regi et inter duas acies versari,
velut incerti, quorum essent, haud dissimiliter navibus sine
gubernaculo vagis. Claudius "quid ergo praecipiti cursu 12
tam longum iter emensi sumus?" clamitans militibus, cum

in adversum collem frustra signa erigere conatus esset,
13 postquam ea regione penetrari ad hostem non videbat
posse, cohortes aliquot subductas e dextro cornu, ubi
stationem magis segnem quam pugnam futuram cernebat,
14 post aciem circumducit et non hostibus modo sed etiam
suis inopinantibus in sinistrum hostium latus incurrit; tanta-
que celeritas fuit, ut, cum ostendissent se ab latere, mox
15 in terga iam pugnarent. ita ex omnibus partibus, ab fronte,
ab latere, ab tergo, trucidantur Hispani Liguresque, et ad
16 Gallos iam caedes pervenerat. ibi minimum certaminis
fuit: nam et pars magna ab signis aberant, nocte dilapsi
stratique somno passim per agros, et qui aderant, itinere
ac vigiliis fessi, intolerantissima laboris corpora, vix arma
17 umeris gestabant; et iam diei medium erat, sitisque et
calor hiantes caedendos capiendosque adfatim praebebat.
49 Elephanti plures ab ipsis rectoribus quam ab hoste interfecti. fabrile scalprum cum malleo habebant; id, ubi
saevire beluae ac ruere in suos coeperant, magister, inter
aures positum, ipso in articulo, quo iungitur capiti cervix,
2 quanto maximo poterat ictu adigebat. ea celerrima via
mortis in tantae molis belua inventa erat, ubi regentes
sprevissent, primusque id Hasdrubal instituerat, dux cum
3 saepe alias memorabilis, tum illa praecipue pugna. ille
pugnantes hortando pariterque obeundo pericula sustinuit,
ille fessos abnuentesque taedio ac labore nunc precando
nunc castigando accendit, ille fugientes revocavit omissam-
4 que pugnam aliquot locis restituit; postremo, cum haud
dubie fortuna hostium esset, ne superstes tanto exercitui
suum nomen secuto esset, concitato equo se in cohortem
Romanam immisit. ibi, ut patre Hamilcare et Hannibale
fratre dignum erat, pugnans cecidit.

5 Numquam eo bello una acie tantum hostium interfectum

The losses on both sides.

est, redditaque aequa Cannensi clades vel
ducis vel exercitus interitu videbatur. quin- 6
quaginta sex milia hostium occisa, capta quinque milia et
quadringenti; magna praeda alia cum omnis generis tum
auri etiam argentique. civium etiam Romanorum, qui 7
capti apud hostes erant, supra quattuor milia capitum
recepta; id solacii fuit pro amissis eo proelio militibus.
nam haudquaquam incruenta victoria fuit: octo ferme
milia Romanorum sociorumque occisa; adeoque etiam 8
victores sanguinis caedisque ceperat satietas, ut postero
die, cum esset nuntiatum Livio consuli Gallos Cisalpinos
Liguresque, qui aut proelio non adfuissent aut inter caedem
effugissent, uno agmine abire sine certo duce, sine signis,
sine ordine ullo aut imperio; si una equitum ala mittatur,
posse omnes deleri: "supersint" inquit "aliqui nuntii et 9
hostium cladis et nostrae virtutis."

Nero returns to his own camp in five days. Reception of the news and revulsion of feeling in Rome.

Nero ea nocte, quae secuta est pugnam ⟨profectus⟩, cita- 50
tiore quam inde venerat agmine die sexto ad
stativa sua atque ad hostem pervenit. iter 2
eius frequentia minore, quia nemo praecesse-
rat nuntius, laetitia vero tanta, vix ut compotes
mentium prae gaudio essent, celebratum est.
nam Romae neuter animi habitus satis dici enarrarique 3
potest, nec quo incerta exspectatione eventus civitas fuerat,
nec quo victoriae famam accepit. numquam per omnes 4
dies, ex quo Claudium consulem profectum fama attulit, ab
orto sole ad occidentem aut senator quisquam a curia atque
ab magistratibus abscessit aut populus e foro; matronae, 5
quia nihil in ipsis opis erat, in preces obtestationesque
versae, per omnia delubra vagae suppliciis votisque fatigare
deos. tam sollicitae ac suspensae civitati fama incerta 6
primo accidit duos Narnienses equites in castra, quae in

faucibus Umbriae opposita erant, venisse ex proelio, nun-
7 tiantes caesos hostes. et primo magis auribus quam animis
id acceptum erat, ut maius laetiusque, quam quod mente
capere aut satis credere possent, et ipsa celeritas fidem
8 impediebat, quod biduo ante pugnatum dicebatur. litterae
deinde ab L. Manlio Acidino missae ex castris adferuntur
9 de Narniensium equitum adventu. hae litterae per forum
ad tribunal praetoris latae senatum curia exciverunt; tantoque certamine ac tumultu populi ad fores curiae concursum
est, ut adire nuntius non posset, sed traheretur a percunc-
tantibus vociferantibusque, ut in rostris prius quam in
10 senatu litterae recitarentur. tandem summoti et coerciti
a magistratibus, dispensarique laetitia inter impotentes eius
11 animos potuit. in senatu primum, deinde in contione
litterae recitatae sunt; et pro cuiusque ingenio aliis iam
certum gaudium, aliis nulla ante futura fides erat, quam
legatos consulumve litteras audissent.

51 Ipsos deinde adpropinquare legatos allatum est. tum
enim vero omnis aetas currere obvii, primus quisque oculis
2 auribusque haurire tantum gaudium cupientes. ad Mulvium
3 usque pontem continens agmen pervenit. legati—ii erant
L. Veturius Philo P. Licinius Varus Q. Caecilius Metellus
—circumfusi omnis generis hominum frequentia in forum
4 pervenerunt, cum alii ipsos, alii comites eorum, quae acta
essent, percunctarentur. et ut quisque audierat exercitum
hostium imperatoremque occisum, legiones Romanas inco-
lumes, salvos consules esse, extemplo aliis porro impertie-
5 bant gaudium suum. cum aegre in curiam perventum
esset, multo aegrius summota turba, ne patribus misce-
6 retur, litterae in senatu recitatae sunt. inde traducti in
contionem legati. L. Veturius litteris recitatis ipse planius
omnia, quae acta erant, exposuit cum ingenti adsensu,

postremo etiam clamore universae contionis, cum vix gaudium animis caperent. discursum inde ab aliis circa templa 7
deum, ut grates agerent, ab aliis domos, ut coniugibus
liberisque tam laetum nuntium impertirent. senatus, quod 8
M. Livius et C. Claudius consules incolumi exercitu ducem
hostium legionesque occidissent, supplicationem in triduum
decrevit. eam supplicationem C. Hostilius praetor pro
contione edixit, celebrataque a viris feminisque est; omnia- 9
que templa per totum triduum aequalem turbam habuere,
cum matronae amplissima veste cum liberis, perinde ac si
debellatum foret, omni solutae metu deis immortalibus
grates agerent. statum quoque civitatis ea victoria movit, 10
ut iam inde haud secus quam in pace res inter se contrahere vendendo, emendo, mutuum dando argentum credi-
tumque solvendo auderent.

Nero's brutal announcement of the news to Hannibal. Hannibal retires into Bruttium.

C. Claudius consul cum in castra redisset, caput Has- 11
drubalis, quod servatum cum cura attulerat,
proici ante hostium stationes captivosque Afros
vinctos, ut erant, ostendi, duos etiam ex iis
solutos ire ad Hannibalem et expromere, quae
acta essent, iussit. Hannibal, tanto simul 12
publico familiarique ictus luctu, agnoscere se fortunam
Carthaginis fertur dixisse; castrisque inde motis, ut omnia 13
auxilia, quae diffusa latius tueri non poterat, in extremum
Italiae angulum Bruttios contraheret, et Metapontinos, civi-
tatem universam, excitos sedibus suis, et Lucanorum qui
suae dicionis erant in Bruttium agrum traduxit.

NOTES

CHAPTER 1

Page 2

§ 1. **hic status rerum**, 'such was the position of affairs.' After a rather rambling history of the war in Italy and Sicily in B.C. 210 Livy had given, in the concluding chapters of Book 26 (41–51), an account of P. Scipio's brilliant capture of New Carthage ending with the despatch of C. Laelius to Rome in charge of the Carthaginian prisoners. See Introduction I. The history of the war in Spain is resumed at Chapter 17 of this book.

Salapia, a small town in Apulia, north of Cannae. Hannibal selected it as his winter quarters in 214 B.C. (Bk 24. 20 *hibernis placebat locus*). Earlier in the present year one of the leading citizens, Blattius, plotted successfully to hand over the town and its Numidian garrison to Marcellus. See 26. 38. 6–14.

Marmoreas et Meles, mentioned only here. From the large amount of provisions captured in them they were obviously important depots.

§ 2. **ad tria milia**. See n. on c. 8. 12.

aliquantum, 'a considerable quantity.' Cp. c. 15. 4.

modium, genitive plural. The older form of the genitive plural in *-um* remained in use alongside the ordinary *-orum* form in a number of words, chiefly technical terms of law, religion, or commerce (e.g. *socium, triumvirum, deum, talentum*). In most of these the form in *-orum* also occurs. For the retention of archaic forms we may compare the diction of the English Law Courts and Church Service.

§ 3. **ceterum**, a favourite word in Livy and affected also by Sallust, but not by Cicero or Caesar. Originally an accusative of respect 'as to the rest,' it easily passed into its use (1) as resumptive conjunction after a parenthesis or digression, like Greek δ'οὖν, 'be that as it may,' 'however' (cp. French *du reste*); (2) with adversative force =*sed* (cp. the development of Greek ἀλλά). That some feeling of the original meaning of *ceterum* remained even when it became a fully developed conjunction, is seen from the fact that in the vast majority of cases it stands at the beginning of the sentence, and examples of the type *longius ceterum commodius* (22. 2. 2) are comparatively rare.

tantum quanta, 'the joy caused by this success was more than counterbalanced (by the gloom occasioned) by a serious disaster to the Roman arms....' *gaudium* is compared, by a slight confusion of thought, not to the *tristitia* resulting from the *clades* but to the *clades* itself. This compressed type of comparison (*comparatio compendiaria*) is common in Latin and Greek. It appears in a variety of forms, the most frequent being that in which something belonging to one person or thing (an action, quality, etc.) is compared to another person or thing or *vice versa*: e.g. Hom. *Il.* 17. 51 κόμαι χαρίτεσσιν ὁμοῖαι, Iuv. 3. 73 *sermo promptus et* Isaeo *torrentior.*

procul, 'far from.' Earlier prose writers use *procul ab.*

Herdonea or *Herdonia*, a town in Apulia, mod. Ordona.

§ 4. **Cn. Fulvius.** See Introduction I.

posita...firmata agree with *castra.*

praesidiis, 'entrenchments,' 'redoubts' (not 'troops'), cp. Tac. *Ann.* 4. 49. 2 *obsidium coepit* per praesidia, *quae opportune iam muniebat.*

§ 5. **spes ea**, 'this hope' = *spes ex ea re.* The *quod* clause explains the source of the hope. *spes ea* would more naturally mean *spes de ea re* or *spes eius rei* (i.e. *recipiendae Herdoneae*). Cp. for the use of the pronoun, 21. 5. 2 *quo metu* = *cuius rei metu*, 2. 21. 6 *eo nuntio* = *eius rei nuntio.* It looks as though Livy had tried to cram too much into his sentence and that what he meant was *augebat spem eam quod ...senserat et spes ea augebat neglegentiam.*

iis, dative of personal interest, lit. 'for them.' Usually it may be translated by a possessive, '*their* loyalty was wavering'; cp. 29. 29. 6 *militanti pro Carthaginiensibus in Hispania pater* ei *moritur* ('he lost his father'). Similarly, *infra*, c. 17. 16 *productae in conspectum* iis, Terence, *Phorm.* 1053 *quod* tuo viro *oculi doleant.*

adversus, 'to' (not in its more usual signification 'against'), cp. 28. 27. 8 *sic me non solum* adversus socios *gesseram sed etiam* adversus hostes.

in Bruttios, 'to the (country of the) Bruttii.' Greek Βρέττιοι. The name of the people is used for the district, for which there was not a special name in classical Latin. So Livy regularly says *Lucani* not *Lucania.*

§ 6. **ea...delata.** See n. on. c. 5. 14.

ita...ut, *ita* looks forward to *magnis itineribus contendit.*

acie instructa, 'in fighting formation'; cp. c. 45. 3 *instructiores.*

§ 7. **sinistra ala.** *ala* means here 'contingent of *socii.*' Originally designed to guard the flanks of the legion, the divisions of the allied troops were hence called 'right and left wings.' For the same reason *ala* is also the name applied to the cavalry of the legion. Fabius kept half his army in reserve, the sixth legion and the *dextra ala* forming the second line (§ 11). Instead of the earlier practice of forming the different lines within the legion (*hastati, principes, triarii*), whole legions now formed the first or second line. Cp. c. 2. 7, c. 12. 14, c. 42. 2 *prima legio et dextra ala proelium inibat,* 25. 21. 6 *prima legio et sinistra ala in primo instructae.*

§ 8. **signo dato ut.** *signum dare,* 'give a signal (for action),' usually implies an order, hence it is followed by an *ut* clause like *imperare*; cp. c. 27. 2. Similarly *auctor est ut* on analogy of *suadet ut* in c. 20. 1.

pugnantium. The text is doubtful. For variant readings see Notes on the Text. From § 7 and § 11 it is clear that when Hannibal gave the order the 5th legion and the left wing were engaged, and that the 6th legion and the right wing were in reserve. The latter would lie between the rear of the fighters (*terga pugnantium*) and the cavalry who rode round. Therefore if Livy wrote *pugnantium* we must suppose that his description—as so frequently with battles—is confused, and that by *pedestres acies* he means the whole of the infantry (as opposed to the cavalry) and in *pugnantium* includes the reserve infantry on the Roman side as well as those he has told us were already engaged. Then *cum occupassent,* etc., would mean 'when the infantry *had their attention entirely occupied* with the conflict they were actually engaged in,' i.e. *oculos animosque* refer to the subject of *occupassent.* To express this we should rather expect *oculi animique occupati* (cp. 26. 46. 4 *intenti omnium non animi solum fuere, sed etiam oculi auresque pugnantium spectantiumque*). Of the various conjectures, Gronov's *terga trepidantium* best explains the MS. reading *oppidantium,* since *tergatrepidantium* would readily become *tergapidantium. spectantium* would make Livy's account consistent and is supported by the parallel passage 26. 46. 4, but it is difficult to see why a scribe should have altered it. I am inclined to think that Livy wrote *certamine ⟨omnium⟩ oculos animosque, circumvecti pars castra hostium, pars terga pugnantium invaderent.*

§ 9. in Fulviis, 'remarking scornfully on the similarity of name in the case of the two Fulvii.' See Notes on the Text. As the regular construction with *increpare* is accusative of the person or thing inveighed against, *in Fulviis* seems the best reading. *in Cn. Fulvi*, however, would also be Latin, in spite of Madvig, cp. 1. 51. 1 *in regem... increpans*. For *in*=in the case of, cp. c. 34. 10, 5. 36. 9 *in tantae nobilitatis viris*.

Cn. Fulvium praetorem. In 212 B.C., in the third consulship of Q. Fulvius Flaccus, Cn. Fulvius Flaccus was praetor in Apulia and sustained, according to the account given in Livy, a severe defeat near Herdonea. See Bk 25. c. 21, where Livy remarks on his *stultitia* and *temeritas*.

devicerat. Livy says that out of 18,000 soldiers only 2000 escaped. Fulvius made off on horseback with a band of cavalry, leaving his army to its fate. Suspicion has been cast on the story of the first defeat of Herdonea. The account of the impeachment of Cn. Fulvius for his conduct (26. 2. 7) gives a materially different story, and the battle is not mentioned in other historians. It is therefore supposed that it is a 'doublet' invented to match the defeat in 210 B.C.

§ 10. comminus acie, 'in hand to hand fight.' *et peditum certamine* is explanatory of *comminus acie*, cp. Virg. *Aen.* 12. 516 *Lycia missos et Apollinis agris*. *Comminus*, an adverb derived from *com-manus*, probably a nominative case originally like *rursus* (=*re-vorsus*), is here used attributively with the substantive *acie*. This use of adverbs or adverbial phrases with a substantive is a favourite construction in Livy, cp. 21. 36. 4 *per invia circa*. The adverb is usually placed between an adjective and substantive, e.g. c. 30. 3 *tutas* circa *stationes*, c. 40. 1 *duo* pariter *bella*, 6. 39. 6 *nullo* publice *emolumento*, 5. 20. 1 *omnibus* ante *bellis*. Livy's free use of this construction may perhaps be due to the influence of the Greek use of an adverb or prepositional phrase with the article, ὁ τότε, οἱ ἐν τῇ πόλει, τὰ ἔξω, etc. Cicero has occasional instances; cp. *Pro Caecin.* 43 *neque conflictu corporum neque* ictu comminus *neque coniectione telorum*.

PAGE 3

ordines signaque, 'the maniples and their standards stood fast,' i.e. the ranks were unbroken; cp. c. 14. 7. The *signa* served to mark out the divisions of the companies in the legion and were thus of importance for the preservation of the formation in carrying out any movement; cp. the very frequent military phrases *signa statuere*, 'halt,' *s. inferre*, 'attack,' *s. referre*, 'retreat,' *s. convertere*, 'wheel,' and many others.

equestris tumultus=*tumultus equitum*, cp. c. 42. 2 *equestris terror*. *tumultus* 'commotion,' 'disturbance.' In the military sphere the word is used generally of any uproar or confused or irregular fighting (c. 42. 1 *excitus tumultu*) and more specifically of an outbreak in Gallia Cisalpina (*Gallicus tumultus*) or other pacified region (c. 24. 6 *Etrusco tumultu*). Thus Cicero distinguishes *tumultus* from *bellum* in *Phil.* 8. 1. 2 (quoted by L. and S. on *tumultus*) *itaque maiores nostri tumultum Italicum quod erat domesticus; tumultum Gallicum, quod erat Italiae finitimus, praeterea nullum nominabant*. But Livy extends the usage, cp. 41. 6. 1 *Istrico tumultu* and 41. 6. 5 *in Sardinia magnum tumultum esse*.

a tergo...a castris. Military expressions such as *a tergo*, *a fronte*, *a latere* show the origin of the use of the ablative of source with *a* giving the direction or point of view from which. Thus in this passage we might translate 'from the rear,' 'from the camp,' but usually we render the *a* by 'on,' 'in,' 'at,' 'on the side of,' e.g. c. 26. 4 *a terra* 'on the land side.' Latin expresses the direction from which the action proceeds, English the point at which the action takes place. So a te *stat*, 'he is on your side,' Plin. *Ep.* 6. 2. 2 *si* a petitore *esset acturus*, 'on the side of the plaintiff.'

ante, bracketed by Mdg. on the ground that *ante—deinde* for *primum—deinde* is not paralleled in Classical Latin. *Ante* may have crept in from a gloss on *prior*. In any case it is redundant with *prior*.

§ **11**. **ad prima signa.** *ad* is normally coupled with an accusative of the terminus, but when the idea of motion in the verb is weakened or disappears, the sense readily approximates to that of an accusative of extent and *ad*, 'at,' is nearly equal to *apud*; cp. *ad forum*, 'at the market.' *ad* in the sense of 'near to,' 'at,' is very common with names of places; cp. c. 2. 1 *ad Herdoneam*. The *prima signa* were the standards of the front division. On the march the standards were carried in front of their companies, but in battle apparently they were in the rear of the first division. The front ranks are spoken of as *ante signa*, cp. 5. 18. 8, and see notes on c. 18. 2 and c. 47. 1.

avertit, 'put to flight,' cp. c. 14. 11, 9. 39. 9 averti *manipuli quidam*; more fully, 26. 44. 4 averterunt...*in fugam hostes*. In c. 25. 14 *averso Locris bello* the word is used of raising a siege.

§ **12**. **et ipse,** 'himself also.' Cicero usually writes *ipse quoque*.

et, 'also,' is very common in Livy and later historians. In Cicero and Caesar it is much more restricted, being confined to a few combinations like *simul et*, *sed et*.

undecim, i.e. all but one, as there were six tribunes in each legion.

§ **13**. **alibi**=*apud alios*. For the use of the local adverb for persons cp. c. 34. 12 *eodem* (=*in eundem*), 2. 2. 5 *unde* (=*a quo*), Virg. *Aen.* 1. 21 *hinc populum...venturum* (=*ab hoc*).

§ **14**. **mansuram**, sc. *esse*. In the direct form the sentence would run *defectura* fuit (or *defecisset*, 'would have revolted') *nec manebit...si hinc abscesseris*.

CHAPTER 2

§ **1**. **nihil admodum**, 'not particularly.' *nihil admodum* generally means 'nothing at all' (=*admodum nihil*). *admodum* is literally 'up to the limit,' hence 'fully,' 'quite,' 'very.' With negatives it may either qualify ('not quite,' 'not very') or strengthen ('not at all') the statement. The former is the rarer usage and is often overlooked. Naturally in many passages with negatives the context is not decisive as to which force *admodum* has. For the qualifying or limiting use cp. 40. 59. 2 *nullam pecuniam admodum*, 'as good as none,' Cic. *De Fin.* 1. 1 *non admodum indoctis* (=*haud ita indoctis*). Similarly in Greek οὐ πάνυ may be a qualified negative ('not quite'), or an unqualified negative ('not at all'=πάνυ οὐ), but οὐδὲν πάνυ and οὐδεὶς πάνυ seem always to be unqualified negatives.

ad Herdoneam, 'in the neighbourhood of H.' Cp. n. on c. 1. 11. *ad* in this sense may be used of a large area; e.g. 24. 11. 3 *ad Picenum*=*in agro Piceno*.

§ **2**. **ceterum**, adversative; cp. n. on c. 1. 3. *duce atque exercitu amisso* is contrasted with *eundem se ire*.

contuderit, 'smashed,' cp. c. 12. 11 *ferociam contunderent*.

post Cannensem pugnam. See Bk 23. c. 16 and 24. c. 17. M. Marcellus was one of the praetors in the year of Cannae, 216 B.C., and was sent with one legion to Apulia to gather the remnants of Varro's army. He took up a position above Suessula about 10 miles from Capua and then at Casilinum, and when Hannibal advanced against Nola, Marcellus drove him back with loss. In the following year (215 B.C.) he again checked Hannibal at Nola. For 214 B.C. he was elected consul with

Fabius and, according to Livy's account, repulsed a third attempt of Hannibal on Nola.

ire...facturum. *facturum* is infinitive not participle. For the asyndeton of the two clauses and the combination of present and future infinitive cp. c. 6. 5 *intercessuros...facere.* With *eo* and its compounds the use of the vivid present for the future is common; cp. the frequent Plautine *iam redeo,* 'I shall be back presently,' and the regular usage of εἶμι in Attic as a future.

§ **3.** **et...quidem** commonly introduces a new point in antithetic form and so is usually followed by *sed,* cp. c. 34. 2.

§ **4.** **Numistronem.** Numistro lay on the borders of Apulia.

loco plano, local ablative. The use without a preposition, apart from names of towns and small islands and some phrases like *terra marique,* is restricted in the best prose to a few words with an adjective in agreement. *Loco* and *locis* are common. Livy extends the list considerably and uses these local ablatives rather freely, even when they are not accompanied by an adjective, e.g. 5. 41. 2 medio *aedium sedere.* See also n. on c. 8. 6.

§ **5.** **addidit et aliam,** 'gave a further proof of his confidence.' *speciem praebere* with genitive of the participle is the usual phrase. *et aliam,* 'another also'; cp. c. 4. 9 *et alios,* c. 18. 6 *et altera* and see n. on c. 1. 3.

detractavit, sc. *certamen.*

ut, 'when.'

portis, sc. *castrorum.*

tamen, i.e. though both generals were confident, *yet* they took due precautions.

cornu in collem erigeret, 'extended his right wing up the slope of a hill.' For the use of *erigeret* cp. *agmen erigere* (2. 31. 5, Tac. *Agr.* 18), 'march an army uphill.' So in c. 48. 12 *in adversum collem signa erigere.*

PAGE 4

§ **6.** **ab Romanis,** 'on the Roman side.' See n. on c. 1. 10.

ab Romanis...acti, explanatory of *primae acies.* The appositional clauses make the sentence clumsy and when he gets to the elephants Livy seems on the point of losing sight of his construction and making a new sentence *acti sunt.* In any case *diu stetit* does not form a very neatly expressed conclusion to *cum ad noctem pugnam extendissent.*

There would have been a distinct gain in clearness had Livy written, as some earlier edd. suggest, *diu pugna neutro inclinata stetit. ab hora tertia cum...acti, primae...subiit*, making *subiit* the conclusion of the *cum...extendissent* clause and taking *ad noctem* as 'towards nightfall.' With the order of the clauses as we have them, it seems necessary to adopt Madvig's insertion of *ut* (which might easily drop out after the similar ending of *stetit*) in order to avoid an awkward asyndeton at *novum*.

pugna stetit, 'the battle stood' or 'hung.' *stare* is used of an evenly balanced or hotly contested combat, cp. 33. 18. 15 *diu* anceps *pugna* stetit, 7. 7. 7 *primo* stetit ambigua spe *pugna*. The metaphor in *stare*, therefore, is probably, like that in *inclinata*, from the scales of a balance. On the other hand it is possible that it is a transference of the ordinary sense of *stare* (cp. § 9) from the fighters to the battle, cp. 26. 44. 4 *primo haud impares stetere acies*, 22. 47. 4 *pugna, primo et viribus et animis par, dum constabant ordines*.

§ **8**. **ex iam segni**, "the fight which had begun to slacken was rekindled into new and fierce vigour by the sudden accession of fresh spirit and fresh strength" (Stephenson). *ex* is used of the change from one state to another, like Greek ἐξ, cp. 6. 23. 5 *cunctatorem ex acerrimo bellatore factum*. The adverb *iam* is incorporated in the phrase without the usual participle (*iam segni* facto), cp. 2. 6. 2 *ex tanto* modo *regno*, Plin. *Ep.* 1. 2. 2 *temptavi enim imitari Demosthenen* semper *tuum*, *Calvum* nuper *meum*. See n. on c. 1. 10.

incerta victoria, abl. of circumstances, 'with the result undecided,' cp. 9. 25. 6 *incerta pace*.

§ **9**. **in multum diei**, 'till well on in the day.' *in* or *ad multum diei* occurs frequently, e.g. 10. 32. 6, 22. 45. 1, cp. 10. 28. 2 in *quam maxime* serum diei. The use of the neuter adjective with a 'partitive' genitive is very free in Livy. He seems to be the first writer who uses it, as here, dependent on a preposition, and he extends the construction to adjectives other than those of quantity, so that the genitive ceases to be very distinctly partitive. See an excellent note by Prof. W. B. Anderson on 9. 3. 1 *adversa montium*.

§ **10**. **silentio**, abl. of manner, equivalent to an adverb. In classical Latin this abl. is regularly accompanied by an adjective except in the case of a few words like *ratione, consuetudine*, cp. c. 5. 10 *ordine*.

vestigiis institit sequi, 'pressed closely on his tracks.' *insistere* with the infinitive is frequent in Livy in the sense of 'set about.' It also takes the dative ('press upon'), cp. c. 13. 4 *fugientibus institistis*, and we find it so construed with *vestigiis*, e.g. 25. 33. 9 *vestigiis abeuntium insistebat*. In c. 12. 9 we have *vestigiis instabat*, 'pressed on his tracks,' and most of the examples of *insistere* with the infinitive in Livy are in the perfect tense *institit*, which, as far as form goes, might be from *instare*. In the present passage *vestigiis* combined with the infinitive construction must of course be ablative. Cp. c. 37. 14 *Iugario vico*, 6. 32. 10 *prope vestigiis sequeretur*, and the use of *via venire*. The ablative is local, but it is so close to the instrumental meaning ('by way of') that it provides a good illustration of the syntactic overlapping by which (among other causes) it came about that the Romans were content in most instances with a single *form* for expressing instrumental and local relations; cp. n. on c. 13. 13 *viribus*.

§ 11. ad Venusiam, 'near Venusia,' cp. n. on § 1. **adeptus est** 'he came up with him,' cp. Lucr. 5. 634 *omnia signa hanc adipiscuntur*; 'reach' is the original meaning of the word.

ab stationibus procursaretur. *procursaretur* is impersonal, 'skirmishing was carried on between the pickets.' *ab stationibus* may be taken as '*from* the pickets (on either side)' or '*by* the pickets.' The former is better, cp. c. 41. 5 *ab stationibus procursantes*. *stationes* is used here in the usual military sense of 'outposts' or 'pickets' in front of an encampment, or concretely 'the men forming the pickets.' It is also commonly used of guards or sentries (*custodes*) set on walls or at gates; cp. c. 15. 12, 5. 48. 6.

tumultuosa. Cp. n. on c. 1. 10.

ferme, 'very nearly.' *ferme* is a superlative of *fere* formed with *-mo-* suffix like *summus* and probably derived from the same root as *firmus* and *fretus*, the idea being that of 'holding fast' or 'close.' For its use with numerals like Gk μάλιστα, cp. c. 15. 2, c. 34. 5.

§ 12. explorato, impersonal ablative absolute. This use of the ablative passive participle becomes common in Livy, e.g. *auspicato, conpecto, litato, audito*, etc. He extends the construction to adjectives, cp. 28. 17. 14 *haud cuiquam* dubio *quin hostium essent*, 28. 36. 12 incerto *quid...peterent*. Where there is a dependent clause following (e.g. *edicto ne..., impetrato ut...*) it may be regarded as the subject, but in other cases the participle becomes practically equivalent to an adverb, cp. *merito, consulto, inproviso* (c. 5. 8), etc.

CHAPTER 3

§ 1. **Flaccus,** Q. Fulvius Flaccus, consul the third time in 212 B.C. and prolonged in command at Capua in 211 B.C. and 210 B.C. He was now there with an army of one legion formed out of two, cp. Bk 26. c. 28. *Flaccus* is out of construction in the principal sentence. It is thrown forward out of the subordinate clause of which it is subject in order to draw attention to the transition to a new theme. Cp. c. 16. 3, c. 17. 1.

bonis vendendis. The punishment inflicted on the Capuans in 211 B.C. was very severe. Livy gives details in Bk 26. c. 34; cp. § 11 *Senatorum omnium quique magistratus Capuae, Atellae, Calatiae gessissent, bona venire Capuae iusserunt.*

agro qui publicatus, cp. 26. 16. 8 *ager omnis et tecta publica populi Romani facta.* The business of letting State lands was usually managed by the Censors, and in the following year this *ager Campanus* was actually let by them, cp. c. 11. 8. Probably, therefore, the arrangements made by Flaccus were incomplete or for temporary occupancy only.

frumento, ablative of price. The rent was to be paid in kind. This was not the usual practice.

ne...deesset. What is really a result is put by Livy as though it were a purpose. Stephenson says "the thought underlying the final clause seems to be a recognition of a divine purpose in misfortunes." But we need hardly read so much into the *ne* clause. In English the same substitution of a final clause for a cause of consequence is quite common, e.g. 'that nothing might be wanting to complete their misery, it began to rain.'

novum, 'yet another.' The fire is called *novum* in reference to the previous one at Rome, supposed to be due to Capuan conspirators, see Bk 26, c. 27, and n. on c. 12. 16.

in occulto. The substantival use of the neuter singular of the adjective in prepositional phrases occurs very frequently in Livy, usually to express temporal or local relations. Phrases with *in* and *ex* are especially common; cp. *in medio, in secreto, in publico, ex occulto, ex composito, per altum, pro dubio, ab alto, de integro,* etc., etc. The usage is an old one, cp. *in oquoltod, in poplicod, in preivatod* on *Senatus consultum de Bacchanalibus.*

protractum, lit. 'dragged forth,' i.e. 'brought to light.'

§ **2.** **simul ut...simul metuens.** The tendency to couple dissimilar expressions for the sake of variety, which is so marked a characteristic of the style of Tacitus, is well developed in Livy also; cp. c. 16. 6, c. 40. 1, 9. 46. 14 *simul concordiae causa, simul ne... comitia essent,* 22. 23. 10 *simul castris praesidio et circumspectans.*

PAGE 5

tecta militariter, 'soldiers' huts,' 'huts constructed in camp fashion.' The adverb may be construed with *tecta,* see n. on c. 1. 10 *comminus acie.* Substantival participles like *tecta* readily retain their verbal nature in this way, cp. 5. 47. 7 *perperam facto,* 'a wrong deed.'

§ **3.** **alimentis,** dative of purpose, with *facta* understood from the previous clause, 'as if purposely made for fuel.' See n. on c. 6. 15.

§ **4.** **principibus Blossiis,** 'headed by the Blossii.'

qui in noxa erant, 'all who were guilty.' *noxa* (cp. *noceo*) 'harm,' 'injury,' had its meaning extended in two ways (1) harm (subjectively), i.e. 'crime,' 'guilt' (=*culpa*), (2) harm inflicted on the guilty, i.e. 'punishment' (=*poena*), cp. the similar extension of meaning in *malum* ('punishment') and in English 'ill.'

§ **5.** **acriter,** i.e. with torture.

aeris, 'of copper,' i.e. 'asses'; so frequently, cp. 1. 43. 1 etc. It is not necessary to understand *assium* as dependent on *aeris.* In English in the same way we speak of 'a copper' meaning 'one penny.' Originally the *as* weighed 12 ounces (*as libralis*) and there are specimens extant weighing nearly that amount. At this period it weighed only one ounce (having been reduced to this weight in 217 B.C. by the *Lex Flaminia minus solvendi*) and from 88 B.C. onwards only half an ounce. The last two changes are generally attributed to the political crises after Trasimene and the Social War, but the history and causes of the earlier reductions have long been a puzzle to scholars. Many have assumed that the successive reductions from 1 lb. were also due to State bankruptcy. The explanation is rather to be sought in the substitution of a silver for a bronze standard. The *as* came to represent merely a certain amount of silver and thus became, like our copper (and silver) coins, merely *token* money, and consequently the reduction in weight was of no importance save as making the coins less cumbrous. The first silver was coined at Rome in 268 B.C., but it appears that Rome had issued silver from a mint at Capua at a much earlier date.

§ **6.** **Acerris...Nuceria,** towns in Campania, both taken by Hannibal after Cannae, see Bk 23. cc. 15 and 17. Nuceria was a place of some importance on the Appian Way. It also was rebuilt later.

§ **7.** **Atellam...Calatiam.** These places had revolted along with Capua and surrendered after the fall of that city. See 26. 16. 5. They shared her fate. Atella is noted in literary history as the birthplace of the fabula Atellana, a species of rude farce popular at Rome about the time of Sulla.

§ **8.** **nunc...nunc,** common in Livy and subsequent writers for the classical *modo...modo*, 'at one time...at another,' cp. c. 39. 4.

Tarentinae...arcis. The Roman garrison still held the citadel and supplies could be introduced by sea. See Introduction I. and note on c. 15. 5.

excidit, rather Perfect than Historic Present.

§ **9.** **de exercitu urbano.** In the disposition of the armies there were regularly two legions, with the usual contingent of *socii*, reserved for guarding Rome. When necessary they were ordered out for service elsewhere.

in praesidium, 'as guard to escort it.' This use of *in* to express purpose is an easy extension of its ordinary use denoting destination; cp. the frequent use of *ad* in a final sense, c. 41. 4 *ad insidias*, 21. 23. 3 *decem milia peditum ad praesidium obtinendae regionis data.*

CHAPTER 4

§ **1.** **aestas.** This word has caused difficulty. At this period the *comitia consularia* were normally held in January and the consuls entered on office on the Ides of March. It is objected that *aestas* could hardly be said to be *in exitu* when January was close at hand, and it does not suit the whole context to suppose that the elections were held unusually early this year, for, as Wb. points out, the year was already far advanced when Laevinus had reached Sicily, cp. 26. 40. 1. But *aestas* in the sense of 'season of the summer campaign' may be used loosely. Cicero more than once, writing in December, uses the phrase *aestivis confectis* in reference to operations extending almost to the end of the year, cp. *ad Att.* 5. 21. 6. And for a similar continuance of the campaign up to the time of the consular elections, cp. 25. 2. 3 *comitiorum consularium iam adpetebat tempus, sed quia consules bello intentos avocare non placebat*, etc.

e re publica, 'to the public advantage.' *ex* in phrases of this kind originally expresses the standard from which a thing is judged, cp. *e re mea*, 'to my interest,' *ex animi tui sententia*, etc. This is closely connected with the modal use seen in adverbial phrases, *ex vano* 'groundlessly' (c. 25. 15), *ex insperato* (1. 25. 9), etc., expressing the circumstances out of which an action or feeling arises.

abscedi, impersonal passive. **vestigium**, accusative of extent, 'a step.' Cp. Plaut. *Aul.* 56 si *hercle tu ex istoc loco* digitum transversum aut unguem latum *excesseris*.

§ **2. curam iniecerant ne**, 'had made them anxious lest they should either have to call away...or else...' *ne aut...aut* emphasises the dilemma in which the authorities found themselves.

res agentem, 'prosecuting the war' (i.e. =*res gerentem*). *res agere* is usually applied to the transaction of public business by an official.

in annum, 'for the following year'=*in proximum annum*.

PAGE 6

§ **3. quamquam esset.** The subjunctive is here due to the oblique. The indicative is normal in *quamquam* clauses, but the subjunctive begins to become frequent in Silver Latin. Certain instances in Livy are scarce, cp. 45. 17. 7 quamquam...mitterentur...*tamen in senatu quoque agitata sunt summa consiliorum*.

§ **5. Syphace**, Prince of the Western Numidians. In Book 24, c. 48 Livy relates the beginning of his friendship with Rome. In 213 B.C. he was at war with Carthage (*subito Carthaginiensibus hostis factus*) and P. and Cn. Scipio sent envoys to encourage him to persevere in his efforts. For his subsequent history see Bk 28. cc. 17, 18, Bk 30. c. 3.

§ **6. imperatores.** Livy regularly speaks of the two Scipios as *imperatores* (e.g. 25. 32. 1, 25. 37. 9). *Imperator* technically means (1) one invested with *imperium*, (2) a general greeted with the title by his soldiers after a victory. The title *imperator* in the first sense apparently belonged properly to P. Scipio only, at least it is nowhere mentioned that Cn. Scipio had the *imperium*. Livy applies the term *imperator* to Cn. Scipio alone in 26. 2. 6, and he may there refer to the period that elapsed between the death of the proconsul and that of Cn. Scipio. See also n. on c. 19. 4.

voluisse, indirect of *voluit*=ἠθέλησε, 'he resolved.'

§ **7. sed et ipse.** See n. on c. 1. 12.

§ 8. **pondo**, 'by weight,' sc. *libris*, an old ablative, the only case which survives of the second declension noun *pondus*. *libra* is regularly omitted in such expressions, just as in English we say 'hundred (sc. pound) weight,' and *pondo* comes to be treated as an indeclinable substantive in neut. plural, cp. c. 10. 12 *quingena* pondo *consulibus data*, or singular, 34. 52. 5 *auri* pondo fuit *tria milia septuaginta* 'there was a weight of....' See note on § 9.

§ 9. **protinus**, 'straightway,' from *pro-tenus*, 'stretching forward' or 'a stretch forward.' It has also the meaning 'straight on,' i.e. 'continuously,' cp. 6. 28. 2.

terna pondo, 'three pounds each in weight.' *terna pondo* is treated as a nominative plural neuter in apposition to *paterae*. In c. 10. 13 *pondo* is treated as neuter singular.

§ 10. **Ptolomaeum**, Ptolemy IV, Philopator. See n. on c. 30. 4.

M'. = Manius. It stands for ΛΛ/, an old five-barred form of the letter found in various Greek alphabets and used in early times in Rome.

commemorandam, 'to recall memory of.' The treaty mentioned was made with Ptolemy Philadelphus in 273 B.C. It is included in the Summary of Book 14. An alliance with Egypt was of importance to Rome on account of the corn supply.

pallam pictam, 'an embroidered cloak.' *palla* was a large wrap worn out of doors by ladies over the *stola*. *Amiculum* or *amictus* appears to be the name of a second mantle thrown over the *palla*. See Becker's *Gallus*, *Excursus* on Dress.

§ 11. **prodigia**. The *prodigia* which occupy a considerable portion of Livy's narrative are of very various kinds. Some resemble medieval (or modern) 'miracles' (*infra* § 14 *signa sanguine multo...sudasse*) or 'silly season' stories (§ 13 *in mari...angues magnitudinis mirae lascivientium piscium modo exsultasse*). Not a few are mistaken descriptions of actual occurrences which modern science explains as due to natural causes, e.g. a river or lake flowing with blood or rain of blood or flesh. Others again are perfectly ordinary phenomena, e.g. places struck by lightning, or, as here, a lamb born *cum ubere lactenti*. Others are quite trivial occurrences, such as birds deserting their nests (§ 12) or mice gnawing articles in a temple (c. 23. 2). Many are cases of physiological monstrosities (30. 2. 11 a foal with five legs) which are frequently exaggerated (§ 14 pig with human head, c. 11. 5 boy with elephant's head). Livy usually contents himself with reporting these various *prodigia* as he found them recorded in the annalists.

cum ubere lactenti. This is not an uncommon phenomenon in the young of sheep and pigs. For *cum* see n. on § 14.

tecto nudatum, 'stripped of its roof,' lit. 'laid bare from its roof,' ablative of separation.

§ 12. **diem ac noctem,** 'for a day and a night,' cp. 24. 17. 7. *die ac nocte* means 'by night and day.'

ad Compitum Anagninum, 'at Cross-roads near Anagnia,' i.e. he spot near Anagnia where the *via Latina* was crossed by another *via* leading from Rome to Labicum. *Compita* is usually plural. Varro explains it as a place *ubi viae competunt.* For *ad* see n. on c. 1. 11. In c. 23. 7 *compita* refers to the chapels of the Lares Compitales built at cross-ways.

PAGE 7

§ 14. **cum ore humano,** 'with human face' (not 'with human utterance'). The ablative of quality normally has no preposition but unnatural qualities are regarded as detached and regularly have the *cum* (cp. 31. 12. 7 *agnus cum suillo capite,* Plaut. *Aul.* 554 *quingentos coquos cum senis manibus*) which is used of external addition, *cum dolabra, cum vestibus,* etc.

Fĕroniae, an ancient Italian or Etruscan goddess, probably of fertility. *Primitiae frugum* were offered to her (cp. 26. 11. 9). If the word is Italic in origin it may be connected with *fero.* Fairs were held at the festivals in the groves dedicated to her cult. The most famous of these was the grove here mentioned, lying at the foot of Mt Soracte near Capena in Etruria.

signa, 'statues.'

§ 15. **hostiis maioribus,** full-grown victims as opposed to *lactentes,* cp. 22. 1. 15 *ut ea prodigia partim maioribus hostiis partim lactentibus procurarentur.*

procurata, 'expiated by sacrifice.' *procurare* is the technical word used for the performance of rites to avoid the evils supposed to be portended by *prodigia. curare* is sometimes used in the same sense. Only those *prodigia* which occurred within the Roman sphere and on public property or on the sea were regarded as *publica prodigia.*

pontificum. In ordinary cases the *pontifices* looked after the atonement ceremonies. Sometimes, where their books and the Sibylline books did not provide a remedy, *haruspices* were summoned from Etruria, cp. c. 37. 6.

diem unum, acc. of extent, with *supplicatio*, instead of the more usual *in diem unum* dependent on the verb, cp. c. 7. 4. Wb. quotes 39. 22. 4 *addita unum diem supplicatio est.*

ad omnia pulvinaria. The *pulvinaria* were cushioned couches of the gods. At the *lectisternium* the statues of the gods were placed upon six couches, two upon each, and tables with food were put before them.

CHAPTER 5

§ 1. **L. Cincio**, cp. Bk 26. c. 28. L. Cincius Alimentus, famous as one of the earliest Roman historians. In his *Annals* of the Second Punic war he wrote of his own personal experiences. Livy does not appear to have used his *Annals* directly. See Introduction II.

§ 2. **decem navibus.** In military phrases the sociative ablative does not require *cum*, though with numbers *cum* is usually added. Even with verbs like *profectus*, ships, like soldiers, may be regarded as instruments.

§ 3. **prope sexaginta**, 54 years, from the outbreak of the First Punic war in 264 B.C.

provinciam confecisse, 'reduced to complete subjection.' Before Laevinus' arrival over 60 Sicilian towns were in revolt against Rome. After the fall of Agrigentum six of these were taken by the Romans and all the rest were either betrayed or surrendered. Laevinus then compelled the Sicilians to devote themselves to corn-growing in order to supply Rome and Italy; see Bk 26. c. 40.

§ 4. **neminem Siculum qui** = *neminem Siculorum eorum qui.* Cp. Sall. *Iug.* 35 *unus ex eo numero qui...erant.* For Madvig's conjectural rearrangement of the text see Notes on the Text.

afuerint, represents *afuerunt* of the direct speech. For the use of primary tenses in oblique see n. on c. 9. 3.

suos, emphatic, 'their own,' cp. c. 35. 4 *sua omnia.*

§ 5. **frugiferam**, cp. Pind. *Nem.* 1. 14 f. ἀριστεύοισαν εὐκάρπου χθονὸς Σικελίαν πίειραν.

fidissimum, 'most reliable.' Along with Egypt and Sardinia Sicily remained one of the main supports of the Roman corn supply.

§ 6. **Muttine.** Muttines was a halfcaste Carthaginian officer sent by Hannibal to Sicily in 212 B.C. He was a man of great ability (*vir impiger et sub Hannibale magistro omnis belli artes edoctus*, 25. 40. 5), and proved a most successful leader of Numidian cavalry. Hanno's jealousy deprived him of his command in 210 B.C. and when Laevinus advanced on Agrigentum Muttines betrayed the city to him. He had now come with Laevinus to Rome to receive the reward of his treachery.

§ 7. **ex auctoritate patrum.** See n. on c. 6. 6. *patrum auctoritas* technically meant the nominal sanction of the patrician part of the Senate given beforehand to acts of the *comitia.* See also n. on c. 11. 8.

ad plebem. This should mean the *concilium plebis* in which originally only plebeians voted, but owing to the fact that after the Lex Hortensia in 287 B.C. the distinction between the *comitia tributa* and the *concilium plebis* seems to have become merely formal, Livy confuses the two bodies and uses the word *plebs* to refer to tribe assemblies.

§ 8. **M. Valerius,** sc. *Messala,* cp. § 1.

PAGE 8

§ 9. **mortalibus,** 'persons.' *Mortalis* occurs fairly commonly in the sense of *homo,* especially in Sallust; cp. *nemo mortalis* in Plautus = 'no mother's son.'

tramisit, 'he crossed over.' *tramisit* is reflexive in force, cp. c. 29. 7 *consul cum classe...in Africam* tramisit; similarly *traicit* frequently = *se traicit* (c. 7. 16, 28. 16. 12). This reflexive use is especially common in military language, cp. *recipere = se recipere, dirigere = se dirigere,* and n. on c. 43. 12. On the interchange of 'transitive' and 'intransitive' verbs see n. on c. 27. 13.

tertio decumo die quam for *tertio decumo post die quam*; *quam* after an expression of time is commonly used in the sense of *postquam,* cp. c. 7. 1, 21. 15. 3 *quinto deinde mense quam ab Carthagine profectus sit,* 3. 8. 2 *tertio die quam interregnum inierat.* In this construction the ablative is best explained as instrumental, giving the 'measure of difference.' Others take it as locatival ablative of time within which.

§ 10. **ordine.** See n. on c. 2. 10.

§ 11. **Masinissa,** son of the king of the Eastern Numidians. He would be about 30 years old at this time. Two years previously, in 212 B.C., he was in Spain commanding the Numidian cavalry on the Carthaginian side; see 26. 34. 1, where Livy describes him as *iuvenis eo tempore socius Carthaginiensium, quem deinde clarum potentemque Romana fecit amicitia.* It was in 206 B.C. after the defeat of the Carthaginian generals at Silpia that he came over to the Roman side. See 28. 16. 11.

Carthagine, locative.

per totam Africam means no doubt Africa Propria, the dominions of Carthage, and also the northern part generally, including Mauretania and Numidia.

§ **12. primo quoque tempore**, 'at the earliest possible moment,' 'as soon as possible.' In this phrase the sense of distribution or succession regularly given by *quisque* with superlatives and ordinals is lost and 'at each first opportunity (as it comes)' comes to mean 'at the first opportunity (whenever it is).' Usually *primus quisque* means 'all the first,' i.e. 'one after another,' 'in succession.' See also n. on c. 51. 1 *omnis aetas currere obvii, primus quisque oculis auribusque haurire tantum gaudium cupientes.*

in eo, i.e. the successful junction of Hasdrubal and Hannibal.

se credere, *se* refers to Valerius Messala and *scripsit* or a similar verb is to be understood from *perscripta* (*sunt*) § 10.

§ **13. traiecturam.** See n. on § 9 *tramisit* and contrast § 11 *qui...traicerentur.*

§ **14. haec recitata**, 'the recital of this news.' This use of a past participle passive with a substantive or pronoun equivalent to a verbal substantive with a dependent genitive or to a substantive clause ('the fact that...') is particularly common and free in Livy; cp. c. 44. 5 *consules interfecti*, 'the death of the consuls,' c. 47. 4 *castra nihil aucta*, 'the fact that the camp was not enlarged,' 2. 20. 2 *ut cuius familiae decus eiecti reges erant*, etc. The present and future participle occurs less frequently in this construction. We have an instance with the gerundive in 2. 13. 2 *moverat eum subeunda dimicatio*, 'the prospect of having to face a conflict.' A similar construction is much more common in Greek than is generally supposed, cp. Hdt. 1. 46 *τὰ μὲν Περσέων πρήγματα αὐξανόμενα πένθεος μὲν Κροῖσον ἀπέπαυσε*, Thuc. 1. 6. 2, 4. 29. 3 *καὶ αὐτῷ ἔτι ῥώμην καὶ ἡ νῆσος ἐμπρησθεῖσα παρέσχε.*

movere, perfect, not historic infinitive; cp. c. 7. 3 *maxime movit.*

dictatore comitiorum habendorum causa, cp. Bk 25. c. 2, when both consuls were *bello intenti* in 213 B.C.

§ **15. illa disceptatio** = *disceptatio de illa re*; see n. on c. 1. 5.

in Sicilia goes with *dicturum.*

eum autem in Italia terminari, 'the title Roman land did not apply to land outside Italy' (whether it was in the possession of Rome or not). *ager Romanus* meant strictly the original territory of Rome and regularly the consul was recalled to Rome for the naming of a dictator, but by a legal fiction the term was extended; cp. c. 29. 5 where Crispinus who is lying wounded at Capua is ordered *si ad comitia venire Romam non posset, dictatorem in agro Romano diceret comitiorum causa.*

§ **16. tribunus...consuleret,** sc. *senatum.* It appears that the tribunes had the right to call a meeting of the Senate and bring motions forward in it; cp. Varro, quoted by Gellius 14. 8. 2, *nam et tribunis plebis senatus habendi ius erat, quamquam senatores non essent, ante Atinium plebiscitum.* When and how they received these powers is obscure. It is clear that the summoning of the Senate was normally confined to the consuls and in their absence to the praetor urbanus, and that it was only in exceptional cases that the tribunes exercised their right. In 216 B.C. Livy mentions a case of a tribune bringing forward a motion in the Senate (22. 61. 7).

decrevit ut, etc. This action was of course unconstitutional. Neither Senate nor Comitia had the right of interfering with the consul's choice. The case of Fabius's appointment by the Comitia in 217 B.C. after Trasimenus was different. It was a substitution of *creatio* by the Assembly for *dictio* by the consul, not an interference with the choice of the consul.

populum rogaret, i.e. in the Comitia.

praetor, sc. *urbanus.* He was the representative of the consuls in their absence, but it is not clear that he had the right of naming the dictator. Cicero indeed says (*ad Att.* 9. 15. 3) *consules roget praetor vel dictatorem dicat, quorum neutrum ius est.*

ad plebem. See n. on § 7. Livy calls the assembly *plebis concilium* in § 18.

§ **17. quod suae potestatis esset,** 'a thing which lay entirely in his own hands'; cp. c. 51. 13 *qui suae dicionis erant.*

PAGE 9

§ **18. censuerunt ut...diceret quem p. iussisset** as compared with § 16 *diceret ut eum quem p. iussisset, dictatorem diceret* illustrates well the inadequacy of the Latin subjunctive for representing the tenses of the indicative in oblique. *iussisset* in § 16 represents *iusserit* (fut. perf.) of the *recta* while in § 18 it represents *iussit.* The context makes this quite clear here, but sometimes the ambiguity remains.

§ **19. a M. Claudio.** When last mentioned (c. 2. 12 and c. 4. 1) Marcellus was following Hannibal in Apulia. Where he was when he nominated the dictator we are not told. It must in any case have been *in agro Romano.*

CHAPTER 6

§ **1. C. Calpurni praetoris.** Calpurnius had been urban praetor in 211 B.C. and had gone on as propraetor in Etruria. See Bk 26. c. 28; for *praetor=pro praetore* cp. 22. 57. 1.

§ **2. in quem diem primum potuit,** i.e. on the first following day on which *comitia* might be held, cp. 25. 2. 4 *primo comitiali die,* 24. 7. 11 *in eum quem primum diem comitialem habuit. Dies festi* and *dies nefasti* were excluded. It is not certain whether at this period the rule that notice must be given 17 days (*trinundinum*) beforehand was in existence. For the attraction of *diem* into the relative sentence cp. 25. 17. 3 *uti ea quae ante dicta prodigia sunt procuraret* and 24. 7. 11 quoted above.

§ **3. Galeria iuniorum**=*centuria iuniorum Galeriae tribus.* The *century* that voted first was called *praerogativa.* It was chosen by lot. Consequently its decision was thought to indicate the will of heaven, and it seems to be the fact that the result was regularly in accordance with its vote, though Cicero may be exaggerating when he says (*Pro Plancio* 20) that *no candidate* who had carried the *centuria praerogativa* ever failed to be elected. Originally the 18 centuries of knights voted first (1. 43. 11 *equites vocabantur primi*). It would appear that in the reorganised *comitia centuriata* the tribe was the basis of division, each tribe containing 5 classes and 10 centuries, and that the *praerogativa centuria* was drawn by lot from the centuries of the first class in the various tribes. In the cases where the *praerogativa* is mentioned it is regularly the *centuria iuniorum,* cp. 24. 7. 12, 26. 22. 13. *Galeria* was one of the rustic tribes.

eodem, adverb with *inclinassent,* 'in the same direction.'

iure vocatae. *iure,* 'in regular order,' as opposed to *sorte.*

§ **4. neque...et,** like οὔτε...τε in Greek, cp. c. 10. 4, 30. 37. 10 *de pace quam nec iniqua et necessaria esset.*

neque satis civile, 'contrary to republican principles.' *civile,* 'what is fitting for a citizen.'

multo foedioris exempli, cp. 3. 72. 2 *orare ne pessimum facinus* *peiore exemplo admitterent iudices*: 'it was an undemocratic proceeding to keep a man in office year after year and the thing became far more scandalous when the man in question had charge of the election.'

§ 5. **nomen...acciperet.** The presiding magistrate at elections had power to disqualify candidates. *Nomen accipere* was the technical expression for allowing a candidate to be voted for. Similarly *rationem habere*='consider a man as candidate,' 'permit his candidature.' Cp. *ne ratio absentis habeatur* in the famous instance where Caesar in 49 B.C. wanted to stand for the consulship while in Gaul without laying down his command.

praeterquam, 'except.' *praeter* ('past,' 'beyond,' hence 'excluding,' 'except') contains a comparative idea, which is enhanced when, as here, we have a comparative word like *alius*, and we get *quam* added, just as in Greek we find πλὴν ἤ e.g. Plato, *Apol.* 42 A ἄδηλον παντὶ πλὴν ἢ τῷ θεῷ. Cp. the use of *praeterquam quod* (c. 34. 10) and *superquam quod.* We might regard the sentence here as a combination of *aliorum praeter ipsum* and *aliorum quam ipsius*, though the later construction in positive sentences is post classical. A comparison, especially where there is a negative, seems to be the most difficult type of statement for a language to keep within decent logical limits. Redundancy and contamination run riot. Greek with its 'sentimental' redundant negatives, Sanskrit with its difficulty in making a comparison in any but the simplest way, English with its dialectal 'better nor,' its Shakespearian double comparatives, its journalese 'equally as well as,' etc., etc., all illustrate this. See also notes on c. 17. 14, c. 44. 3, c. 48. 5.

intercessuros...non facere. For the tenses see n. on c. 2. 2. *non facere* in the direct speech would be *non facimus*.

§ 6. **causam comitiorum,** 'the case of the elections,' i.e. the procedure in the elections, a curious extension of the legal *causam tutari*, as though the *comitia* were on trial.

auctoritate senatus, *not* in the technical sense of a resolution passed by the Senate but vetoed by a tribune, but, as frequently, equivalent to *senatus consultum*, cp. the non-technical use of *ex auctoritate patrum* in c. 5. 7. The decree is that implied in c. 5. 18 *censuerunt ut.*

§ 7. **namque** refers to *exemplis*; cp. the similar use of γάρ in Greek.

§ 8. **in eam rem,** 'bearing upon this point,' cp. Plaut. *Most.* 99 *argumenta dum dico ad hanc rem.*

vetus...**recens**, in distributive apposition to *exempla*, cp. 29. 2. 5 *cornua dextrum*...*laevum*, Hom. *Od.* 12. 73 f. οἱ δὲ δύω σκόπελοι ὁ μὲν... τὸν δ' ἕτερον. See Notes on the Text.

Postumi Megelli, in 291 B.C.

interrex. In cases where the consuls' year of office had come to an end before the election of new consuls, an *interrex* was nominated by the Senate for five days.

Q. Fabi, in 215 B.C. See 24. 9. 3.

Page 10

bono publico, 'involving the public advantage,' 'to the advantage of the public interest,' an ablative expressing accompanying circumstances as result. *publicum* occurs frequently as a substantive with *bonum*, *malum*, *pessimum*, *optimum*; cp. 2. 1. 3, 2. 44. 3, Varro *R. R.* 1. 13. 7 *villis pessimo publico aedificatis*, Gell. 7. 3. 17 *quicquid optimum esse publicum existimabant*. Others take *bono* as substantive and *publico* as adjective.

nisi fieret may stand for *nisi fieret* of the direct speech, but I think it is rather the oblique of *nisi fit*, 'unless it is a thing which is done to the advantage of the state,' i.e. a general protasis with nothing implied as to fulfilment and not directly related to the apodosis, which implies non-fulfilment. A similar combination in English would be: 'unless it is generally rougher on this side of the channel than on the other side, he would not have crossed in such a small boat.'

sisset=*sivisset*, cp. c. 40. 4 *delesset*=*delevisset*. The ready dropping of *v* between two vowels in Latin is cited as one of the many pieces of evidence that show that its pronunciation was not like English *v* but like English *w*.

§ **9**. **censuisset**, indirect for *censuerit* (fut. perf.).

eo...**staretur**, 'that they should abide by whatever the senate decided.' With *stare* in this sense ('be content with,' 'abide by') the instrumental ablative is the regular construction but *in* with the locatival ablative also occurs. For the former cp. 28. 45. 7, 34. 22. 13, 3. 36. 8 *decreto stetisse*, Cic. *Tusc.* 2. 63 *eius iudicio stare nolim*.

§ **10**. **expertos**, 'tried,' 'experienced.'

non placere, historic infinitive. The origin of this common construction remains a puzzle in spite of all that has been written on the subject. The view in antiquity was that there is an ellipse of *coepit*, etc. Cp. Quintil. 9. 3. 58 'stupere gaudio Graecus.' *simul enim auditur* '*coepit*'; but to understand *coepit* would in hosts of instances give a wrong meaning to the historic infinitive. Modern suggestions that it was originally an imperatival infinitive or that it was really a 3rd plur. perf. in the 1st conjugation (e.g. *laudare*=a contracted form of *laudavere*) extended to the sing. and by analogy to the other conjugations, are equally or more unsatisfactory.

§ **11.** **quintum...quartum.** The accusative is one of extent. In specifying the number of consulships above two the adverbial accusative of the ordinal is the accepted usage, but the Romans themselves hesitated between this form and the locatival ablative in *-o*. For the interchange of *primum* and *primo* see n. on c. 14. 7. Aulus Gellius has an amusing story about Pompey's doubt whether he should inscribe on his theatre *consul tertium* or *consul tertio*. After consulting all the best scholars and finding them divided in opinion he finally appealed to Cicero and was advised to write *consul tert.*! Later restorers of the inscription evaded the difficulty also by writing *consul III*. The five consulships of Fabius were in B.C. 233, 228, 215, 214, 209.

§ **12.** **in annum,** see n. on c. 4. 2.

§ **13.** **extremo,** substantival use of adjective=*exitu*. See n. on c. 3. 1.

classis traiecta, pass. of *classem traiecit* which is not so freq. as *classis traiecit*. See n. on c. 5. 9.

§ **14.** **Olbiensem...Caralitanum.** The territory of Olbia lay on the N.E. and that of Caralis on the S. coast of Sardinia.

§ **15.** **suffectique,** sc. *novi*, cp. 26. 33. 7, or *alii in eorum locum*. Properly the priests were elected by cooption, cp. 40. 42. 11 *pontifex in locum eius a collegio cooptatus Flaccus*, but Livy frequently uses *factus* and *suffectus* loosely for *cooptatus*; similarly *creatus*, 25. 2. 2 *pontifices suffecti...augur creatus*.

T. Otacili Crassi. He had died at the end of the previous year, but his place had not been filled up at once. See Bk 26. c. 23.

decemvir sacris faciundis, or *decemvir sacrorum*. This board had charge of the Sibylline books, cp. 10. 8. 2 *carminum Sibyllae ac fatorum populi huius interpretes*. *Sacris faciundis* is dative of purpose, often called dative of 'work contemplated.' This dative occurs most frequently in this gerundival construction in technical phrases specifying the sphere of an official, or with *comitia*, *dies*, etc., e.g. *tresviri coloniae deducendae*, *comitia censoribus creandis*. Livy uses it more freely, cp. notes on c. 3. 3, c. 42. 13.

item. Two priesthoods were frequently held by the same man, e.g. *pontifex* and *augur* (30. 26. 10 *nam duo sacerdotia habuit*), *pontifex* and *decemvir sacris faciundis* (40. 42. 11). Similarly priestly and civil offices were combined, e.g. *pontifex* and *censor* (§ 17), *flamen* and *praetor* (37. 50. 8).

§ **16.** **rex sacrorum**, or *rex sacrificulus*, 'sacrificial king,' an old title surviving from the days of kingship. On the abolition of the monarchy the priestly functions of the king were carried out by this official who retained the kingly title and held the office for life. His wife was called *regina*. The duties of the office were trivial.

maximus curio. This official presided over the 30 *curiones* who had the superintendence of the religious rites of the *curiae*. He was elected in the *comitia tributa*, cp. c. 8. 1.

neque may have slight adversative force, 'but not,' as freq., cp. 9. 46. 2 *cum...fieri se pro tribu aedilem videret neque accipi nomen*, or it may mean 'also...not' referring to the similar delay in the previous year, cp. 30. 3. 3 *nec Scipio ullo tempore hiemis belli opera remiserat*.

§ **17.** **Crassum**, cp. c. 5. 19. **ex aedilitate.** He was elected to the curule aedileship in 212 B.C. over the heads of Q. Fulvius Flaccus and T. Manlius Torquatus. See 25. 5. 4. Livy there remarks that for 120 years previously there had been only one instance of a man being elected *pontifex maximus qui sella curuli non sedisset*, and election to the censorship before the consulship was equally rare.

PAGE 11

§ **18.** **diremit**, 'interrupted,' 'stopped,' sc. *censuram*.

et, 'also.' See n. on c. 1. 3.

§ **19.** **ludos Romanos.** The *ludi Romani* were at the outset probably *ludi votivi*, i.e. games held at irregular times to fulfil vows of generals, and afterwards became established as annual games, held in September under the presidency of the Curule Aediles. In 6. 42. 12 they are called *ludi maximi* and they are first called *ludi Romani* apparently in 8. 40. 2, if we except 1. 35. 10, where their first institution is described, *Romani magnique varie appellati*.

diem unum instaurarunt. *instaurare* is used of the repetition of any ceremony the celebration of which had been vitiated by some religious informality. Cases of *instauratio ludorum* occur very frequently. In 2. 36. 1 f. Livy tells what the vitiating circumstance was which gave rise to the repetition. The number of days on which repetition took place is usually expressed by the numeral adverb *semel*, *bis*, *ter*, etc. (*septiēns* being the highest number recorded, 33. 25. 1, 29. 11. 12). *per biduum*, *per triduum* occur also and *biduum* alone like *diem unum* here. If the whole performance is repeated *toti* is added. We find this combined with *semel* (28. 10. 7), with *ter* (30. 50. 2, 31. 4. 7 and often), with *quinquiens* (38. 35. 6).

ex multaticio, 'money from fines,' cp. 10. 23. 13 *ex multaticia item pecunia quam exegerunt pecuariis damnatis.* The word occurs frequently in Livy and is regularly applied to the money fines exacted by the plebeian aediles. We find *multaticus* in inscriptions in the same sense, e.g. Q. A. [C]aidicio Q. f. T. Rebinio Q. f. aidile moltatico. For the formation cp. *adoptaticius*, *emissicius*, *suppositicius*, *novicius*. The quantity of the first *i* in the termination *-icius* is sometimes long, sometimes short. The rule usually given is that those formed from nouns (e.g. *tribunicius*) or adjectives (e.g. *natalicius*) have ĭ, while those from past participles (e.g. *conducticius, surrupticius, missicius*) have ī. If this rule were true we should pronounce *multatīcius*. But metric evidence is available in only a small percentage of the words in *-icius* and, even where it is, does not always bear out the rule, *novīcius* being a notable exception. Besides Priscian gives a number of the 'past partic. formations' with ĭ. Therefore we cannot be certain that *multatĭcius* is not right, alongside *multatĭcus.*

ad Cereris, cp. Hor. *Sat.* 1. 9. 35 *ventum erat ad Vestae*; so in Greek, εἰς Ἀπόλλωνος, εἰς Αἴδου. It is usual to suppose an ellipse of *aedem*, etc.; others call it a local genitive and deny that there is an ellipse. It only occurs after a preposition. In English the usage is much more free, cp. St Paul's, Liberty's, Christ's, Queens'.

dedere, 'dedicated,' cp. *dedit*, *dedere*, etc., or *dono dedit*, etc., in inscriptions *passim.*

ludos, sc. *plebeios.* These are first mentioned in 23. 30. 17 (216 B.C.). They were held annually in November.

pro temporis eius copia, cp. 25. 2. 8 *ludi Romani pro temporis illius copiis magnifice facti. pro*, 'in proportion to,' 'considering,' cp. 27. 11 *pro aetate*, 'for a man of his age.'

CHAPTER 7

§ 1. **exitu anni huius.** According to Livy's account Scipio arrived in Spain in the autumn of 211 B.C. (26. 19. 11) and captured New Carthage in the spring of 210 B.C. (26. c. 41–51). He despatched Laelius to Rome with some of the prisoners on a quinquireme to announce the news of his victory (26. 51. 2 *nuntium victoriae Romam mittit*). In 26. 51 Livy agrees closely with Polybius's account, cp. Pol. 10. 19 ἐξέπεμψε...Λαίλιον ἐπὶ πεντήρους εἰς τὴν Ῥώμην. It is very strange therefore that he should now make Laelius arrive in Rome at the *end* of the year from Tarraco, not from New Carthage, and with *ships* (§ 4), not with a single quinquireme. It is impossible to suppose that Laelius would have landed at Tarraco and stayed there several months. There was every reason for him to travel with his news as speedily as possible. The very fact that Livy mentions the number of days spent on the voyage shows this. The usual explanation of the inconsistency is that Livy is here following a different authority. See further nn. on § 2 and § 5.

quam. See n. on c. 5. 9.

isque...ingressus, 'his entry,' see n. on c. 5. 14.

§ 2. **receptasque aliquot urbes.** Hesselbarth (*Historisch-kritisch Untersuch. zur III[ten] Dekade des Livius*, p. 413) thinks that this is an invention of Livy's in order to fill the gap between the capture of New Carthage in spring and the end of the year. If Laelius left directly from New Carthage he would have no further news to report.

in societatem adscitas, 'enrolled as allies.'

§ 3. **transitus in Italiam,** the verbal substantive retains the construction of the verb, cp. 37. 10. 5 *reditum in patriam*; see also n. on c. 11. 9.

obsistentem. See Notes on Text.

§ 4. **et,** 'also.' **productus** is the regular word used when an envoy is brought forward to address the people, as **introductus** (§ 2) is the expression when one is given an audience in the senate.

in unum diem. See n. on c. 4. 15.

primo quoque tempore. See n. on c. 5. 12.

quibus venerat navibus. See n. on § 1.

§ 5. **in hunc annum contuli.** We cannot say who the *multis auctoribus* were. Soltau (*Livius' Quellen in der III[ten] Dekade*) argues that this notice of Laelius is taken from Coelius Antipater. According to Polybius the capture of New Carthage took place in 209 B.C. It has been thought therefore that Livy followed the Polybian narrative (cp. n. on § 1) but had made a mistake of a year in his chronology, and Hesselbarth's theory is that he only discovered his error at this point, and realising that these events belonged to the summer of 209 B.C. in Polybius's account, he fits them in at the very end of his own 210 B.C. The notice comes in an unusual position, *after* the sections dealing with the priests and games which regularly wind up the account of a year. Soltau has shown, however, that in the sections dealing with the Spanish history Livy is not using Polybius directly, and he argues in favour of Claudius Quadrigarius being the Roman writer who took the account from Polybius and was followed by Livy. The mistake in the chronology would arise from the fact that this writer followed Polybius in making 219 B.C. the first year of the war, whereas elsewhere than in the Spanish sections Livy takes 218 B.C. as the beginning (e.g. in c. 22. 1 208 B.C. is the 11th year). Thus Spanish events assigned to the 10th year of the war get put down to 210 B.C. instead of 209 B.C.

§ 6. **quod**, 'because,' giving the reason for *in hunc annum contuli*. There is a *v.l.* '*sed*.'

minus simile veri, 'not very likely'; for the force of the comparative see n. on c. 13. 13. With *similis* the dative is used of particular or partial likeness ('similar to'), the genitive of general or complete resemblance ('the like of,' 'the match of'). Livy, however, uses *vero simile* also.

integrum nihil gerundo. As Wb. points out, Livy fails to observe that on *his* dating Scipio spends the whole of 208 B.C. *nihil gerundo*.

PAGE 12

§ 7. **provincia**, 'official sphere.' The word probably originally meant 'lordship' from a stem *prōv* (cp. Goth. *frauja*, 'lord'). Another derivation connects it with *provincere* as the 'sphere one goes forth to conquer.' As a technical term it was specially applied to the sphere of duty assigned to a magistrate holding *imperium* outside Rome. It is also used of the official sphere of duty inside Rome (cp. § 8, *urbanam*), and of sphere of duty generally, but the military sense was regularly felt: cp. the scene in the *Stichus* of Plautus (produced a few years after this time), 698 f. ST. *cape provinciam*. SA. *quid istuc est provinciae?* ST. *Utrum Fontine an Libero imperium te inhibere mavis?* As the Roman dominion extended the word acquired its geographical meaning denoting the conquered district administered by a magistrate holding *imperium*.

ad Tarentum. See nn. on c. 2. 1 and c. 3. 8.

rem gereret, 'conduct the war.' The subjunctive is jussive, the indirect form of *gerat* which might appear in the actual decree.

§ **8. M. Claudio.** *Dat. commodi* with *prorogatum*. Marcellus had his consular army at Venusia.

prorogatum. The development of meaning in *rogo* and its compounds is interesting. *rogo* is a frequentative of *rego* ('stretch,' cp. *pergo*, *surgo*) and meant originally 'apply (oneself) to,' hence 'ask.' The political sense (*rogatio*, 'bill,' *comitia consulibus rogandis*, etc.) is derived from the magistrate's 'applying' to the people to decide. Hence in the passive it is used of the decision given and in the active of the people who decide. Consequently a number of the compounds of *rogo* are regularly used as technical terms of the action of the *comitia*, e.g. *prorogo*, 'prolong a command,' *abrogo*, 'deprive of command' or 'annul a law,' *subrogo*, 'appoint an official in the room of another,' *irrogo*, 'fine' (sc. *multam*), *erogo*, 'disburse from treasury,' etc. See also n. on § 17 and c. 21. 3.

peregrinam cum Gallia. Not infrequently the *praetor peregrinus* was given a *provincia* outside Rome, leaving his duties there to be carried out by the *praetor urbanus*. Sometimes this was decided at the time of the partition of the spheres of duty, sometimes the *praetor peregrinus* was put at the disposal of the senate. See n. on c. 22. 3 *peregrina et quo senatus censuisset*. In 207 B.C. urban and peregrine praetorship were combined in one man (c. 36. 10).

§ **9. exercitus...divisi.** See Bk. 26. c. 28. The construction of the following clauses is rather mixed. For the sake of variety, when he is giving the contents of a decree or decrees embodying the arrangements of provinces and armies, Livy frequently blends direct narrative and oblique. The words from *Fulvio* to *acciperet* are in the *form* of an oblique command, except the clause *qui tum Arimini erat*, which is a remark of the historian and does not belong to the decree. *praeesset*, *obtineret*, *acciperet* are indirect jussives varied by an equivalent *ut succederet*. Then we return to the statement form in *gesserat*, *decretae*, etc. Further, since the mood of *haberet* and *praefuisset* in § 9 shows that their clauses belong to the oblique, strict syntax would demand that with *Fulvio* and *Fabio* we should understand *ita ut darentur* or the like, rather than *datae* or *decretae*. A comparison, however, of passages like 26. 28. 3 *exercitus eis duo decreti, qui in Etruria Galliaque* essent, or 26. 1. 9 *duae legiones quas P. Cornelius* habuisset *decretae* with 26. 28. 12 *totidem legiones...praetore decretae quibus L. Cornelius*...praefuerat, shows that in the relative clause after *decreti* (*sunt*) etc., Livy sometimes writes indicative as his own statement of fact, sometimes subjunctive, confusing the direct statement of *decreti* (*sunt*) with the content of the decree, (*decrevere ut darentur* or the like). See also c. 22. 6.

§ **10**. **ut succederet**. Some editors put a comma at *praefuisset* and take *ut* to mean 'with the proviso that,' a sense that *ut* clauses very frequently have in passages like the present, cp. c. 22. 4.

§ **11**. **C. Hostilius**. If the text is correct, Livy has apparently made a mistake, for Hostilius did not go to Etruria till the following year; see c. 22. 4.

C. Laetorio. See 26. 28. 5. **Arimini**, on the Umbrian coast, mod. Rimini.

§ **12**. **Cannensis exercitus**. The survivors of Cannae were sent to Sicily to serve there without release so long as the war in Italy lasted, cp. 23. 25. 8. Later they were debarred from having their winter-quarters in a town or within 10 miles of one (cp. 26. 1. 10).

qui superessent. The survivors of the defeat at Herdonea who had taken refuge with Marcellus. See c. 1. 15.

§ **13**. **ignominia**. See note on previous section.

praetoris Cn. Fulvi, see n. on c. 1. 9.

ob similis iram fugae, 'anger at.' *fugae* is objective genitive, cp. c. 28. 6 *ab ira defectionis*, 1. 5. 3 *ob iram praedae amissae*. The order of the words is unusual.

eo, to Sicily.

§ **15**. **P. Sulpicio**. P. Sulpicius Galba, consul with Cn. Fulvius Centumalus in 211 B.C., was sent in 210 B.C. to succeed Laevinus in the Greek command, see Bk. 26. c. 28.

§ **16**. **praedatum** goes both with *traicere* and *mittere*.

traicere. See n. on c. 5. 9.

PAGE 13

§ **17**. **nec**, 'also...not,' i.e. as well as in the East and in Sicily; see n. on c. 6. 16.

non in annum...prorogatum, cp. Zonaras, 9. 10 *ὁ δὲ Σκιπίων μέχρις ἂν πάντα τὰ ἐν τῇ Ἰβηρίᾳ καταστήσῃ ἄρχειν τῶν ἐκεῖ προσετάχθη*.' Prolongation of command was usually for one year, but might be made for an indefinite period, as here. Cp. the first recorded instance (327 B.C.), Bk 8. 23, *pro consule rem gereret quoad debellatum cum Graecis esset*, and 30. 1. 10 *donec debellatum in Africa foret*. As the name implies (*prorogo*, see n. on § 8) originally no doubt the prorogation was decided by the people. In several cases both senatorial decree and plebiscite are mentioned (e.g. 10. 22. 9) but at this period Livy regularly mentions the senate only. Cp. Polyb. 6. 15. 6 τοῦ ἐπαποστεῖλαι στρατηγὸν ἕτερον, ἐπειδὰν ἐνιαύσιος διέλθῃ χρόνος, ἢ τὸν ὑπάρχοντα ποιεῖν ἐπίμονον· ἔχει τὴν κυρίαν αὕτη (sc. ἡ σύγκλητος).

nisi quod, 'save for the fact that.' Cp. c. 36. 4.

forent=*essent*. See n. on c. 25. 8.

CHAPTER 8

§ **1**. **maximi curionis**. See n. on c. 6. 16. "Livy describes this inaccurately as the election of a *sacerdos*. It was the election of one of the *curiones* (already *sacerdotes*) to be president of them." (Stephenson.)

§ **2**. **patriciis negantibus**. Religious offices were very gradually opened to the plebs. In 367 B.C. they had gained admission to the college of the *decemviri sacrorum* and in 300 B.C. the *lex Ogulnia* threw open to them the pontificate and augurship, but the *rex sacrorum* and various other priestly officials remained patrician. *patriciis negantibus* may mean *patricii se auctores futuros negabant*, i.e. the patrician members of the senate refused their formal sanction (*patrum auctoritas*, now regularly given beforehand) to the acts of the *comitia*.

habendam rationem. See n. on c. 6. 5.

quia...habuisset. The subjunctive is due to the oblique. For the mood in causal clauses see n. on c. 28. 16.

§ **3**. **tribuni appellati**, i.e. by Atellius.

rem. See Notes on Text. *rem reicere* is the regular phrase for the shifting of a decision by a competent magistrate or body to another authority, cp. 5. 22. 1 *qui ad senatum...rem arbitri sui reiecisset*.

potestatem, 'empowered the people to decide the question.' With *potestatem facere* the dative is usual.

§ **4**. **flaminem Dialem**, the flamen of Juppiter. For the form *dialis* cp. *diespiter*=*Iuppiter*. Prof. Ridgeway (*Proc. Brit. Acad.* Vol. III) argues that *dialis* is connected not with *diespiter* but with *Ianus* and that the three *flamines maiores* (*Dialis*, *Martialis*, *Quirinalis*) were the priests of Sabine deities. The etymology of *flamen* is disputed. The attractive equation Skt *brahman* = *flamen* is now generally given up, and the root may be that seen in *flagro*, *flamma*, φλέγω.

⟨in⟩augurari, an early correction of the MSS. *augurari*. An important part of the ceremony of formal consecration of a priest was the solemn taking of the auspices to see whether the gods approved the election. Hence the ceremony itself came to be called *inauguratio* and *inaugurari* meant 'to be installed ceremoniously.'

coegit. The edd. cite a parallel case from Bk. 40. c. 42, where the *pontifex maximus* insisted on appointing a man *rex sacrorum* against his will.

decemvirum, genitive plural, 'as one of the decemvirs.' See Notes on Text. It appears that the *pontifex maximus* had the right of selecting (*capere*) certain of the other priests as well as the vestals.

§ 5. **causam coacti flaminis**, 'the reason why the flamen was forced to let himself be consecrated.'

captus, 'chosen,' cp. αἱρεῖσθαι.

fratri germano. *germanus* is probably for **genmanus* with the root of *gigno* γενέσθαι, etc. If so, the *r* may have come in through a popular connexion with *creare*.

§ 6. **antiquos mores**, 'his former ways.' More usually *antiquus* (ἀρχαῖος) is used in a good sense of something with an added quality on account of age, as contrasted with *vetus* (παλαιός) which regularly denotes lapse of time.

tota iuventute, 'among all the young men,' like the local ablative, § 17 *omni ambitu*, Cic. *Pro Leg. Man.* § 31 *quis enim* toto mari *locus?* See n. on c. 2. 4. With *totus*, *omnis*, *cunctus*, *medius* the preposition *in* is regularly omitted as these words in themselves suffice to make the locatival sense clear.

probatior primoribus, 'more highly approved by the leading men.' The dative of the agent and the 'dative of person judging' become practically indistinguishable in phrases like this. *primores* is apparently formed from *primus* on the analogy of *prior*. An ingenious suggestion is that it is formed from *primo ore* (cp. its use to denote 'front ranks' in battle), just as we find in Greek a suffix -οψ which originally was the substantive ὄψ.

§ 7. **rem intermissam**, 'a right that had been in abeyance.'

ut in senatum introiret, 'namely that he should have a seat in the senate.'

§ **8**. **L. Licinius.** Livy seems to be anticipating. In the following year *P.* Licinius Varus was *praetor urbanus* and *P.* Licinius Crassus *praetor peregrinus*. So perhaps L. is a mistake here for P. In inscriptions of this period these letters would appear as L and Γ.

curiam. See n. on c. 50. 9.

datum...esse, dependent on a verb of saying implied in *repetebat*.

toga praetexta, 'the purple bordered gown' was the robe of curule magistrates and was also worn by boys till they assumed the ordinary toga of manhood. The distinctive part of the dress of the *flamen dialis* was a curious high conical cap with an apex called *albogalerus*.

PAGE 14

sella curulis. *curulis* for **currulis*, 'a chair to be carried on a chariot,' the official seal of the higher magistrates. It was a square stool inlaid with ivory. The epithet *curulis* is thought to imply that the office was not confined to one place.

ei flaminio, 'assigned to that office of flamen,' i.e. by Numa, who was the traditional founder of the three *flamines maiores* and the first holder of the office of *flamen dialis*, cp. 1. 20. 2 *flaminem Iovi adsiduum sacerdotem creavit, insignique eum veste et curuli regia sella adornavit.*

§ **9**. **volebat,** 'would have it that.' *repetebat* and *volebat* are descriptive imperfects. Thus *repetivit* (§ 7) states the fact, *repetebat* pictures the scene.

exoletis...exemplis, 'precedents from historical records that were out of date and forgotten.' *vetustate* goes with *exoletis*.

stare, 'rest on,' 'depend on.' The ablative is instrumental.

recentissimae cuiusque, 'the actual practice of late years in each case.' *consuetudinis usus* is a curious phrase.

§ **10**. **rem obliteratam,** 'the fact that the right had fallen into abeyance'; cp. n. on c. 5. 14.

damno, 'to the prejudice of the individuals holding the priesthood rather than of the office.' *damno*, predicative dative.

fuisse. Note the tense. The effect of *rem obliteratam* on *ipsis* was *past*, but the tribunes' judgment (*aequom censuissent*) has to deal with its effect on *sacerdotium* lasting into the present (of the speakers). English can bring this out by means of a clumsy 'should prove to have been'; Latin with its delightfully ambiguous *fuisse* (both 'was' and 'has been') is simpler.

obtinuisse, 'had gained his point,' 'had maintained his right.'

§ **11. priusquam irent,** 'before going.' In earlier writers *prius-quam* and *antequam* take the subjunctive (apart from *oratio obliqua*) only when there is some idea of purpose or anticipation on the part of the subject of the leading verb expressed in the temporal clause. Thus we find the subj. frequently used of an action that is prevented, 'before they could go.' In Livy, however, the subjunctive steadily encroaches on the indicative, and we find these temporal conjunctions used not infrequently with the subjunctive where, as here, mere priority in time is expressed. Cp. c. 18. 2 *priusquam castris locum caperent...impetum fecerunt.*

legiones, in supplementum. The troops for reinforcing the other legions are in addition to the two urban legions; so in full the sentence would be *duas urbanas legiones et tantum militum quantum opus erat in supplementum. ceteris exercitibus* goes rather with *opus erat* than with *in supplementum scripserunt.* For *in* expressing purpose see n. on c. 3. 9.

§ **12. urbanum veterem exercitum.** Note the two adjectives with one substantive. Accumulations of adjectives unconnected by *et* are avoided by Latin writers except (1) in rhetorical asyndeton, (2) as here, where *urbanus exercitus* is treated as one idea and qualified by an adjective. Similarly *res gesta*, 'an exploit,' may have an adjective. Cp. c. 22. 8 *magnum navalem apparatum*, c. 22. 12 *naves longas triginta veteres.* Cicero (*Verr.* 5. 52) has three epithets in *privata navis oneraria maxima*, 'very large private-merchantman.'

§ **13. Fulviani.** See n. on c. 7. 12.

fuere ad quattuor milia trecenti, 'they amounted to as many as 4344.' Cp. c. 12. 16, 22. 50. 11 *ad sescenti evaserunt*, 26. 16. 5 *ad mille et ducenti erant. ad* is used by Livy frequently with numerals without effect on the case, in the sense of 'as many as' or (more rarely, of the number to which anything is reduced, cp. Tac. *Ann.* 15. 39) 'as few as.' Originally no doubt, as in *ad unum*, 'to a man,' the preposition was used with the accusative as a phrase in apposition with the subject of the verb (cp. ἔπιπτον ἐξ ἑκατέρων 'men on both sides fell'). Then being felt as subject and helped by the analogy of *fere* with numerals it was put into the nominative and thence the 'adverbial' use of *ad* was extended freely to the other cases. Cp. Caes. *B. C.* 3. 53 *ad duorum milium numero ceciderant*, Caes. *B. G.* 2. 33 *occisis ad hominum milibus quattuor.* Edd. frequently say that *ad*='about'; but it has not the same meaning as *fere* ('approximately'). We do not say in

English '*about* 4344.' Latin uses the *ad* freely where the exact number is specified, cp. 23. 37. 11 *signa militaria* ad quadraginta unum *cepit.*

duas legiones et triginta quinqueremes. The two legions for the consul Fulvius and the 30 quinquiremes for Fabius; see c. 7. 9 and 15.

§ **14.** **nihil...nec.** *nemo* and *nihil* are usually continued with *nec...nec* rather than *aut...aut.* Similarly *nego,* 6. 23. 9.

§ **15.** **veteres legiones** = *Cannensis exercitus.*

haberet, sc. Valerius.

Epicydis, a Syracusan, one of two brothers who had served with Hannibal in Spain and Italy, and sent by him to negotiate an alliance with Hieronymus of Syracuse. In the reaction against the blood-thirsty conduct of the party that murdered Hieronymus, Epicydes and his brother Hippocrates were elected generals by the Syracusans. When the fall of Syracuse became inevitable Epicydes withdrew to Agrigentum and two years later (210 B.C.) he hastily fled with Hanno when that city was betrayed by Muttines.

§ **17.** **qua regnum Hieronis fuerat.** Hiero's kingdom included a considerable stretch of territory on the E. coast of Sicily from Tauromenium to the S.E. corner of the island. After the murder of Hieronymus, Hiero's grandson and successor, the kingdom rapidly fell to pieces.

divisam quondam. We know nothing of any such division. Stephenson suggests that it is 'a historical impromptu on Livy's part.'

PAGE 15

§ **18.** **notaret**, ('mark and) distinguish.' **perinde**, 'accordingly.'

dominos, 'the farmers,' not 'owners' in the strict sense.

§ **19.** **tantum** goes with *frumenti* as subject of *provenit* 'grew,' and *ea cura* is abl. 'by means of'; 'there was such a fine crop.'

aestiva acturus, 'carry on the (summer) campaign.' Cp. n. on c. 4. 1.

CHAPTER 9

§ **1.** **Latini nominis sociorumque.** For the use of *nomen* = 'those who bear the name' cp. 5. 22. 8 *Etruscum nomen.* Originally the *nomen Latinum* had been the Latin communities forming the old confederation in Latium. By the end of the 3rd cent. B.C. however, these had received the full franchise of Rome and the 'Latin Name' was applied to the *Coloniae Latinae* (who had not received the franchise), i.e. colonies throughout Italy consisting of mixed bodies of Romans and Latins, such, for example, as Venusia (291 B.C.), Brundusium (242 B.C.), Placentia (218 B.C.). These were the *socii Latini nominis* or *Latini*. As distinguished from these the non-Latin or Italian allies, including the various Italian communities, Etruria, Umbria, Samnium, Apulia, etc., subdued by Rome, were called *socii* or *civitates foederatae* in the special sense. Thus on the copy of the famous *Senatus consultum de Bacchanalibus* addressed to those *quei foideratei esent* and applying to all classes in Italy, we have the phrase *vir nequis...ceivis Romanus neve nominus Latini neve socium quisquam*. When Livy uses the term *socii* he sometimes means all the allies, Latin and Italian (cp. 23. 17. 9 *Romanis sociisque*), sometimes the latter only. Both classes had to furnish troops to Rome. The amount of the contingent to be sent by each was arranged by the consuls after the senate had fixed the total number of men to be sent by the *socii*. The chief distinction between them lay in the fact that each Latin community enjoyed *commercium* and, in most cases, *conubium* with Rome but not with any other community, while the Italians had no rights of *commercium* or *conubium* with Rome but had them with one another.

ex parvis, 'great and decisive issues are often directly brought about by insignificant events.' The metaphor is taken from the scales of a balance, and is a favourite one in Livy. *momentum* is 'what causes movement (of the scale),' hence 'determining cause,' 'decisive factor'; cp. 2. 7. 10 *tam levi momento meam apud vos famam pendere*, 9. 1. 11 *rerum humanarum maximum momentum*, 32. 17. 9 *bellum quod ex momentis parvarum rerum penderet*, Lucan 4. 819 *momentum...curio rerum*.

§ **2. in conciliis**, 'gatherings,' i.e. mass meetings held to protest.

decimum annum, since 218 B.C.

stipendiis. *stipendium* stands for *stipi-pendium, as Eng. idolatry for *idolo-latry. *stipendiis* is generally taken here as =*pecunia*, 'taxes,' 'money contributions,' cp. § 7 *milites pecuniamque darent* and § 13 *nec miles qui legeretur nec pecunia quae daretur in stipendium*. We might expect it to have the common meaning of 'military service' or 'campaigns' (as e.g. in c. 11. 14, Cic. *Pro Leg. Man.* 26 *stipendiis confecti*) since the following sections, 3–7, which describe what was discussed in the *concilia*, all deal with the hardships of the service, with the exception perhaps of *egestatem* in § 5. However, for this we should expect *fessos* or *confectos* rather than *exhaustos*. *exhaurire* is regularly applied to the draining of money resources, cp. 37. 19. 4 *exhauriant commeatibus praebendis socios.*

quotannis, an adverb which has crystallised out of a phrase *tot annis quot sunt*; cp. *quot Kalendis.*

§ **3**. **magis perire sibi**, 'the citizens levied by Rome to serve in her army were lost to them more surely than those taken prisoners by the Carthaginian.'

Romano...Poeno, singular in collective sense, like *militem* and *hostis* in next section. Livy most commonly uses the name of the people in the singular to designate the army of that people. Cp. 22. 14. 5 *Romanus conserere pugnam...contra eludere Poenus.*

lectus sit. The use of primary tenses of the subjunctive (cp. *excedat, redeant, legantur, negatum sit, perveniant, videant*) in *oratio obliqua*, or *repraesentatio*, as it is called, is a device very freely used by Livy. As in using the historic present the historian assumes the standpoint of the spectator of the past events, so in *Repraesentatio* he adopts the point of view of the speaker. The effect in both is to give greater vividness to the narrative. The most remarkable characteristic of Livy's treatment of the oblique discourse is the manner in which he shifts from one point of view to the other and uses primary and secondary tenses of the subjunctive in quick succession, in a fashion quite unciceronian. It is natural to suppose that these deviations from the normal sequence do not depend merely on 'the taste and fancy' of the writer, but only recently has a reasonable explanation of the principles which guided Livy been offered. This is due to Professor Conway, who in an appendix to his edition of Book 2 makes out a strong case for the theory that Livy's *rule* was to retain the primary tenses of direct speech wherever the subjunctive had a primary tense to correspond. Thus *facit, fecit* (prest. perf.), *faciat, fecerit* (perf. subj.) are regularly reported by Livy as *faciat, fecerit, faciat, fecerit*, whereas *fac, faciet, fecerit* (fut. perf. indic.), which have no corresponding tense in the subjunctive, usually become *faceret, faceret, fecisset*, though even here Livy allowed himself to write *faciat, faciat, fecerit*. The chief exception to this rule of *Repraesentatio* is in the case of subjunctives depending directly on the main verb introducing the *oratio obliqua*. These Livy makes secondary. There are, however, many instances which cannot be brought under Professor Conway's rules or the classes of exceptions which he draws up, so that the problem cannot be regarded as solved. Note that Cicero can and frequently does employ *Repraesentatio* where he has the leading verb in the historic present. The peculiarity of the usage in Livy and the historians is the shift of tenses following a verb in a secondary tense. See also nn. on § 6, § 12, c. 17. 14, c. 34. 13, c. 44. 2.

gratis remitti. Cp. Hannibal's conduct, 22. 58. 2 *cum captivis productis segregatisque sociis sicut ante ad Trebiam Trasumennumque lacum sine pretio dimisisset. gratis* (for *gratiis* which appears in Old Latin) used here as an adverb is originally instrumental plural of *gratia* 'with (mere) thanks.' Cp. § 13 *alternis.*

§ **4.** **ibi**=*extra Italiam*, i.e. in Sicily.

nunc cum maxime. *nunc* is retained in the oblique for vividness, as often, cp. c. 40. 6 and the similar retention of *hic* for *ille* and the use of *adhuc* for *ad illud tempus. nunc cum maxime* (νῦν γε μάλιστα) means 'now especially,' 'at this time particularly,' and is equivalent to an emphatic *nunc.* Similarly *tum cum maxime*='just then.' The phrase is often explained as arising from *nunc* ut *cum maxime* ('now as when most'), cp. Cic. *ad Q. Fratr.* 2. 6 *domus celebratur ut cum maxime* (sc. *celebratur*), but the *ut* is not necessary to explain the ellipse, as is shown by cases where the verb is supplied with the *cum* clause, e.g. 2. 59. 7 *cum maxime agmen...explicaretur.* So here, *cum maxime* (*floret*) *nunc florens.* Frequently the *nunc* or *tum* is omitted and we find *cum maxime* meaning 'just now' or 'just then,' cp. 29. 17. 20 *omnia...passi sumus et* cum maxime *patimur*, Cic. *de Orat.* 1. 18. 84 *sed* cum maxime *tamen hoc significabat*, Tac. *Ann.* 3. 59 *litora et lacus Campaniae* cum maxime *peragrantem.*

§ **5.** **res ipsa**, 'the pressure of circumstances.' 'Therefore before their population and their resources were absolutely exhausted they must refuse to Rome the service which the force of circumstances would soon make it impossible for them to perform.'

§ **6.** **si videant.** The *recta* would be *si videbunt* more probably than *si videant*, so that on Prof. Conway's theory, *si viderent* would be more usual here.

acta, 'debated,' cp. *actio*='pleading,' 'speech,' and *agere cum populo* used of a magistrate bringing business before the assembly.

§ **7.** **triginta tum coloniae populi Romani.** This means the *coloniae Latinae*, colonies planted by Rome with Romans and Italians. See n. on § 1. *triginta.* After this date only four (five, if L. is right in adding Luca) more Latin colonies were founded, Copia, Valentia, Bononia, Aquileia.

negaverunt consulibus, 'declared to the consuls that they had not the means to provide.'

PAGE 16

Nepete, Sutrium, in Etruria, colonised in 383 B.C. They were the 'gates' of Etruria (*cum...loca opposita Etruriae et velut claustra inde portaeque essent*). **Alba,** sc. *Fucensis* on the lacus Fucensis to the E. of Latium. **Cora,** an ancient Latin town. *Sora,* which is read by some edd., is a town in N. E. Latium colonised in 299 B.C.

§ **8.** **profecturos rati,** sc. *se*. *profecturos* from *proficio.*

§ **9.** **in animum inducere non possent,** 'could not think of.'

§ **10.** **itaque,** like *namque,* regularly put at the beginning of the sentence in classical prose but often second word in Livy. See also n. on c. 15. 15.

tamquam integra re, 'as though no step had been taken.' *integra,* lit. 'untouched.' **locuti magis.** The force of *tamquam* is carried on, 'as though they had not really dared to commit such a crime but had merely spoken of it.' *locuti magis, etc.* explain *re integra.*

Romanos, a rhetorical exaggeration. They are called *coloniae populi Romani* in § 7 and of course there was a proportion of Roman citizens in them, though this proportion was very small in the early Latin colonies and the latest of these 12 settlements, *Carseoli,* dated from 298 B.C.

§ **11.** **inde,** sc. *ex Roma.*

oriundos, 'sprung,' cp. *secundus* ('following') *volvendus* ('rolling'), words which show that the meaning of obligation attaching to the nom. of the gerundive is not original.

§ **12.** **temere,** 'in the dark,' locative of a substantive **temus* (cp. Skt. *tamas*), 'darkness,' hence 'blindly,' 'rashly.'

agitassent. The *recta* would be *agitavistis,* so that according to the 'rule' mentioned in § 3 we might expect *agitaverint.*

ea prodendi...esse, predicative genitive describing the sphere, lit. 'these things belong to the betraying.' Trans. 'the design you have rashly set on foot simply means the betrayal of our empire and giving Hannibal the victory.' Note the rhetorical *prodendi...tradendae.*

§ **13.** **alternis** = *alternis vicibus.* See n. on § 3 *gratis,* and cp. 2. 2. 9 *agere...rogando alternis suadendoque coepit.* *alternis* might mean 'first one consul and then the other discussed,' but it more probably refers to the interchange of argument between the consuls and the envoys.

senatum suum, i.e. the assemblies in the various colonies. The constitutions of the *coloniae* were modelled on that of Rome.

§ **14**. **socios**. See n. on § 1.

CHAPTER 10

§ **1**. **hortari, consolari, dicere**. Historic infinitives. See n. on c. 6. 10.

alias, 'the rest.' *alii* = οἱ ἄλλοι is very common in Livy.

fide atque officio, 'would remain true to their allegiance and duty.' *fides* is the pledge given in treaty (*foedus*), *officium* is the service due in consequence of the treaty. It is not a hendiadys 'in loyal allegiance to their duty.'

PAGE 17

§ **2**. **agerent facerentque**, oblique command where we should expect *ut agerent facerentque* after *permissum esset*; cp. c. 22. 11. *agerent* 'engage in,' *facerent* 'perform.'

ut, 'in whatever way,' 'as.'

e re publica. See n. on c. 4. 1.

ecquid, 'whether,' equivalent to *num* in indirect question.

§ **3**. **ex formula**, an official list, i.e. *formula togatorum* (κατάλογος), specifying the size of the contingent to be sent by each state of the allies, cp. 22. 57. 10 *ad milites ex formula accipiendos mittunt*.

§ **4**. **neque...et**. See n. on c. 6. 4. **deesse...superesse**, another bit of Livy's rhetoric, 'for this we have money enough, for this we have spirit enough—and to spare,' or 'we have the money and we are ready, aye more than ready.'

§ **5**. **parum sibi videri**, 'it seems to us that commendation from us is less than you deserve (and that your merits will not be adequately recognised) unless, etc.' The *recta* would be *parum videtur...nisi egerint* (fut. perf.) and the apodosis and protasis do not logically correspond, since the apodosis is condensed.

§ **6**. **ipsis...suis**, includes of course the people; in the direct it would be *nobis...nostris* 'us and our ancestors.'

§ **7**. **ne...sileantur**, 'we must not omit to record.' The subject of *sileantur* is *ei* not *merita eorum*.

saecula, 'generations.' **tot**, i.e. about six.

§ **8.** **ab altero mari**, 'on the western side.'

mediterranei, 'inland.' It is curious that Livy does not include at least Venusia in the inland towns. It was about as far from the E. coast as Beneventum from the W. *Pontia* was a small island opposite Formiae. **Lucerini**, another reading is *Nucerini.* **Cosani.** There were other *Cosas* besides the one in Etruria. Weissenborn thinks the colony referred to here is *Cosa* in Campania. **Placentini et Cremonenses.** *Placentia* and *Cremona* had been settled less than 10 years previously, in 218 B.C. The last seven colonies are given in chronological order.

§ **10.** **illos**, i.e. the envoys from the 12 colonies.

ex dignitate. See n. on c. 1. 4.

§ **11.** **expedientibus**, conative present participle, 'endeavouring to get together.'

quae opus erant. The nominative construction with *opus* as predicate is frequent, as well as the instrumental ablative (*quibus opus erat*); the construction of *opus* with a dependent genitive seems to occur in Livy only.

aurum vicensimarium. This was the proceeds of the *vicensima manumissionum*, a 5 % tax on the value of slaves manumitted, imposed by the *lex Manlia* which was passed in the camp at Sutrium in 357 B.C.; see Bk 7. c. 16. This reserve fund had been hoarded for nearly 150 years and was kept in gold ingots (*lateres aurei*) in the temple of Saturn. Fifty years later the gold reserve had mounted to 17,000 lbs.

sanctiore, 'not to be touched,' 'inviolable.' There may have been a special inner chamber or safe in the temple. On the financial difficulties of these years see Mommsen, *Rom. Hist.* Bk III. c. VI. Eng. Trans.[2], p. 343.

PAGE 18

§ **12.** **pondo.** See n. on c. 4. 8.

quattuor milia, '4000 pounds weight,' about £180,000. The first issue of gold coins from the Roman mint had taken place, probably in 217 B.C., according to Pliny, on the scruple standard, i.e. the 20 sesterce piece weighed one scruple. Gold was not again coined at Rome till 49 B.C. when Caesar seized the gold in the state treasury and coined it into *aurei* of 25 denarii each. On the scruple standard 4000 pounds of gold should amount to $4000 \times 288 \times 20$ sesterces. But this standard of 217 B.C. was a forced one, and it appears that the value of 1 lb. of gold at this period was 4000 sesterces, i.e. about £45. See Hultsch, *Gr. u. Röm. Metrol.*[2] p. 300 f.

inde = *ex eo auro*.

§ **13**. **additum...praecipuum**, 'given as a special grant.' For the construction see n. on c. 4. 8.

praesenti pecunia, 'for ready money payment.' Among the many financial shifts to which Rome was reduced after Cannae, the state had taken supplies from contractors on credit in order to provide the Spanish army with rations and clothing; see 23. 48. 10–12. Usually the Roman soldiers had to pay for these things. The *socii* on the other hand received their rations free and were paid and clothed by their own states; cp. Polybius 6. 39 *δίδοται δὲ τοῖς μὲν συμμάχοις τοῦτο ἐν δωρεᾷ· τοῖς δὲ Ῥωμαίοις τοῦ τε σίτου καὶ τῆς ἐσθῆτος κἄν τινος ὅπλου προσδεηθῶσι πάντων τούτων ὁ ταμίας τὴν τεταγμένην τιμὴν ἐκ τῶν ὀψωνίων ὑπολογίζεται.*

exercitui, 'for the army.' For the dative cp. 5. 23. 7 *tum Iunoni reginae templum...locavit.*

CHAPTER 11

§ **1**. **prodigia quoque**. On *prodigia* see n. on c. 4. 11. Note the alliteration. Alliteration is very common in Livy, no doubt usually quite unconscious, as it may be even here. With *p* it seems to be especially common (as is π alliteration in Greek), cp. 33. 42. 3 *pensionem pecuniae in bellum conlatae persolvi placuerat privatis*, 37. 3. 1 *priusquam consules in provincias proficiscerentur prodigia per pontifices procurari placuit.*

priusquam proficiscerentur. See n. on c. 8. 11. The subjunctive here may be taken as normal, due to dependence on *procurari placuit*, cp. c. 37. 1.

§ **2**. **Ostiae lacus**. Weissenborn suggests that this may have been a tank made for the purposes of the salt works at Ostia. The emendation *lucus* would give excellent sense, but it is difficult to see why a scribe should have altered it to *lacus*. See Notes on Text.

§ **3**. **auctores erant**, 'averred,' 'vouched for the fact.'

aquam Albanam. For the famous legend of the Alban Lake see Bk 5. c. 15 f. The tunnel for carrying off the overflow still exists.

cella aedis. The combination *cella aedis* is curious, and possibly Luchs is right in bracketing *aedis* as a gloss.

Fortis Fortunae, genitive of *Fors Fortuna*. *Fors* and *Fortuna* both contain the same root *bher* seen in fero, φέρω, bear, etc. The Romans were fond of making abstract ideas into deities, very often with a double title, as here, e.g. *Aius Locutius* (*aio-loquor*), *Anna Perenna* (which Roman popular etymology connected with *annus*).

signum, 'a statuette.' **de capite,** 'from the head of the goddess.'

§ **5.** **androgynos,** 'hermaphrodites.'

faciliore ad duplicanda, 'which forms compounds more freely.' By *duplicanda verba* Livy probably means compounds in which two nouns are put together, as in *androgynos*, or a noun and adjective. Greek undoubtedly shows greater facility in forming substantival compounds with nouns and adjectives of the type of Latin *meridies*, but compounds like *androgynos* are not common in either language.

lacte pluvisse. The instrumental ablative is regular in this construction, cp. *lapidibus* (1. 31. 1 and often), *sanguine* (24. 10. 7), *carne*, *terra*, *creta*. The accusative occurs less frequently, *lapides pluere* (28. 27. 16), *terram* (10. 31. 8), etc.; cp. English, 'rain fire,' etc. The coloured appearance of rain described as blood or milk is explained by modern scientists as due to the presence of millions of tiny living organisms. Red snow is not infrequent in the Alps and proves as alarming to the inhabitants of the Swiss villages as a similar *prodigium* did to the Romans. They think it portends war and bloodshed.

cum capite. See n. on c. 4. 14.

§ **6.** **maioribus.** See n. on c. 4. 15.

obsecratio, used of a solemn prayer recited by a magistrate or priest and repeated by the people.

iis annis, 'in the last few years.' The *ludi Apollinares* were established in 212 B.C. and from 208 B.C. onwards were held each year in the beginning of July. See c. 23. 5.

§ **7.** **et,** 'also.'

censoribus creandis, cp. n. on c. 6. 15 *decemvir sacris faciundis*, dative of 'work contemplated.' These censors were to take the place of those elected in the previous year; see c. 6. 17–18.

§ **8.** **agrum...locarent.** See n. on c. 3. 1.

ex auctoritate patrum. *auctoritas patrum* is here used in the technical sense. See n. on c. 5. 7.

PAGE 19

§ **9. contentio inter...de.** The use of prepositional phrases or their equivalent in dependence on a noun unaccompanied by a participle or attribute (e.g. here, *orta* or *magna*) is common in Livy, and occurs in all periods of Latin. The usage in Cicero is more restricted but he has the construction not infrequently when the dependent phrase denotes place or time (e.g. *ad Att.* 9. 5. 1 *mansio Formiis* 'at Formiae'). See notes on c. 1. 10 and c. 7. 3.

de principe legendo. The *princeps senatus* was the Senator whose name was first on the roll. The position carried no power with it but it was regarded as an honourable distinction. It was formerly thought that in later times the Emperor's title of *princeps* meant *princeps senatus*, but it is more probable that it stood rather for *princeps civitatis*; see Bury, *Student's Rom. Empire*, Chap. II. note C.

tenuit, 'held back,' 'delayed,' cp. c. 5. 15.

Semproni lectio erat. The revision of the Senate was carried through by the two censors together. From this remark it would appear that in some cases (probably when there was a difference of opinion) the censors cast lots to decide which should appoint the *princeps*; in other cases certainly they joined in the appointment.

morem...traditum. The custom of appointing the senior of the *censorii* was not invariable, as we see from 34. 44. 4.

§ **11. T. Manlius Torquatus** had been elected censor in 231 B.C. **Q. Fabius Maximus** had been censor in 230 B.C.

vel, 'even.' *vel* is an old imperative of *volo*, originally meaning 'choose,' or possibly a 2nd singular **vels*, 'you choose.' German *wohl* has a similar development.

victurus esset, 'would succeed in proving.' *vincere* has two idiomatic meanings, (1) 'prevail in argument' (=*vincere verbis*), hence 'victoriously prove that,' usually with acc. and infinitive of the fact, as here; cp. Hor. *Sat.* 2. 3. 225 *vincet enim stultos ratio insanire nepotes*: (2) 'prevail on a person to do' or 'be decisive that,' followed by *ut* or *ne* with subjunctive; cp. c. 35. 9 *vicit auctoritas senatus ut administrarent*, 2. 36. 3 *verecundia vicit ne...abiret*. On the tense of *victurus esset* see n. on c. 35. 5 *haberet*.

§ **12. alius,** see n. on c. 10. 1.

octo praeteritis, 'with the omission of eight names.' *praeterire* in this connexion may mean either 'drop out' or 'omit to include.'

auctor, 'author of the proposal.' A number of young nobles headed by Caecilius Metellus conspired *Italiae deserendae causa*. See 22. 53. 5 and 24. 18. 3. Metellus had been disgraced for this in 214 B.C., being removed from the *centuriae equitum* and also from his tribe.

§ **13**. **notis.** *nota* was the mark put by the censors opposite a man's name on the list; hence the meaning 'brand,' 'stigma.'

eadem servata causa, 'the same offence was made decisive.' *causa* is the offence of being in the conspiracy to leave Italy.

attingeret. The subjunctive here has probably consecutive force 'for this disgrace to attach to,' as is frequently the case in relative sentences giving a description of a class. The subjunctive in descriptive clauses of fact started no doubt from cases where the relative clause contained a potential subjunctive, e.g. *nihil est quod* malim, 'nothing which *I should prefer*' comes to be used for 'nothing which *I prefer*.'

§ **14**. **omnibus adempti**, 'taken from all.' The dative of the person interested is by no means always a *dativus commodi*. An excellent illustration of the difference occurs in Plautus, *Aulul.* 635 S. *nil equidem* tibi ('from you') abstuli. EVC. *at illud quod* tibi ('for yourself') abstuleras *cedo*.

equi, i.e. *equi publici*, so that they had to serve *equis privatis*.

tempus, "the severity of the sentence was increased by an additional term of service, for the past campaigns were not to count" (Stephenson). The regular term of service was 10 years.

ne procederent...facerent, indirect jussives put loosely after *addiderunt tempus* which contains the idea *decretum est* or the like. *procederent* lit. 'go on,' i.e. 'count,' 'be reckoned,' cp. 5. 7. 12 *aera procedere* 'pay should be reckoned.'

iis, 'for them'; *quae* goes with *stipendia*.

§ **15**. **neque.** See n. on c. 6. 16.

aerarios, 'passive citizens.' The *aerarii* were citizens who paid taxes but had no political rights, i.e. they had no vote and could not hold office or serve in the army. The name is derived from *aes* 'poll tax,' the *aerarii* being taxpayers *capite censi*. *referre in* (or *inter*) *aerarios* or *aerarios facere* was the usual phrase for the action of the censors. They might inflict additional punishment on a man they degraded by assessing him for *tributum* at double (or more) the usual rating.

§ **16. incendio.** See Bk 26. c. 27. The fire broke out in several places at once (*pluribus simul locis ortum*) and burnt a row of seven shops on the S. side of the Forum, the fish market, and the *atrium regium*, a building at the S.W. corner adjoining the temple of Vesta, which was with difficulty saved.

atrium regium, or *regia*, was so called from its having been built and occupied by Numa.

CHAPTER 12

§ **2. consecutus**, 'overtook,' cp. c. 20. 1, 1. 48. 4 *fugientem consequi*; similarly *adsequi* as in § 10 *adsequitur*.

PAGE 20

obtestatus. Some editors take this as participle and put commas only after *oppugnaret* and *fore*. It is better to understand *est* and put a full stop at *fore*. This somewhat lightens a sentence that needs it. Otherwise the period would be extremely clumsy, with the most important piece of argument tacked as a parenthesis on to *Tarentum* and such a weight of detail piled on *praesidii* that it disappears beneath it and has to be rescued with a *hanc manum* in § 6.

Marcellum. Marcellus was in Apulia with his consular army of the previous year. c. 7. 11.

§ **3. hosti** may go with *adempta* 'taken from the enemy' or with *causam fore* or with both.

§ **4. Regium**, 'to Rhegium.'

pars maxima, 'the majority of them,' in partitive apposition to *milia*.

§ **5. ab Agathyrna**, in the N. of Sicily. **ante dictum.** See 26. 40. 17. Laevinus had shifted the *incondita multitudo* of debtors and criminals to the number of 4000, thinking that if left in Sicily they might disturb the peace.

rapto vivere, 'maintain themselves by plunder.' They were *latrociniis adaucta manus* and so proved useful to the Rhegines for ravaging the Bruttii. *rapto.* For the neut. participle as a substantive cp. *opus est maturato* 'there is need of haste,'

hominum. The repetition is clumsy.

indidem = αὐτόθεν, 'from there,' i.e. from the country of the Bruttii. *indidem* is regularly used with *ex* and an ablative of the place whence. Cp. 5. 26. 6 *indidem ex agris*, 28. 1. 6 *ducibus indidem ex Celtiberia transfugis*.

§ **6**. **Cauloneam**. The name of this town is variously spelt *Caulonea*, *Caulonia*, *Caulon*. It lay on the E. coast of Bruttium.

§ **7**. **ita induxerat in animum**, 'he had convinced himself.' *in animum inducere*, here with accusative and infinitive, in c. 9. 9 followed by *ut*. **ita**, 'to this effect, namely,' merely anticipatory of the infinitive.

ad Canusium, 'before Canusium.' Canusium had remained steadfastly loyal to Rome, and had afforded a refuge to the remnants of the Roman army after Cannae.

§ **8**. **ceterum**. See n. on c. 1. 3.

§ **9**. **vestigiis instabat**. See n. on c. 2. 10. **conferebat, educebat,** imperfects of repeated action. *castra castris conferre*, 'pitched camp by camp' like *gradum conferre*, 'go along with,' cp. c. 27. 1, c. 47. 6 *cum quo castra conlata haberet*; similarly *castra castris coniungere* of two hostile camps (3. 69. 9).

opere perfecto, 'as soon as the camp fortifications were complete.'

turmatim, 'in squadrons,' properly applied to the *equites* only. Adverbs in *-tim* originate in the adverbial use of the accusative of abstract nouns in *-ti*, cp. Greek βάσις, στάσις. Thus *statim*, *partim*, *strictim*, *raptim*. *-tim* was much extended by analogy and with collectives and concrete terms acquired a distributive force, as here, cp. *guttatim*, *gradatim*, *catervatim*.

levia certamina, 'skirmishes.'

serere. The phrase *serere certamina* occurs several times in Livy, cp. c. 41. 5. *serere* is from *sero*, *sertum*, 'join,' 'twine,' 'set in rows' (Gk. ὅρμος 'necklace'), *not*, as Stephenson takes it, from *seri*, *sevi*, 'sow,' in the sense of 'raising crops one after another.' The use with *certamina* or *proelia* may arise in two ways: (1) an extension from *manus* (*con*)*serere*, 'join hands (in conflict),' to *pugnam* (*con*)*serere*, cp. English, 'join battle'; or more probably (2) from the sense of 'making a series'; cp. 21. 10. 4 *ex bellis bella serendo*, 'joining war to war,' Tac. *Hist.* 5. 11 *crebra...proelia serebant*.

casum, 'risk a general engagement.'

§ **10**. **adsequitur**, 'comes up with,' cp. c. 2. 11 *adeptus est*.

PAGE 21

§ **11**. **contunderent.** See n. on c. 2. 2.

§ **12**. **quietos**, sc. the Carthaginians.

§ **13**. **haud incruentus.** Livy is fond of using this negative figure (litotes) for rhetorical purposes, cp. *haud vanus*, *haud dubie*, etc. **uno proelio** is instrumental with *incruentus*. This epithet is more often applied to the battle or the victory than to the participants, e.g. 2. 56. 16 *haud incruento proelio*.

abeat, 'retire,' like ἀπαλλάττεσθαι in Greek.

quietius...tranquilliusque, 'in a quieter and more restful fashion,' a rhetorical pair frequently combined, cp. Cic. *De Fin*. 1. 18. 5 *nihil quieti...nihil tranquilli*. The words really contain the same root, cp. Eng. 'while.'

§ **14**. **amplius duabus horis**, i.e. *amplius quam duas horas*; but with *plus*, *minus*, *amplius* the *quam* is often dropped without affecting the construction, cp. c. 25. 13 *minus*.

ab Romanis, 'on the Roman side.' See n. on c. 1. 10.

extraordinarii, the name given to one-third of the cavalry and one-fifth of the infantry selected from the whole body of the *socii* in each army to attend on the general.

duodevicensimam. The legions are renumbered each year, those of the consuls being the first to the fourth.

§ **15**. **alii...cedunt**, the *dextra ala*; **alii...subeunt**, the legionaries.

dabant, descriptive imperfect or inchoative, 'began to.'

§ **16**. **ad septingenti.** See n. on c. 8. 13.

CHAPTER 13

§ **1**. **proelio...tolerato.** This may be ablative of comparison but it is best taken as ablative absolute, 'though they had had to maintain an unsuccessful fight.'

tristior, 'caused them greater distress.'

§ **2**. **ut in tali re**, 'so far as one may in such a situation.'

grates ago, regularly used, instead of *gratias ago*, of solemn thanks to the gods, cp. c. 51. 7.

victor hostis. *nomina agentis* in *-tor*, *-trix* are very freely used as adjectives, cp. c. 18. 14 *levem et* concursatorem *hostem*, Cic. *de Sen.* 5. 14 *equi fortis et* victoris.

incidentibus, used of hasty and confused entry, 'tumbling in.' Elsewhere we have dative, *incidere portis*, cp. 5. 11. 8.

PAGE 22

§ 3. qui...pugnaretis, dependent on *oblivio.*

nempe, 'why,' (Irish) 'sure.' It explains the surprised tone of the previous question.

§ 4. per hos dies, 'during the last few days.'

institistis. See n. on c. 2. 10.

§ 5. cuius et ipsius, 'a thing which in itself should cause you no less shame and regret' (i.e. than your actual defeat). *et ipsius.* The fact that on the previous day Marcellus' soldiers had stood up to the same enemy shows that they had only themselves to blame for their defeat that day. For *et* see n. on c. 1. 3.

diremistis, 'you parted battle,' an extension of *dirimere pugnantes* (cp. c. 2. 8) to *dirimere pugnam.* See n. on c. 12. 9 *certamina serens.*

§ 6. eadem sunt, i.e. 'the same as they were on the previous day,' rather than 'the same as Roman soldiers.'

§ 7. an. In Classical Prose where *an* occurs in a single question it usually expresses impatience or indignation, as here. This use of *an* is usually described as elliptical ('is it not so? or...') since *an* is regularly used to introduce the second member of a *disjunctive* question. Possibly, however, *an* is the same word as Gk ἄν and originally denoted simply doubt or uncertainty. Thus the disjunctive force would be a development from its use in the second of two questions and the numerous instances in which the disjunctive or adversative force seems to be suppressed would really be survivals of the earlier usage; cp. Plaut. *Stich.* 549 *quis istuc dicit? an ille quasi tu? Most.* 489 *quis homo? an gnatus meus?*

alicui. As the question *signa ademisset?* implies a negative, we should expect *ulli* here. *aliquis* and *ullus* are used normally where in English we use 'some' and 'any' respectively; i.e. the former in sentences that are affirmative, the latter in negative or virtually negative sentences.

cohorti. § 9 **cohortibus**, § 11 **cohortes**, c. 14. 3 **sinistra ala et cohortes.** It is not entirely clear from these passages what Livy means in each case by *cohortes.* Editors have taken *cohorti* in § 7 to refer to the allies and *manipulo* to the legionaries, and *cohortibus* in § 9 to apply to both allies and legionaries. In c. 14. 3 *cohortes* as opposed to *sinistra ala* obviously means the legionaries. It is uncertain at what period the division of the legion into cohorts (consisting of three maniples) was introduced, but it is generally supposed to be a century later than this. We cannot depend on Livy, for he frequently speaks of cohorts at a period when this formation certainly did not exist and also applies the term to other armies than the Roman. It seems likely in any case that the word was applied to divisions of Roman troops earlier than the time of Marius. Cp. Polybius λαβὼν τρεῖς σπείρας (τοῦτο δὲ καλεῖται τὸ σύνταγμα τῶν πεζῶν παρὰ Ῥωμαίοις κοόρτις). The *socii* at this time were perhaps organised in the same way as the legions. It is generally supposed that the cohort system existed in the allied troops earlier than in the legions.

§ **9.** **hordeum**, barley instead of wheat. As a punishment they received as rations the grain on which the baggage animals were fed.

discinctos destitui, 'be left standing without their belts.' Weissenborn quotes Suet. *Oct.* 24 *ut stare per totum diem iuberet ante praetorium interdum tunicatos discinctosque*. For the reading see Notes on Text.

§ **10.** **neque virum quemquam.** *virum* is emphatic, 'not a single soldier on their side had played the man that day, except the general alone, and to him they must make amends, etc.' Beware of translating 'there was not a man in the army (except the general) who was not bound to make amends.'

ornati, 'smartly equipped.' *orno* stands prob. for **ord*(*i*)*no*, 'put in order,' 'fit out,' and has not necessarily the idea of some extra or addition to set off attire, etc.

§ **12.** **iam**, sums up, 'my orders now to every man are: "fight and win; strive one and all."'

omnibus is contrasted with *cohortes* and so may be taken with *edicere*. But it may go with *pugnandum* or with both.

PAGE 23

§ **13.** **ut viribus sufficerent**, 'that their strength might hold out.' *viribus* 'by reason of strength' (instrumental ablative) or 'in respect of strength,' 'from strength' (true ablative of source), cp. n. on c. 2. 10.

longior, 'somewhat long.' The comparative is very often used absolutely, i.e. with reference to a normal standard rather than a particular case. Thus it may denote a considerable degree ('more than usual,' i.e. 'rather much') or excessive degree ('more than right,' i.e. 'too much'). Cp. c. 7. 8 *minus*, c. 16. 16 *gravioris*, c. 17. 8 *nihil maioris rei*, etc., and see also n. on c. 48. 7.

CHAPTER 14

§ **1. possit**, generic subjunctive. See n. on c. 11. 13.

seu vicit...seu victus est, general suppositions, 'if at any time he has won, etc.' Unlike Greek, Latin does not distinguish formally between general and particular suppositions. But see n. on c. 17. 8.

ferociter instat, e.g. after the capture of Syracuse in 212 B.C. See Bk 25. c. 40, 26. cc. 29–32.

§ **2. ad obtinendum adnitentibus**, 'exerting themselves to maintain.'

§ **3. ab Romanis**, 'on the side of the Romans,' cp. c. 12. 14. Similarly, *ab dextro cornu* and § 5 *ab Hannibale.*

sinistra ala...vicensima legio. Yet it was the *dextra ala* that began to give way on the previous day and lost its standards, and the 18th legion, not the 20th, should have been in front, cp. c. 12. 17 and c. 13. 11.

§ **4. hortator testisque**, cp. 42. 34. 7 *virtutis spectator.* 'Marcellus commanded the centre in person and so confirmed the courage of his men who had their general to urge them on and felt that they were fighting under his eye.'

§ **5. primam frontem**, 'forefront'=*primam aciem.*

id roboris erat, 'these formed the best troops in all his armies,' lit. 'there was this (much of) strength in all his armies.' This is a curious way of expressing *ii robur erant.* In examples like c. 20. 8 *ex omni equitatu quod roboris esset*, c. 28. 8 *quod roboris in praesidio erat.* c. 43. 11 *sociorumque quod roboris esset*, the phrase means 'what strength there was,' *not* 'which was the strength,' and *roboris* is an ordinary instance of the partitive genitive dependent on *quod.* But in cases like *id roboris erat* here and 9. 19. 5 *hoc roboris erat*, the *id* or *hoc* is logically subject and *roboris* predicate, and we have an analogical (and illogical) extension of the partitive genitive into the predicate, cp. 37. 23. 11 *loci nihil relicti erat* (where *relicti* is logically predicate), Caes. *B. G.* 1. 21 *quod consilii sui sit*, Cato, *R. R. hoc erit signi.* This manner of expressing 'this was the strength' as 'there was this strength' is really parallel to the common attraction of the subject pronoun to the gender of the predicate *hoc lumen est* ('*he* is your light'), *hic labor est* ('this is toil'). That the Romans felt the latter expression as 'there is this labour' seems to be shown by the fact that they do not say *hic non est labor*, since 'this is not toil' and 'there is not this toil' mean quite different things.

§ **6.** **si quem...posset,** 'in case this movement might, etc.' *si* often means 'to see whether' or 'in the hope that.' *si forte* and *si qua* (εἴ πως) are common in this construction. In sentences of this kind the protasis and apodosis do not correspond as condition and result. This is explained by the fact (1) that the true apodosis is suppressed or implied in the leading verb, e.g. 26. 9. 9 *alii offerunt se si quo usus operae sit*, where the apodosis is equivalent to *dicunt se iturum*, 5. 1. 9 *frons in Etruscam spectans si qua forte inde venirent, obstruebatur*, i.e. *si venirent, prohibitura obstruebatur*. Thus in 31. 8. 11 *legiones scribere iussi quae si quo res poscerent, mitterentur*, if *quae mitterentur* had been left out we should have a sentence of the same type. Or (2) the protasis is equivalent to a wish. 5. 42. 1 *ostentari quaedam incendia terroris causae si compelli, ad deditionem...possent*, 6. 3. 7 *cum...tenderent ad portas si qua forte...possent*.

§ **7.** **primo,** 'at first' corresponds to *deinde* or *postea* 'afterwards'; *primum* 'for the first time' or 'in the first place' corresponds to *iterum* 'again' or *deinde, tum*, 'in the second place,' but not infrequently *primo* is used in the sense of *primum* 'in the first place.' See also n. on c. 6. 11.

signa ordinesque. See n. on c. 1. 10.

qui circa erant, vaguely 'those near (the point of attack),' not *qui circa signa erant*.

nudaverant, lit. 'had made the line bare,' i.e. 'made a break in the line.' *nudare* is used of the removal of something which covers or protects, and the *acies* is regarded as the position defended by the soldiers composing it.

manasset, 'would have spread.' The metaphor is from a liquid pouring through a mass. It is frequent with words like *rumor, fama, malum*.

§ **8.** **signo arrepto.** Cp. the action of the centurion in 26. 5. 15 and the prefect of allied cavalry in 25. 14. 4.

primi hastati, 'of the first (maniple of the) hastati.'

§ **9.** **ex propinquo** and **in tanta corpora** depend on *haud difficili* *ictu*. *difficili* carries the prepositional clauses easily as being equivalent to a participle. See n. on c. 11. 9.

et tum, 'and the more so on this occasion when they were crowded together.' *haud difficili*, i.e. 'easy at any time'; *et tum* 'then especially,' adds a further reason why it was easy on this occasion.

ut...ita, 'though...yet,' as often; cp. 9. 13. 1 *sicut...ita*.

anceps, 'uncertain,' 'untrustworthy.' The word literally means 'two headed,' ambi-caput.

PAGE 24

avertere. See n. on c. 1. 11.

§ **10.** **tantoque maiorem...imperio regitur.** A rather involved sentence on account of the fact that within each member of the comparative clauses (*tanto...quanto*) there is inserted a second comparison *maiorem quam...acrius quam*; 'the havoc they made was proportionately greater than they had caused among the enemy, as the beast when in panic is driven by his terror with sharper goad than when controlled by the rider on his back.' **edere,** 'caused,' cp. *caedem, cladem edere*. *edo*, 'put forth,' 'produce,' is a compound, not of *do* 'give,' but of *do* corresponding to Gk τίθημι, Eng. *do*, √dhē; cp. *condo* (lit. 'put with'), *abdo* ('put away'), and *stragem dare* (Lucr. 1. 288). **consternatam agit.** The singular refers to elephants as a class, 'the elephant.'

§ **11.** **avertunt.** See n. on c. 1. 11.

§ **13.** **super alia quae facerent,** 'as a crowning cause of terror and confusion.' *super*, 'on top of.' Livy uses *super* in the sense of *praeter* 'besides,' 'beyond,' in various phrases, *super haec*, *super ceteros*, etc. See also n. on c. 40. 4. **quae facerent,** 'such as to cause.' See n. on c. 11. 13.

corruerant...ruere, 'fall...rush.' The extraordinary variety of meanings exhibited by Latin *ruo* and its compounds ('fall,' 'rush,' 'rake up') is due to the fact that there are really three different verbs, one parallel prob. to ἔχραον, another to ὄρνυμι, and a third to ἐρυσίχθων.

ad octo milia, 'as many as 8000.' See n. on c. 8. 13.

§ **14.** **supra,** 'more than,' for the Ciceronian *plus*.

§ **15.** **cupientem...prohibuit.** Marcellus' subsequent inactivity at Venusia led to an attempt to deprive him of his command. See cc. 20–21.

CHAPTER 15

§ **1.** **Bruttios petere**, i.e. to the relief of Caulonea. c. 12. 6.

§ **2.** **isdem ferme diebus**, 'during the same days,' ablative of time within which, cp. c. 11. 6, c. 30. 12. For *ferme* cp. c. 34. 5 *octavo ferme...anno* and see n. on c. 2. 11.

et, 'also,' i.e. in addition to Marcellus' victory.

Hirpini. They had revolted after Cannae. **Volcientes.** Weissenborn notes that this cannot refer to *Vulci* in Etruria and suggests that it means the *Volcentani* in Lucania mentioned in inscriptions and elsewhere, though he cannot explain their being specially mentioned along with the Lucanians among whom they were included.

clementer accepti. They wisely surrendered at the opening of the campaign and got easy terms.

§ **4.** **in Sallentinis.** Manduria lay to the East of Tarentum.

PAGE 25

in ipsis faucibus, 'close to the narrow entrance of the port.' Tarentum was situated at the entrance of the long landlocked inlet known as the 'Port' of Tarentum (Mare Piccolo) on an isthmus which stretched N.W. from the E. side almost across the mouth. Fabius encamped on the west side of the mainland opposite it. The citadel was placed on a rocky hill at the point of this isthmus and the city lay to the S.E. of it.

§ **5.** **Livius**, *Macatus*, the Roman commander in the citadel. He had been despatched from Brundusium to Tarentum by Laevinus in 214 B.C. just before Hannibal reached the city. Bk 24. c. 20.

tutandis commeatibus. See n. on c. 6. 15.

machinationibus apparatuque means towers, rams, scaling ladders, etc. **tormentis**, 'engines for hurling missiles.' These might have been included in the *machinationibus apparatuque* but the *ut alii* clause explains why Livy separates them. *tormentum* is also used for the 'missile hurled by the engines.'

onerarias as opposed to *naves* alone, which means war galleys (*naves longae*). Apparently in merchantmen oars were only used as an auxiliary to sails, cp. Greek δεύτερος πλοῦς proverbial of the second best means, i.e. rowing when wind fails.

agerentur, generic subjunctive. See n. on c. 11. 13.

§ **6.** **alii...alii**, i.e. the crews of the ships.

§ **7.** **ab aperto mari**, 'on the S. side,' 'from (the direction of) the open sea.' See n. on c. 1. 10.

classe Punica tramissa, ablative absolute, not ablative dependent on *liberum*.

Corcyram, cp. c. 30. 16 and see 26. 20. 7. The *cum* clause follows *tramissa*.

§ **8.** **sub adventum.** See n. on c. 37. 2.

a praesenti impetu tutum, 'secure from an immediate attack.'

§ **9.** **leve dictu**, 'insignificant in itself.' **momentum.** See n. on c. 9. 1. 'A circumstance apparently insignificant turned out to be of considerable moment and aided, etc.'

deperibat amore, 'was deeply enamoured of,' cp. Eng. 'be dying of love for.' In Early Latin *pereo* and *depereo* in this sense are construed with the accusative on the analogy of *amo*.

mulierculae. The diminutive is contemptuous. An old translator renders it 'a small baggage.'

§ **10.** **consuetudine**, 'love affair,' '*liaison*.'

quolibet impelli, 'be induced to do anything,' 'be influenced to any extent.'

§ **11.** **haud vana cogitatio visa**, 'the idea seemed feasible.'

conciliatus, 'introduced.'

blanditiis muliebribus goes with *perpulit* rather than with *explorata levitate*.

§ **12.** **convenit**, 'were agreed on.' The verb agrees with *tempus*.

ratio et tempus, 'plan and time,' do not form a true hendiadys in which one of the two ideas is logically subordinate and attributive to the other.

stationum=*custodiae*, 'sentries.' See n. on c. 2. 11.

Page 26

§ **13.** **ab regione**, not 'away from' but 'on the side of that quarter of the city.' "Fabius marched round the harbour...to the base of the tongue of land on which the city was built, at the apex of which was the citadel" (Stephenson).

§ **14.** **a portu**, i.e. the position opposite the citadel occupied by the Roman troops *in ipsis faucibus portus* (§ 4).

de industria, 'with a purpose,' i.e. to draw the attention of the enemy away from the real attack on the E. side.

§ **15. igitur.** Cicero avoids putting *igitur* first word but in the historians it is normally at the beginning. Quintilian remarks on the difference of opinion among authors as to its proper position. The derivation is disputed. Originally it probably meant 'thereupon.' See also n. on c. 9. 10.

Democrates, the Carthaginian admiral. See Bk 26. c. 39.

illo loco praepositus. Note the local ablative, 'in command *at* that point.' *loco* is not governed by *praepositus*. See Notes on Text.

§ **16. captae urbis clamor**, not 'a shout that the city had been taken,' but 'such shouting as *takes place* in a city that has been taken' =*clamor, ut captae urbis* or *qualis esse in capta urbe solet*, cp. 29. 28. 4 *prope ut captae urbis tumultus fuit*. The word of comparison is omitted here probably because of the presence of the *ut* in a different sense.

interdum, 'at intervals.'

traducit, i.e. across the city.

§ **17. ex temporis spatio**, 'from the time that had elapsed,' i.e. the moment arranged for had arrived, cp. § 12 *tempus convenit*.

praesidium agitare, 'were on guard,' cp. *custodiam* or *vigilias agitare*.

conciliator, 'the man who had engineered.' Gk ὁ κατασκευάσας.

§ **18. ea**, sc. *parte*, 'at that point.'

ut...inferrentur, 'that they might march in.' For *signa inferre* (usu. ='attack') in this sense cp. § 16 and c. 42. 10. **frequenti agmine**, 'in a regular body,' 'in full line.'

§ **19. sub ortum.** See n. on c. 37. 2.

omnesque, accusative gov. by *converterunt*.

ad, 'at,' 'by.' See n. on c. 1. 11.

CHAPTER 16

§ **1. proelium maiore impetu**, 'a sharp struggle ensued but it was soon over.'

vigore...viribus. See n. on 11. 1. The alliteration is here no doubt intentional, cp. the rhetorical repetition of *non* and the repeated *a* in *animo, armis, arte*.

Romano Tarentinus. See n. on c. 9. 3.

§ **2. prius...quam consererent**, 'before they could come to blows,' not merely temporal. See n. on c. 8. 11.

nota. See n. on c. 47. 9.

in domos, 'to their several homes.' Livy frequently omits the preposition with the accusative plural as well as with the accusative singular of *domus*, cp. c. 35. 4.

§ **3**. **Philemenus**, thrown forward out of the subordinate sentence to which it is subject. See n. on c. 3. 1.

proditionis ad Hannibalem. See n. on c. 11. 9.

PAGE 27

§ **4**. **vacuus**, 'riderless.'

praecipitasse. The subject *eum* is understood. *praecipitasse* is reflexive in meaning. If the act is unintentional this reflexive sense readily becomes passive, cp. c. 40. 3. When used of intentional action, 'throw oneself into,' *se* is regularly added, cp. 23. 19. 6.

§ **5**. **miles**, 'a soldier,' not 'the soldiers.'

§ **6**. **alii alios**. Not the ordinary use as in c. 40. 4 *alia super aliam*, but *alii*='other than the slayer of Carthalo,' *alios*='other than Carthalo.'

seu per errorem, seu vetere odio, etc., a mild example of the coupling of words and phrases of different type noted on c. 3. 2.

§ **7**. **servilium capitum**, '30,000 *head* of slaves,' spoken of as cattle, cp. the use of σώματα in Greek. The sing. σῶμα is very frequently used in later Greek manumission inscriptions, e.g. γυναικεῖον σῶμα='a female slave.'

signatique, 'stamped,' cp. *aes signatum*. The earliest issue of stamped silver coins from the Roman mint was in 268 B.C., but Greek silver coinage was of course in use in Magna Graecia and Sicily long before this, and Rome had established a mint at Capua for the issue of silver as early as 335 B.C. See n. on c. 3. 5.

octoginta tria milia, between £3,000,000 and £4,000,000, an immense sum, scarcely credible.

signa ac tabulae, 'statues and paintings.'

prope ut aequaverint, 'almost to equal,' lit. 'so that they have equalled.' The sequence of tenses in clauses of result is exceptional. After a past the perfect subjunctive is used regularly to express (*a*) a perfected result (pure perfect), as here, or (*b*) a result which took place once for all, i.e. regarded as a whole or as a point attained (aoristic perfect, as opposed to imperfect of continuance, equivalent to Greek ὥστε with aorist). Thus in this type of clause the perfect subjunctive is given the two tense meanings of the perfect indicative. In clauses other than consecutive the aoristic perfect subjunctive is rare in classical Latin, cp. c. 44. 2. For contrast between perfect and imperfect see c. 34. 4.

§ 8. **maiore animo**, 'with more magnanimity.'

interroganti scriba. Drachenborch's emendation *scriba* for the MSS. *scribae* is generally adopted by editors. The dative with *iubeo* is unusual, but it occurs in Tacitus combined with an accusative of the thing, with a subjunctive clause, and with an *ut* clause (*Annals* 4. 72. 2, 13. 15. 3, 13. 40. 3). These instances are to be explained on the analogy of *impero*. Dative and infinitive would be a mixture somewhat similar to that seen in the use of δεῖ with dative and infinitive in Greek. Here, however, *iussit* is far removed from *scribae* and the dative may possibly have been written by Livy in careless anticipation of a *respondit* or the like. Wb. suggests *interrogatus a scriba* as the original from which the reading of P is derived. See Notes on the Text. *interroganti*. The *i* form is unusual in the ablative of the present participle except when used as an adjective. In the ablative absolute we have regularly the ablative in *e*, and editors usually alter instances like 1. 54. 6 *sequenti nuntio* to *sequente nuntio*.

fieri signis, 'done *with* the statues.' Cp. *quid me fiet?* 'What will become of me?' The ablative is instrumental. So with *esse* (cp. 33. 27. 11 *quidnam se futurum esse*) and *facere*. The construction runs parallel with the dative *quid mihi fiet?* etc. It might also be regarded as a true ablative of source, 'made from' or 'out of,' since we find also *de* used with the ablative (cp. 5. 20. 3).

sunt, i.e. in Livy's time.

habitu, 'dress,' 'guise,' instrumental ablative of manner.

pugnantium. Plutarch (*Life of Fabius*, c. 22) mentions a colossal statue of Hercules brought from Tarentum and set up in the Capitol.

Tarentinis goes with *iratos*, not with *relinqui*, cp. Plut. *l.c.* ἀπολείπωμεν τοὺς θεοὺς Ταραντίνοις κεχολωμένους.

§ 10. **cursim agmine acto**, 'marching at full speed.'

PAGE 28

§ 12. **fidem...accepturos** might mean 'sent two men who were to obtain a pledge from the consul that, etc.' or 'with a letter to the effect that they would accept the pledged word of the consul.' The difficulty about the second interpretation is that it implies previous negotiations of which we have heard nothing from Livy.

iis=*principibus eius civitatis*.

§ **13.** **diem qua.** Livy has *dies* frequently feminine. Most of the other fifth declension words (exc. *res* and *meridies*) are feminines in *-yē* parallel with first declension *-ā*, cp. *luxuries* beside *luxuria*, and owing to their influence *dies*, which is a masculine like Gk Ζεύς, was made feminine. The analogy of words of similar meaning, like *tempestas*, no doubt also helped.

§ **14.** **enimvero,** 'indeed,' 'naturally.' The old asseverative or corroborative use of *enim* is preserved in this word and in *etenim*, *sed enim*, *neque enim*. *enim* in Plautus regularly means 'indeed' rather than 'for,' cp. *Most.* 1113 *non enim ibis*, *ibid.* 1144 *enim istic captiost*. The word is probably the same as Oscan *inim*, '*et*,' and Umbrian *enom*, '*tum*.' The causal sense of Classical Latin was an easy development of the corroborative force, cp. German *denn*, 'for.' Instances of *enim* asseverative survive, e.g. in Virgil. *enimvero* often marks a contrast 'but really' (5. 25. 6), or an indignant statement 'truly' (6. 14. 12).

si fuisset, virtual oblique expressing Hannibal's thought. *fuisset* might stand for *fuit* or for *fuerit* (fut. perf.) of the direct. In the first case it means 'delighted to think that even Fabius had been outwitted,' in the second 'delighted at the success of his strategy—and successful it would be if it should prove that even Fabius had been outwitted.' Weissenborn prefers the latter.

§ **15.** **priusquam egrederetur.** See n. on 8. 11. There is an idea of purpose in *auspicanti*, 'taking auspices to see whether the omens were in favour of his going.'

aves non addixerunt, 'the fowls were unfavourable,' i.e. 'the sacred chickens refused to eat,' cp. 10. 40. 4 *cum pulli non pascerentur*. *addicere* is the technical term to express propitious omens from birds, cp. 22. 42. 8, and often.

§ **16.** **postquam non venerat.** *postquam* usually takes the (aoristic) perfect or historic present, but when emphasis is laid on the completion of the action before the time of the main clause the pluperfect is used. Thus we find it commonly when the verb of the main clause is in the imperfect (e.g. 9. 45. 6), or when the interval between the two actions is definitely specified (e.g. Cic. *ad Att.* 12. 1. 1 *undecimo die postquam a te discesseram*). Here *venerat* is *venit* (true perfect 'now that he has come') thrown into the past. See also n. on c. 48. 13.

gravioris quaestionis, i.e. examination with torture. For the comparative see n. on c. 13. 13.

CHAPTER 17

§ **1.** **P. Scipio.** For the position see n. on c. 3. 1.

§ **2.** **velut fortuita,** 'which had somehow arisen,' 'without any apparent reason.'

§ **3.** **principibus.** They were the chiefs of the Ilergetes, a tribe north of the Ebro in Tarraconensis.

secedendi, depends on *causa.*

per continentia iuga, 'along a chain of hills.' *continens* = *continuus* as freq., cp. c. 51. 2 *continens agmen.*

PAGE 29

§ **4.** **audendo aliquid moveret,** 'produce an effect by a bold move.'

qua, 'as,' or 'in the direction in which,' for *qua ratione* or *qua parte.*

fluerent. The subject is *res suae,* 'his power would continue to melt away.'

§ **5.** **a spe** = *propter spem,* causal, as is shown by the parallel clause *quod malebat.* The ablative of cause, more commonly without a preposition, here originates, as the *a* shows, from an ablative of source, cp. 2. 49. 12 *ab insita levitate.* More frequently the causal ablative is instrumental.

priusquam iungerentur, 'before they could unite,' i.e. with the idea of preventing their uniting. See n. on c. 8. 11.

§ **6.** **ceterum,** 'however.' See n. on c. 1. 3.

etiamsi...foret, 'in case he should *actually* be obliged to fight.' Virtual oblique. The thought in Scipio's mind would be *si dimicandum erit.* The true apodosis is omitted. See n. on c. 14. 6. For a similar sentence with the apodosis expressed cp. 31. 8. 11 quoted there.

quia...erat. The causal clause is put in the indicative as the remark of the historian. We should have expected *esset* as giving the reason in the mind of Scipio.

navales socios, 'sailors' as opposed to marines. The term is used for both sailors and rowers (e.g. 24. 11. 9) or for rowers alone (e.g. 26. 35. 10). The name *socii* points to their having been originally supplied by the allies, while the regular soldiers on board (*epibatae* or *classiarii*) were Romans, but *socii navales* came to be the general term for sailors; e.g. in 21. 50. 2 it is applied to the Carthaginian fleet.

§ 7. **adfatim.** See n. on c. 48. 17.

Carthagine, sc. *Nova.*

fecerat, 'had had made,' cp. c. 34. 1, 4. 11. 3 *senatus consultum fecerunt*, 'got passed,' 6. 1. 8 *creat*, 'gets appointed.'

tanto opificum numero. See 26. 51. 7 *urbs ipsa strepebat apparatu belli fabris omnium generum in publica officina inclusis.* **incluso** (sc. *officinis*) does not mean 'shut into,' but 'gathered.' There were 2000 craftsmen at New Carthage and Scipio promised them liberty if they worked energetically to supply war material, cp. 26. 47. 2.

§ 8. **ab Tarracone...ab Roma.** *Ab* with names of towns for 'place whence' is chiefly used for the point from which a distance is measured, e.g. *decem milia passuum ab Roma distat*, but Livy generally adds the preposition to towns also to denote 'motion from.' On the other hand, for 'motion to' he has regularly the simple accusative, but to express 'towards' or 'in the direction of' *ad* is added, cp. c. 41. 1.

Laelius. See c. 7. 4.

nihil maioris rei, 'no considerable operation,' partitive genitive. For the comparative used absolutely see n. on 13. 13. **motum,** 'set going,' 'started.' For the p. part. with *volo* cp. *factum volo*, 'I want it done.'

ducere, 'lead,' without object expressed is very common. That the object (*copias*, *exercitum*, etc.) is no longer felt is seen by the addition here of *cum copiis.* Cp. a similar development with ἐμβαλεῖν in Greek. ἐμβαλεῖν is used for κώπας ἐμβαλεῖν 'dip in the oars,' 'row,' and then κώπαις is added, κώπαις ἐμβαλεῖν, 'row with the oars,' e.g. Hom. *Od.* 9. 489.

§ 9. **per omnia pacata,** 'through districts entirely subjugated.' For the use of the neuter plural denoting region, etc., cp. c. 18. 9, c. 39. 7 *per munita pleraque*, 21. 35. 7 *per omnia nive oppleta.* The usage is common in Greek, cp. Xen. *Anab.* 3. 4. 49 ἕως μὲν βάσιμα ἦν, ἐπὶ τοῦ ἵππου ἦγεν κ.τ.λ.

ut, 'as' or 'when.' The clause depends on the ablative absolute following.

transiret. The use of the imperfect or pluperfect subjunctive to denote repeated or customary action is characteristic of Silver Latin, though it begins in Cicero, cp. c. 48. 2, 1. 32. 13 *id ubi dixisset* (whenever he had said) *hastam in fines eorum emittebat*, 5. 42. 4 *quocunque clamor...avertisset, paventes oculos flectebant.* Except with the indefinite 2nd person this iterative subjunctive rarely occurs with the present.

excipientibus, 'welcoming.' See n. on c. 27. 3.

§ **10**. **glorianti eam.** It seems best to construe *glorianti eam* (*occasionem*) *raptam* (*esse*) *velut primam occasionem*, 'not boasting that they had taken the first chance of coming over but rather pleading in excuse that they had been compelled to change sides.' Others understand *transitionem* with *eam* and take *raptam* as equivalent to *raptim factam*. Gronov reads *ea velut ad primam occasionem rapta.*

velut primam, 'pretending it was the first.'

§ **11**. **scire enim se**, etc. Gronov suggests that this is a reminiscence of Thuc. 3. 9.

veteribus...novis. See n. on c. 8. 6.

morem, not 'the practice of changing sides,' but 'the practice of regarding deserters as odious.'

si tamen, 'provided that.' **anceps** with *odium*, 'on either side,' i.e. felt by old and new allies alike. **causa**, 'motive in changing sides.'

§ **12**. **merita in...iniurias in.** See n. on c. 11. 9.

superbiamque. Weissenborn quotes Polyb. 10. 36. 3 *ὑπερηφάνως ἐχρῶντο τοῖς κατὰ τὴν χώραν.*

§ **13**. **dumtaxat**, 'merely,' is a sentence which has crystallised into an adverb. *taxat* is subjunctive from an old verb *taxo* parallel to *tango* (or perhaps to Old Latin *tongere*), and the phrase was used originally in formulae setting a limit to the amount of fine which a magistrate could impose, e.g. *C.I.L.* 1. 48 *eum qui volet magistratus multare*, dum minore parte familias taxat, *liceto*, 'in so far as (or 'provided that') he levies it at less than half the estate.' Hence *dum taxat* came to be used as an adverbial modifier meaning on the one hand 'at most,' on the other 'at least.'

animum, 'their hearts.' **ius ac fas...coli**, 'where the law of man and the law of God are regarded.'

quoque, i.e. 'just as those who, etc.' **hominum**, subjective genitive, 'inflicted by men.'

PAGE 30

§ **14**. **quales...perinde**, 'such as he should find them to be...he should value their services accordingly.' *quales...perinde* is a mixture such as we often get in comparative clauses for *quales...tales* or *ut... perinde*. See n. on c. 6. 5 *praeterquam*.

cognorit...faceret stand for *cognoveris* (fut. perf.) and *fac* of the direct speech. *cognorit* therefore would be an exception to one of Prof. Conway's rules: "Imperfect subjunctive which is regularly used to give a past command throws any verbs that may depend upon it into secondary tenses." See n. on c. 9. 3. Similarly for *sanctum esset* § 15, according to Prof. Conway's rules, we should expect *sanctum sit*.

§ **15**. **facturum**, sc. *se*, cp. c. 9. 8.

ratam, 'valid.'

§ **16**. **productae...in conspectum iis**, 'led forward into their presence,' see n. on c. 1. 5. *productae in conspectum...in hospitium abducti* seems to be an artificial rhetorical antithesis on a par with 'Miss Bolo went home *in a flood of tears and a sedan chair*.'

§ **17**. **foedere...fides**, 'pledge obtained under formal bond of alliance.' *foedere* is an ablative of manner, 'by way of a treaty.' Note the combination of *fides* and *foedus*, words from the same root.

isdem...tendebant, 'they shared the same camp.' *tendere* (sc. *tentoria*) 'encamp.' Distinguish the use of *tendere* (sc. *cursum* or *iter*), 'march.'

ducibus iis, 'under these men's guidance.' *dux* frequently = 'guide,' cp. c. 47. 9.

CHAPTER **18**

§ **1**. **Hasdrubalis**, 'namely Hasdrubal's.'

Baeculam. This town lay to the N. of the Baetis (Guadalquivir) and in the district of the important town of Castulo, the scene of the defeat of P. and Cn. Scipio in 212 B.C.

§ **2**. **antesignani**. The word has caused difficulty here. As in battle array the *signa* were apparently in front of the second line (see n. on c. 1. 11), *antesignani* meant the front companies of the first division, but the word does not appear to be used elsewhere in reference to a skirmishing attack. It seems doubtful, however, what the meaning of *antesignani* was in reference to a marching column (*agmen*) since the standards were carried in front of the army on the march. See also n. on c. 47. 1.

priusquam caperent seems to be purely temporal. See n. on c. 8. 11.

§ **5**. **plano campo...patentem**, 'with an extensive plateau on the top.'

ante circaque, adverbs, 'in front and at the sides.'

velut ripa, 'what resembled a steep river bank.' **oram eius**, 'the edge of the plateau.' *ripa* and *oram* are no doubt suggested by *fluvius*.

§ **6**. **inferior**, 'at a lower level.' **summissa fastigio**, lit. 'let down by a slope,' i.e. 'which sloped gradually down.' Weissenborn cps. Curtius 6. 22. 23 *rupes...leniore summissa fastigio*. For *fastigium* see n. on c. 31. 6.

altera crepido, 'a second steep slope.' *crĕpīdo* (borrowed from Greek κρηπίς), properly 'a base,' is used of any steep elevation or bank.

faciliori ascensu. See Notes on Text.

§ **7**. **leviumque armorum**, 'of the light armed troops,' partitive genitive. *arma=armati*, cp. our use of 'arms' for the various branches of the army.

§ **8**. **ordines signaque.** See n. on c. 1. 10.

praedamnata spe, 'because they recognised there was no hope for them if they fought on level ground.'

PAGE 31

quae transcendisset. *quae* is continuative, i.e. equivalent to *et ea*, and so Livy might have written the clause in the accusative and infinitive. See n. on c. 33. 10.

§ **9**. **nec...nec...ne quidem.** Instead of a third *neque, ne quidem* adds the emphasised point in asyndeton, cp. Tac. *Germ.* 7 *neque animadvertere neque vincire, ne verberare quidem*.

ad id. The sentence begins as if to introduce a clause of purpose but ends in one of consequence, 'the heights would serve the purpose of compelling the enemy in their flight to leap down, etc.' **per praecipitia.** See n. on c. 17. 9.

§ **10**. **cohortesque.** *que* 'and so,' 'accordingly.' Cp. Caes. *B.C.* 2. 26 *praemittit equites...ipse aciem instruit...equitesque committunt proelium*. This explanatory *que* continues the account and thus frequently as summing up is used to give the natural consequence arising from what precedes. In Greek τε is used commonly in the same way, cp. Thuc. 1. 12 (after an account of the various ethnic movements in Greece after the Trojan war) μόλις τε πολλῷ χρόνῳ ἡσυχάσασα ἡ Ἑλλὰς κ.τ.λ., 'and so.' Thuc. 4. 4. 11 (after a description in detail of the Athenian soldiers fortifying Pylos) παντί τε τρόπῳ ἠπείγοντο φθῆναι τοὺς Λακεδαιμονίους.

alteram...alteram, in partitive apposition to *cohortes*, cp. c. 6. 8, c. 12. 5, etc.

fauces vallis. Livy has not mentioned this before. As usual his description of the battlefield is lacking in clearness.

insidere, from *insīdo*, 3rd conj. 'settle into,' 'occupy,' not *insĭdeo*, 'be settled into,' 'be in occupation of.' In many cases, however, either meaning would suit, and outside the present stem the conjugation of the two verbs is the same. Cp. the difference between *possīdo* and *possĭdeo.*

ab urbe, i.e. Baecula.

per tumuli obliqua, 'at a slant across the slope,' cp. 9. 3. 1 *per adversa montium* and see n. on c. 2. 9.

ferret, 'led,' intransitive. It is usually said that *viatorem* is understood as object in such cases but it is unlikely that the Romans felt this. See n. on c. 17. 8 *ducere*, and cp. Gk ὁδὸς φέρει and Eng. 'the road bears to the right.'

infimo...supercilio, 'at the bottom of the slope.' *supercilium*, metaph. like Eng. 'brow' (of hill).

§ **11.** **per aspreta,** 'over rough ground.' *per aspera* is the reading of several MSS.

nihil aliud quam, adverbial accusative, 'in no other wise than.' Cp. 2. 20. 3 *nec quicquam equo retardato.* With this phrase sometimes a verb may be supplied, e.g. *nihil aliud* (*facit*) *quam*, but usually it is to be treated as an adverbial accusative = 'simply,' 'only,' cp. οὐδὲν ἄλλο ἤ in Greek.

via, i.e. 'the difficulty of the ground.'

sub ictum venerunt. With *ictus* usually *teli* is added. Here it is omitted probably because of the following *telorum.* For 'come within range' *ad coniectum teli venire* is the common phrase; cp. also *ad ictum teli venire* and *sub ictu esse.*

§ **13.** **succedendi muros,** 'climbing walls.' With the dative c. 42. 11 *successit vallo* means 'marched up to the rampart.'

§ **14.** **concursatorem,** 'light-armed skirmishers who keep at a safe distance and evading a regular battle discharge volleys of missiles from long range.' See n. on c. 13. 2 *victor.* For *eluditur* cp. Tac. *Ann.* 2. 52. 5 *ne bellum metu eluderent, ibid.* 3. 74. 1 *pluris per globos concursaret eluderetque. pugna eluditur* may mean 'they make feints,' 'keep up an evasive fight.' It is better to take the present tense as applying to light-armed troops in general than as historic present like *dum...volunt* in § 16. Note that *missilibus* is not governed by *procul*.

eundem, *idem*, as regularly, contrasts two acts or characteristics of the same person, cp. the use of the article in Homer.

impegere, 'drove them back upon.'

§ **15**. **evadere**, 'make their way up against,' 'get up the slope against.' *evadere* is frequently used of making one's way through and out of difficulties, 'win clear,' cp. 9. 39. 8 *ut equites...per arma per corpora evaserint*; hence of surmounting a height c. 27. 5 *evadere in iugum*, 2. 17. 5 *ut in muros evaderet miles*.

parte dextra, 'by the right,' ablative of route. *dextra* and *laeva* refer of course to the right and left of the Romans.

in transversos, 'charge the enemy on the flank.' As regularly with *transversus* we have the adjectival construction instead of the adverb; cp. c. 42. 6 *in transversa latera*.

§ **16**. **flectere...obvertere**, 'wheel...face.' Hasdrubal's left wing was to wheel to the left to face Laelius and the right wing to the right to face Scipio. *volunt* seems to imply that the wheeling movement was not actually carried through (cp. § 19 *in nuda latera*). Before it was completed the enemy, finding Laelius in their *rear*, fell back (*pedem referunt*) and consequently the formation of their line was broken and space was left for the Roman *expediti* in the centre to mount to the upper plateau.

§ **17**. **hoc tumultu**, 'in the midst of this confusion.' The ablative may be either locatival or instrumental in origin. See n. on c. 2. 10.

et Laelius. He had made a longer detour and did not come in touch with the enemy as soon as Scipio.

pedem referunt. The subject of *referunt*, as of *volunt*, is apparently *hostis* generally.

ad evadendum. See n. on § 15.

et mediis, i.e. the *expediti*, referred to in § 15 as *victoribus*.

PAGE 32

§ **18**. **stantibus...locatis**. Ablative absolute equivalent to a conditional sentence, 'if the ranks had been standing unbroken.'

ante signa. See n. on § 2.

§ **19**. **maxime**, 'chiefly,' 'particularly,' cp. 9. 40. 5 *alia maxime plebis turba*.

nuda latera, i.e. on their right, the side uncovered by the shield.

§ **20.** **vias**, cp. § 10.

porta castrorum...fuga clausa. *fuga* is causal ablative, 'owing to the flight.' Livy has not told us the position of the Carthaginian camp in relation to the *tumulus* and he does not now explain why the flight of Hasdrubal should have closed the gate of the camp.

CHAPTER 19

§ **1.** **antequam dimicaret.** The subjunctive may denote Hasdrubal's purpose, but it may be purely temporal here. See n. on c. 8. 16.

rapta, 'hurriedly got together.'

excipiens. See n. on c. 27. 3.

praeter, 'along,' 'past.' Cp. *praeter pedes*, *praeter oram Italiae*, *praeter ora*, etc. **tendit**, 'marches.' His march was nearly due N. Hasdrubal crossed the Pyrenees at the W. end, cp. Appian, Bk 6. c. 28 παρὰ τὸν βόρειον ὠκεανὸν τὴν Πυρήνην ἐς Γαλάτας ὑπερέβαινεν.

§ **4.** **quo se...appellassent.** It appears that the general, though holding the *imperium*, did not receive this title until he had won a considerable victory and was saluted as *imperator* by his soldiers on the field. This is called by Tacitus (*Ann.* 3. 74) *priscus erga duces honor*. We have here the earliest mention of the custom. The first instance of a general calling himself *imperator* on an inscription is Aemilius Paulus in 189 B.C. See Mommsen, *Staatsr.* 1². p. 124 f. In later times the title was reserved strictly for the Emperors, though Augustus occasionally gave special permission for the general to receive it, cp. Tacitus *l.c.* *concessit quibusdam et Augustus id vocabulum ac tunc Tiberius Blaeso postremum.*

§ **5.** **amplissimum ducerent**, 'regard as most worthy of recognition.'

§ **6.** **cuius miraculo nominis**, 'a title the magnificence of which proves dazzling to the minds of most men.'

tam alto fastigio, 'from such a lofty height.' See n. on c. 31. 6 and Notes on Text.

PAGE 33

§ **9.** **cuias**, 'from what country he was.' *cuias* (O.L. *quoiatis*) is formed from the possessive adjective *cuius* ('whose,' Gk ποῖος) with the suffix *-āti* denoting the place of birth, cp. *Arpinas* a native of Arpinum, *nostras*, etc.

id aetatis, 'so young,' the accusative of extent of time where we should expect the ablative, *ea aetate*. This usage is colloquial in origin. Cp. Plaut. *M. G.* 618 *tibi istuc aetatis homini*. We find it extended in later prose to other accusatives of extent, cp. Tacitus *nemo id auctoritatis aderat*.

fuisset. With *quis* and *cuias* we must understand *esset*.

§ **11.** **in praeceps,** 'headlong.' See n. on c. 3. 1. Third declension adjectives are rarely used thus even in Livy, cp. 6. 40. 18 *in commune*, 42. 66. 7 *per praeceps*, 3. 8. 9 *in facili*.

pro tribunali. In the camp the *tribunal* was a raised platform placed at the corner of the *praetorium* from which the general addressed his soldiers and administered justice. *pro tribunali* is locatival 'forward on the tribunal,' i.e. 'on the front of,' not ablatival 'in front of,' cp. *pro rostris* and 21. 7. 8 *non pro moenibus modo atque turri tela micare*. Gk πρὸ ὁδοῦ 'forward on the way.'

§ **12.** **cupere vero.** *vero* is vividly retained from the direct ('I do *indeed* wish it'), cp. 28. 9. 8.

anulum...lato clavo. The ring and the *latus clavus* ('broad purple band on tunic') were the badges of a senator.

ornatum, 'caparisoned.'

CHAPTER 20

§ **1.** **auctoribus ut.** *auctor est=suadet* and consequently takes the same construction. Cp. n. on c. 1. 8.

consequeretur, 'endeavour to overtake,' the *con* gives the perfective idea in 'overtake' and the imperfect tense the conative idea.

§ **2.** **ne...iungerent.** *ne* depends on the idea of 'precaution' in *anceps ratus*. Editors point out that this remark is an attempt to excuse Scipio's serious blunder in allowing Hasdrubal to slip past him into Italy.

alter Hasdrubal=Hasdrubal, son of Gisgo.

§ **3.** **Castulonensi.** See n. on c. 18. 1.

serum...opportuni. The antithesis is heightened by the chiastic order and the asyndeton, 'too late to help but in good time to advise.'

exsequenda. Madg. reads *exsequendi* agreeing with *belli* and takes *in cetera* (? =*per reliquum et in posterum*) as dependent on it and *belli exsequendi* objective genitive with *consilio*. The MSS. reading, however, may be retained. *belli* is partitive genitive with *cetera*, like 25. 15. 20

ad subita belli and *in cetera* depends on the phrase *consilio opportuni*, 'in-good-time-with-counsel for.'

haud parum. See n. on c. 12. 13.

PAGE 34

§ 4. quid...animorum, partitive genitive, 'what was the state of feeling among the Spaniards?' **in cuiusque provinciae regione,** 'in their several districts.' *cuiusque* is masculine and dependent on *provinciae*. Madvig's reading *cuiusque provincia et regione*, which involves a very slight correction of the MSS. may be right. He suggests that Livy added *et regione* to show that Carthaginian Spain was not divided into regular provinces.

Hasdrubal Gisgonis, 'Gisgo's Hasdrubal.' The omission of the formal *filius* is common in the case of foreigners. Cp. the omission of *servus* and *uxor* in the case of slaves and women.

adhuc, 'up to this time.' *adhuc* is often used vividly of past events for *etiam tum* or *ad id tempus* (cp. c. 40. 8), just as *hic* is retained in oblique for *ille* and *nunc* for *tum*. See n. on c. 9. 4.

§ 5. publice privatimque in sense may go with *beneficiis*, 'his kindness to them as states and as individuals.' Cp. Caes. *B.G.* 5. 55 *amicitiam publice privatimque petere.*

§ 6. senatus...censuisset. See c. 5. 11 f. *censuisset...eundum fuisse* is oblique of *censuisset...eundum fuit.*

ubi belli caput rerumque summa, 'which was the main centre of the war and the place where the supreme issue was to be decided.'

§ 7. repleri, 'have gaps filled up.' The infinitives depend on a *statuerunt*, or the like, to be gathered from *constabat*, and implied in *his decretis* and *statuerant* at the end of § 8.

§ 8. quod roboris esset, 'the pick of all the cavalry.' See n. on c. 14. 5. The phrase is in apposition to *tria milia equitum.* **expleri,** 'be made up to full number.'

vagum, 'ranging up and down.'

agros populari. *populari*, 'harry,' means originally 'fill with people' hence, 'overrun.' Cp. Eng. 'harry' which is the same root as Germ. Heer, 'a host.'

§ 9. astu magis. See 15. 9 f.

senescere, 'was on the wane.' **Fulvi,** i.e. Q. Fulvius Flaccus. He had been in command of armies each year since the fall of Capua but had not added to his laurels by any considerable achievement.

§ **10.** **superquam quod,** used by Livy for the more usual *praeter-quam quod*; cp. 22. 3. 14 and see n. on c. 6. 5.

PAGE 35

quia...abduxisset, subjunctive of virtual oblique implied in *adverso rumore.*

in tecta, i.e. into the shelter of buildings. In camp they would be *sub pellibus.* Cp. c. 21. 3 *aestiva Venusiae sub tectis agere.*

§ **11.** **a prima pugna.** See c. 12. 14 f.

contionibus, 'harangues.'

§ **12.** **cum tamen,** 'his friends however succeeded in getting permission for him to come to Rome.' Cp. Cic. *Verr.* 5. 29 *fit gemitus omnium et clamor cum tamen...continuit populus Romanus se et repressit.* *cum tamen* adds a fact adversatively, and the use is similar to that of *cum inversum*, where what would normally be the *cum* clause is made the main clause and *cum* introduces what is logically the leading verb. In both constructions *cum* always takes the indicative. Distinguish *cum tamen*, 'although,' introducing a concessive clause and followed by the subjunctive. "*Claudi* and *Marcellus* are the same person. The use of the *nomen* in the first clause suggests the strong family interest at work" (Stephenson).

§ **13.** **venit,** sing. agreeing with *Fulvius* only.

CHAPTER 21

§ **1.** **circo Flaminio.** The *prata Flaminia* lay along the Tiber in the S. of the *Campus Martius.* We hear of assemblies being held there as early as the fifth century B.C. The *circus Flaminius* was constructed in this meadow by the Consul Flaminius who was defeated and slain at Trasimene.

§ **2.** **nobilitatem** = *nobiles.*

provinciam habeat. See n. on c. 7. 7. Edd. quote 21. 5. 1 *velut Italia ei provincia decreta* and 22. 44. 6 *velut usu cepisset Italiam.*

diutius. This is actually true. Hannibal had been taken to Spain by his father, Hamilcar Barca, at nine years of age.

§ **3.** **prorogati Marcello,** *dat. commodi*, 'prolonged for Marcellus.' This is part of the attack on the *nobilitas* (§ 2) since it was by decree of the Senate that a command was regularly prolonged at this time. See n. on c. 7. 17.

aestiva. See n. on c. 4. 1.

§ **4.** **obruit,** 'overwhelmed,' 'swamped,' cp. n. on c. 14. 13.

antiquaretur, 'was rejected.' This sense of *antiquare* (*legem*) is derived from the voting phrase '*antiqua volo*,' 'I prefer the old.'

§ **5.** **P. Licinius Crassus,** cp. c. 6. 17.

§ **6.** **C. Calpurnius.** C. Calpurnius Piso was praetor with *urbis iurisdictio* in 211 B.C. In 210 B.C. he held Etruria as propraetor and was continued in the command of the same province in 209 B.C. Cp. c. 7. 10.

Arretinis. Arretium, mod. Arezzo, was one of the chief cities in N.E. Etruria.

PAGE 36

§ **7.** **eo metu.** See n. on c. 1. 5.

§ **9.** **Ludi Romani et plebei.** See n. on c. 6. 19.

in singulos dies instaurati, 'repeated each for a single day.' The expression here is unusual. See n. on c. 6. 19.

Caudinus. See Bk 9, c. 4 and c. 15. "L. Cornelius Lentulus was legate in the Caudine campaign and recommended the consuls to accept the terms offered by the Samnites. He was dictator the next year and, as his descendants claimed, was the general who avenged the Caudine disaster. L. Cornelius Lentulus, consul in B.C. 237, was the first who assumed the cognomen" (Stephenson).

§ **10.** **negabant.** The subject is indefinite 'people declared it illegal.'

quod patrem...vivere. Livy does not explain here how the holding of these offices while his father was alive was illegal, nor does the fuller phrase in Bk 30. c. 19. 7 (*quod patre qui sella curuli sedisset vivo...*) make it any clearer. It has been suggested that C. Servilius was a patrician and became a plebeian in order to hold the tribunate and plebeian aedileship and that for this his father's consent would be necessary. But if this explanation is correct, what is the point of adding *qui sella curuli sedisset* in Book 30?

triumvirum agrarium. The usual phrase is *triumvir agris dandis assignandis* or *agro dando* (in Inscriptions IIIVIR · A · D · A). When a colony was established a law was passed (*lex coloniae*) containing regulations for the foundation, and commissioners (usually three in number) were appointed to see to the carrying out of these regulations.

a Boiis circa Mutinam. In 218 B.C. Livy tells the story in 21. 25. 3 but mentions that the facts are doubtful. Six years after this date (203 B.C.) C. Servilius was consul with Etruria as his province and released his father and his fellow triumvir, C. Lutatius, from captivity. Cp. 30. 19. 7 *privato magis quam publico decore insignis.*

CHAPTER 22

§ 1. **ut numeretur,** 'provided that we count.'

quem vitio creatus. See 23. 31. 13. In 215 B.C. Marcellus had been elected consul in the place of L. Postumius who when consul designate was slain in battle in Gaul, but on account of an inauspicious peal of thunder on his entry into office he retired and Q. Fabius Maximus was elected suffect consul.

§ 2. **utrisque consulibus** = *ambobus consulibus.* Properly the plural of *uterque* is employed to denote two classes or parties each consisting of a number of individuals. Livy, however, not infrequently uses it of individual persons or things, cp. 9. 12. 2 *utraque consilia,* 30. 8. 7 *utraque cornua* (where Cicero would write *utrumque consilium, utrumque cornu*).

Sallentini. This district embraced the S. of Calabria and the Iapygian promontory. It was subdued after the Pyrrhic wars but revolted in the 2nd Punic War.

§ 3. **divisae,** 'apportioned.' The *provinciae* were apportioned by lot among the praetors after the Senate had specified the spheres to be held by them.

quo...censuisset. See n. on c. 7. 8. The same phrase is used of the consul in 35. 20. 7. Cp. 42. 28. 7 *ita decretae ut uni sors integra esset quo senatus censuisset. censuisset* is of course oblique of *censuerit* (Fut. Perf.) not of *censuerat.*

prorogatum...ut. See notes on c. 7. 8 and c. 21. 3. *ut* means 'with the proviso that.' Cp. c. 7. 10. Note the constant necessity for the prolonging of commands. It became obvious in the 2nd Punic War that the two consuls and the two extra-urban praetors were not sufficient to fill the necessary military commands. Shortly after the end of the war (in 197 B.C.) the number of praetors was raised to six.

quae...fuerat, indicative, a remark of Livy's. See n. on c. 7. 9.

§ 5. **quibus obtinuisset,** subjunctive as belonging to the decree.

PAGE 37

§ **6.** **in L. Veturio,** 'in the case of,' cp. c. 1. 9 *in Fulviis.* **latumque...ad populum.** This was exceptional. See n. on c. 21. 3 and cp. 29. 13. 7. In this case perhaps the *plebiscitum* was required because Sardinia was one of the four fixed *provinciae* (urban, peregrine, Sicily, Sardinia) to which praetors were assigned.

naves quas misisset. See n. on c. 7. 9. **additae,** equivalent to *decretum est ut adderentur.*

§ **7.** **suae...sui,** emphatic. The provinces had been assigned to them indefinitely, c. 7. 17, hence they are called 'their own.' This must have been a formal renewal of the *prorogatio.*

Carthagine, sc. *Nova.* In § 8 *Carthagine* is Carthage in Africa.

§ **8.** **impleturos,** sc. *Poenos,* 'invest.'

§ **9.** **exercitus Cannensis.** See n. on c. 7. 12.

obtineret, adderet...traiceret. Past jussives, i.e. oblique of the imperative.

eo=*ad eam.* See n. on c. 1. 13.

§ **11.** **quo.** Weissenborn rightly takes this as=*ad quas legiones.* Cp. *unde*=*ex quo* or *ex quibus* and see n. on c. 1. 13.

scriberent. See n. on c. 10. 2.

una et viginti. The number of legions varied. In 214 B.C. it was as low as 18; in the following year it was 23. The size of the army in Spain is not mentioned here but it must have been 4 legions, as 17 are accounted for in §§ 1–10, and cp. c. 36. 12, where the number is given as 4.

§ **12.** **sociis.** See n. on c. 17. 6.

naves longas triginta veteres. See n. on c. 8. 11.

compleret, 'man,' πληροῦν. Another reading is *impleret.*

PAGE 38

§ **13.** **idem imperatum,** 'Tubulus also received similar orders, to the effect that.' *idem,* explained by *ut...caveret,* is used somewhat loosely to express the same general meaning as that of the clause *vetitus movere.*

inde, probably=*ab Arretio* (Weissenborn).

nova consilia caperentur, 'revolt.' See n. on c. 24. 7.

CHAPTER 23

§ **1. litabant.** *litare*=‘sacrifice with favourable omens,’ ‘make atonement.’ *litare* perhaps contains the same root as λιτή, λίσσομαι, etc. If the derivation which makes it a frequentative from the same root as *lino* be accepted, the second meaning, ‘appease,’ ‘atone’ (i.e. ‘erase,’ ‘blot out’), would be the earlier and from it would come the idea of favourable omens.

§ **2. prava religio inserit,** ‘superstition sees God's hand in the smallest trifles.’ **minimis rebus** does not mean the mice but the fact of their gnawing the gold.

§ **3. Casini.** The names are obviously arranged geographically. *et* before *Ostiae* corresponds to the *et* before *ex Campania. Casinum,* however, is not in Campania but in Latium. *Casilinum* (Bk 22. 15, 23. 17) in Campania would suit. The emendation *Cas*[*il*]*ini* is therefore probably correct.

Vulsiniis, in Etruria at the N.E. end of a lake of the same name.

sanguine. This phenomena was due no doubt to the nature of the soil. Cp. n. on c. 11. 5.

§ **4. hostiae maiores.** See n. on c. 4. 15.

§ **5. ludi Apollinares.** See n. on c. 11. 6.

§ **6. evasit in,** ‘issued in,’ ‘resulted in.’

§ **7. compita.** See n. on c. 4. 12.

in statam diem. Games held each year on a fixed day were called *ludi stati.* If the day of celebration was fixed annually they were called *ludi conceptivi,* e.g. *Feriae Latinae.*

a. d. tertium nonas=July 5th; but in 37. 4. 4 (190 B.C.) Livy gives the date as July 11th (*a. d. quintum idus*), so perhaps *nonas* is a mistake here. The 13th remained the day on which the games ended.

CHAPTER 24

PAGE 39

§ **1. in dies,** the *in* has prospective force, (‘from day) to day.’ Hence *in dies,* ‘daily,’ may be used where there is a notion of change, whether increase or diminution, or looking forward *to,* cp. c. 36. 1 *cura in dies crescebat,* 21. 11. 11 *minorem in dies urbem,* 22. 39. 15 *qui senescat in dies,* 22. 43. 2 *nova consilia in dies...oriebantur,* 34. 11. 4

in dies exspectat, 38. 37. 3 *incertus in dies terror* (i.e. *terror* renewed each day).

gravior, sc. *esse*.

§ 3. **[tempus]** is probably a gloss. See Notes on Text.

dare...sumpturum edixit. *edicere* in a double sense 'ordered' and 'announced.' We should expect *ut darent* in the first clause. The infinitive may be explained as due to the analogy of *iubere*. We may compare the double sense of ἔδοξε in Eur. *I. T.* 279 ἔδοξε δ' ἡμῶν εὖ λέγειν τοῖς πλείοσι, | θηρᾶν τε τῇ θεῷ σφάγια τἀπιχώρια ('he seemed to us and we resolved').

§ 4. **priusquam...locarentur,** 'before the guards could be placed.' See n. on c. 8. 11.

§ 5. **citari coeptus esset.** *coepi* is generally attracted into the passive where a passive infinitive depends on it; similarly we find *desitus est* with a passive and in Old Latin *nequeo* and *queo* are attracted, cp. Plaut. *Rud.* 1064 *ut nequitur comprimi!*

desiderati, 'missed.'

omnia suspectiora fecit, 'made the Senate think the danger more threatening than they had previously done.' Cp. 9. 13. 11 *artiora fecit omnia*.

§ 6. **Etrusco tumultu.** See n. on c. 1. 10.

alteram, in apposition to *unam*, 'viz. one of the urban legions.'

§ 7. **novare cupientibus.** The construing order is *occasio daretur cupientibus res novare*. The position of *res* is curious. For *res novare*, 'cause a revolt,' cp. Gk νεωτερίζειν.

§ 8. **intercidisse,** 'got lost.' *intercidere*, lit. 'fall between,' i.e. 'drop short of mark,' and so 'fall to the ground.'

§ 9. **intentius,** 'earnestly.' See n. on c. 13. 13.

in eo spem...poneret si. The *si* clause explains *in eo*, 'to depend for security against a rising in Etruria simply and solely upon the timely measures he took to prevent the possibility of it.'

CHAPTER 25

PAGE 40

§ 1. **aequantibus.** Conative present, cp. § 3 *notantibus...decernentibus*. 'Who wanted to make their guilt as great as that of the Campanians and to mete out to them the same punishment.' For the *comparatio compendiaria* see n. on c. 1. 3 and cp. 9. 10. 3 *eum...devotioni*

P. Deci aequabant. *eos* stands for *eorum noxam poenamque,* since it is really the *noxa Tarentorum* and not the *Tarentini,* that is put on a level with the *noxa Campanorum.*

noxae. See n. on c. 3. 4.

poenae. See Bk 26, c. 15 f. The Capuan Senators were scourged and beheaded, the citizens were transported and the lands forfeited.

§ **2.** **in sententiam,** 'in accordance with,' cp. *in sententiam dicere* (Eng. 'speak *to* a motion'). *in* means 'towards,' 'in the direction of,' and this usage is probably an extension from cases like *in sententiam pedibus ire.*

§ **3.** **M. Livio.** *M. Livius Macatus.* See n. on c. 15. 15.

notantibus, 'wanted to pass a vote of censure on.' **decernentibus,** 'were for voting rewards.' See n. on § 1.

socordia proditum. For the story of the capture see Bk 25, c. 8 f. According to Polybius (8. 28. 29) Livius was drunk. Livy gives him a good character in 24. 10. 13. In 25. 10. 3 he tells of his being roused by the tumult and shouting and making his escape by boat to the citadel.

§ **4.** **quinquennium,** from 214 B.C. to 209 B.C.

esset...foret. See n. on § 8.

§ **5.** **mediis,** 'the more moderate.' Cp. the use in Greek of *οἱ μέσοι* or *οἱ ἐν μέσῳ* to denote 'moderate oligarchs' as opposed to democrats and extreme oligarchs.

notionem. *notio* is a legal term 'the taking cognisance of,' 'inquiry' (=*cognitio*). Early editors altered it to *notationem* or *cognitionem,* but *notio* is frequent in Cicero in this sense, cp. especially *notio censoria.*

de eo. See n. on c. 7. 3 and c. 11. 9.

neque enim. Cicero (*Cato Maior* 4. 11) quotes the same sally, *certe, inquit, ridens, nam nisi tu amisisses, nunquam recepissem.* Cp. Plut. *Fab.* c. 23 (Λίβιος) εἶπεν ὡς οὐ Φάβιος, ἀλλ' αὐτὸς αἴτιος γένοιτο τοῦ τὴν Ταραντίνων ἁλῶναι· γελάσας οὖν ὁ Φάβιος, Ἀληθῆ λέγεις, εἶπεν, εἰ μὴ γὰρ σὺ τὴν πόλιν ἀπέβαλες, οὐκ ἂν ἐγὼ παρέλαβον. *neque enim* might be taken in its ordinary sense 'and indeed...not,' but more probably *enim*='for' here. See n. on c. 16. 14.

§ **6.** **cum supplemento.** See c. 22. 11.

§ **7.** **aliae atque aliae,** 'various,' 'a succession of.'

bello Gallico ad Clastidium. Clastidium, mod. Casteggio, was S. of the Po on the road from Placentia. In the war against the

Insubres in N. Italy in 222 B.C. Marcellus as consul slew their chief Viridomarus and won the *spolia opima* at the battle of Clastidium. The poet Naevius made this the subject of a Roman tragedy in his play *Clastidium*.

Honori et Virtuti. We find many instances of temples dedicated to personifications of this kind, e.g. *Fortuna*, *Fides*, *Mens Bona*, *Pavor*, *Salus*, *Spes*, *Valetudo*, etc. Scipio adorned his dedication with works of art taken in 212 B.C. at the sack of Syracuse.

quod...quod...quia...quod. The sentence is clumsily constructed. Livy is giving a string of reasons each dependent on the one preceding. The first *quod* is explanatory of *religiones tenebant*. The last *quod* gives the reason for *difficilis procuratio* which in its turn is the reason for *negabant recte dedicari* which again is the reason for *impediebatur*.

§ **8.** **quia difficilis.** If the direct form was *si factum erit*, *difficilis p. erit*, we should expect here *futura esset* instead of the imperfect subjunctive. See n. on c. 35. 5 *haberet*. In Cicero the forms *forem*, etc. are very rare but Livy uses them freely for *essem*, etc. without any apparent distinction of meaning. Cp. § 4 *tutatus esset...receptum foret*, I. 46. 3 *ut...ultimumque regnum esset quod scelere partum foret*. It appears likely, however, that originally *forem*, etc. were equivalent to *futurus essem* etc., just as *fore* is regularly used for *futurum esse*, and it is suggested that *foret* here is a survival of this meaning. But it is not necessary to take it so, for the *oratio recta* may have been in the ideal condition form, *si factum sit*, *difficilis sit* ('if we should find that anything...has taken place, it would be difficult'), and the indirect form of this would be imperfect subjunctive.

utri deo, i.e. 'Honor' or 'Virtus.' **res divina** 'sacrifice.' Cp. CIL. IX. 4766 *quo die res deina anua fiet*.

fieret, 'should be offered,' oblique of 'deliberative' subjunctive.

PAGE 41

§ **9.** **una hostia**, 'with one victim,' instrumental ablative, cp. *bovid piaclom datod*, 'let him make atonement with one ox,' on the inscription just mentioned. We also find the accusative of the thing sacrificed by an analogical extension somewhat similar to that noted on c. 17. 8 *ducere*.

fieri. Understand *rem divinam*. The omission is so common that we find *facere* frequently = *sacrificare*; cp. Plaut. *Stich.* 251 *quot agnis fecerat*, Virg. *Ecl.* 3. 77 *cum faciam vitula pro frugibus*.

certis deis. *certi dei* is perhaps used in a technical sense. We are told that Varro mentions this appellation as denoting the gods who presided over the various functions and stages of life. Others take *certis* as meaning *quibusdam* or 'certainly specified.'

ab ipso. The dedication was carried out by his son, cp. 29. 11. 13.

§ **10.** **priore anno.** See c. 20. 12.

§ **11.** **Locros.** In 215 B.C. Locri, after allowing its Roman praefect to escape, surrendered without resistance and was admitted to alliance with the Carthaginians *eo iure ut Poenus Locrensem, Locrensisque Poenum pace et bello iuvaret* (24. 1. 13).

indidem = *ex Sicilia.* See n. on c. 12. 5.

§ **12.** **Lacinium,** sc. *promunturium*, the Lacinian promontory near Croton, now called Capo delle Colonne from the columns of the famous temple of the Lacinian Juno which stood upon it. Cp. Virg. *Aen.* 3. 552 *diva Lacinia.* It marked the treaty boundary between Rome and Tarentum in earlier days. *Lacinium* is terminal accusative without preposition as with names of towns.

§ **13.** **Bantiam,** mod. *Banzi*, known to modern scholars in connexion with the *Tabula Bantina*, an inscription written in Oscan and Latin.

minus, with *trium milium p.* See n. on c. 12. 14.

§ **14.** **si...commisisset sese,** 'if he should venture to engage.' We have *se committere* with dative of the conflict (*pugnae* or *proelio*) several times in Livy (cp. 10. 16. 2, 5. 32. 4 etc.), but here *duobus exercitibus c. iunctis* is probably ablative absolute. Edd. compare 3. 42. 4 *se aequo certamine committentes.*

debellari, impersonal passive.

CHAPTER 26

§ **1.** **ex vano,** 'on insufficient grounds,' i.e. he had good reasons to hope for success and also to fear defeat. Cp. 2. 37. 8 *ex supervacuo* and see n. on c. 3. 1.

ut...habebat. See Notes on Text. The MSS. *ut...haberet* would mean 'as he would have.'

§ **2.** **totus,** 'wholly'; cp. Horace, *Sat.* 1. 9. 2 *totus in illis.*

suas, emphatic 'characteristic of him'; cp. 21. 34. 1 *sed suis artibus fraude et insidiis.*

inter bina castra, not the *bina castra* of the two consuls (c. 25. 13) but the camps of Hannibal and the Romans.

§ **3.** **L. Cincio.** See c. 5. 1, and c. 8. 17.

§ **4.** **ab terra,** 'on the land side.' See n. on c. 1. 10.

PAGE 42

§ **5.** **Hannibali,** dative of agent, originating in an ordinary dative of the 'person interested or affected,' 'Hannibal had received information that...,' cp. c. 27. 13 *sibi comperta*. This construction maintains itself as against the ablative with *ab* chiefly with the perfect passive participle and gerundive where the original force can be more readily felt. With other tenses it is rare (e.g. Virg. *Aen.* 1. 440 *nec cernitur ulli*). See n. on c. 8. 6 and cp. the usage in Greek with perfect and pluperf. passive.

mittit, sc. *milites*. Cp. c. 47. 2, but see n. on c. 17. 8.

ab Tarento viam, not 'on the side of Tarentum,' but 'from Tarentum,' sc. *ferentem*.

Peteliae, on the road from Thurii to Tarentum.

in occulto. See n. on c. 3. 1.

§ **6.** **inexplorato.** See n. on c. 2. 12. **ad duo milia.** See n. on c. 8. 13.

saltus, 'forests,' 'passes.' The word is commonly used of wooded country, fit for pasturing cattle but not for agriculture, and it often means 'defile,' 'ravine.' The derivation is uncertain. Varro says it is so called *quod in eo pecora saliunt!*

§ **8.** **ad id** = *ad insidias struendas*.

§ **9.** **fremebant.** The subject is indefinite, cp. c. 21. 10.

in cervicibus. Cp. 22. 23. 6 *bellum ingens in cervicibus*.

§ **10.** **quin imus?** 'let us go.' *quin*, 'why not?' is regularly used in rhetorical questions which easily pass into commands. *quin* stands for *qui ne* and the *qui* is an old instrumental case of the pronoun, surviving also in *atqui*, *qui fit ut*, etc.

subiecta res, etc., 'when we see the position for ourselves we shall be able to decide on a plan with greater security.'

§ **13.** **iocur,** a by-form of *iecur* with *o*-grade vowel. Greek shows a lengthened grade in ἧπαρ (= yēqʷr̥).

sine capite. The *caput iecinoris* was a protuberance on the right side of the liver. If it was absent or undeveloped it was a sign of bad omen. Cp. 41. 14. 7 *in iocinere caput non inventum*. Paul. Diac. 244 *pestifera auspicia esse dicebant, cum...caput in iocinere defuisset*.

auctum may be accusative of the substantive *auctus*, 'a swelling,' 'an enlargement.'

§ **14**. **nec sane**, 'by no means.'

quod secundum trunca, 'the fact that the defective and ill-formed parts exhibited by the first victim were followed by signs all too favourable.' *trunca*, i.e. *iecur sine capite* and therefore *turpia*. **laeta**, 'boding good.'

CHAPTER **27**

§ **1**. **ceterum** = δ' οὖν, resumptive, 'however.' See n. on c. 1. 3.

PAGE 43

§ **2**. **signum**. See n. on c. 1. 8.

§ **3**. **exiguum campi**, 'a short space of level ground,' cp. c. 41. 4 *nihil silvae*, 22. 24. 8 *exiguum spatii*.

ferebat. See n. on c. 18. 10. **conspecta**, 'in sight,' 'visible.'

in spem tantae rei, 'posted in expectation of a movement so important.' *in spem*. See n. on c. 3. 9. Livy uses *spes* frequently in this neutral sense and even of things not desired (e.g. 2. 3. 1 *spe omnium serius*); similarly *spero* = 'think,' 'expect,' especially of past events, cp. Cic. *ad Fam.* 9. 18. 4 *video te bona perdidisse; spero idem istuc familiares tuos*.

si quos...possent. See n. on c. 14. 6.

excipere, 'catch,' 'capture,' cp. c. 47. 2, 40. 7. 4 *ad has excipiendas voces speculator missus...exceptus a iuvenibus* (with a play on two slightly different meanings of the word). In *excipere* the force of *ex*, 'out of,' 'from,' is variously extended. Thus the common meaning 'receive,' 'welcome' (e.g. c. 17. 9, c. 46. 5) implies *ex itinere*, *ex fuga*, etc. Again the sense 'receive from' gives the idea of succession and we get *excipere* commonly in the sense of 'follow,' 'succeed' (e.g. 5. 13. 4 *hiemem aestas excepit*). A use like c. 19. 1 *de fuga excipiens*, 'picking up from,' paves the way for the meaning 'catch,' in which the sense of removal is often very slightly felt. In *voces excipere* 'overhear' (cp. the passage quoted above) the *ex* seems to express distance off, 'catch from (a distance).'

§ **4**. **quibus obviis**, 'those who were to rise and oppose the enemy from (the direction of) the hill itself.' **ab iugo** is best taken like *ab tergo* and with *obviis*, not with *consurgendum erat*. *obviis*, proleptic, 'so as to face.'

§ **5**. **valle**. This seems to be the *saltus* mentioned in c. 26. 8.

Plutarch (*Life of Marcellus*) in his account speaks of 'a wood and hollows' (τὴν ὕλην καὶ τὰς κοιλάδας).

evadere. See n. on c. 18. 15.

receptum, '(way of) retreat.' **ab tergo** goes with *circumventi*.

potuisset ni...iniecisset. The indicative is the more usual construction in the apodosis of unreal conditions with verbs denoting possibility, necessity, and the like. Livy might have written *extrahi potuit*. This would have given the possibility as a *fact* ('could have' = '*was* able to'). When the subjunctive is used the *possibility* is made conditional ('could have been' = 'would have been possible'). Cp. 4. 12. 6, 39. 37. 8, etc.

§ **6.** **donec**, 'so long as.' **integri**, 'unwounded.'

ipsi pugnando. In Livy the ablative of the gerund is very frequently equivalent to the nominative present participle. That Livy felt the equivalence is shown very clearly by his practice of attaching to the ablative gerund a numeral or pronoun in the nominative, treating it as the logical subject of the action denoted by the gerund. The usage reminds one of the common Greek construction τῷ αὐτὸς ποιεῖν, and some editors take it to be a direct imitation of this. In Livy, however, the usage is much more restricted than the construction is in Greek. He confines it to *solus*, *quisque*, *ipse* and numerals. Cp. 4. 31. 2 tendendo *ad sua* quisque *consilia...aperuerunt*, 9. 29. 8 gerendo solus *censuram*, 24. 5. 8 tendendo *autem* duo *ad Carthaginienses*, 25. 23. 11 aestimandoque ipse *secum*.

ex parte means usually 'in part,' but here it is equivalent to *pro parte* or *pro virili parte*, 'as part,' i.e. 'taking their part.'

§ **7.** **et ipsi...et ipso.** See n. on c. 1. 12.

§ **8.** **lictores quinque.** Each consul had twelve lictors.

§ **10.** **tumultuatum**, impersonal passive, 'there had been a bustle.' *tumultuari* is used of hasty and usually disorderly or confused movements. Cp. c. 42. 15 *tumultuaria pugna*, 25. 1. 3 *tumultuario exercitu*, 'a hastily levied army.' See also n. on c. 1. 10.

cum...cernunt, an instance of *cum inversum*. See n. on c. 20. 12.

exiguas reliquias is rather exaggerated. The band was over 200 strong (cp. c. 26. 11); 43 fell and 18 were captured.

PAGE 44

§ **11.** **miserabilis**, 'deplorable.' **alioqui**, 'in other respects.' See n. on c. 26. 10 *quin*.

pro aetate, 'for a man of his years,' goes with *tam improvide*; 'with a rashness which one would not expect from a man of his years and experience as a leader.'

in praeceps, cp. c. 19. 11. **dederat**. See n. on c. 14. 10.

§ **12**. **fecerim si...velim**. The perfect tense in the apodosis of the ideal condition marks the result, 'the result would be,' 'it would mean my writing many pages on a single incident'; cp. Plaut. *Cas.* 424 *si nunc me suspendam meis inimicis voluptatem creaverim*. **ambitus** = *ambitus verborum*. *si exsequi velim* is slightly illogical for *si exsequar*.

circa unam rem, 'round a single incident.' In Cicero *circa* is regularly 'local' (e.g. *Verr.* 2. 1. 48 *quos circa se haberet*). The transference to the sphere of mental action begins with Horace and the metaphorical use 'concerning,' 'in reference to,' becomes common in Silver Latin. Cp. Tac. *Ann.* 11. 29 *iam mihi* circa necem *C. Caesaris narratus*. Livy also frequently uses *circa* with numerals for the classical *circiter*, e.g. c. 42. 8 *circa quingentos*.

auctores, 'authorities.' *auctor* is applied to a writer as the 'promoter' of or 'voucher' for a statement or version, not merely as the narrator.

variant. *variare*, like Eng. 'vary,' may be either transitive, as here, or intransitive, as in § 14. 'Transitive' and 'intransitive' are of course merely convenient terms to denote that a verb normally belongs to the class which requires or does not require an accusative of the direct object. The distinction is quite a fluid one, as any verb may by development of meaning attach itself to the class to which it does not belong. E.g. *perire* is a transitive verb in *illam perit*, 'he is dying of love for her.'

§ **13**. **Coelius** = Coelius Antipater, a lawyer and writer of Annales who lived in the time of C. Gracchus. See Introduction II.

alios. Weissenborn suggests Valerius Antias and Claudius. See Introduction II.

edit, 'publishes.'

laudatione, 'funeral oration delivered by his son.' See Introduction. **qui...interfuerit**. The oblique subjunctive shows that *qui...interfuerit* is a note of Coelius.

sibi. See n. on c. 26. 5.

§ **14**. **ita...ut**, 'amid the varying accounts, however, we find all agree...which most etc.'

variat. See n. on § 12.

CHAPTER **28**

§ **1**. **extemplo**, 'forthwith,' 'on the spot,' from the old meaning of *templum*, 'place,' 'region' (in augury), lit. 'section,' from √tem seen in τέμνω, τέμενος, etc. Cp. *tempus*, 'a section (of time)' like Eng. *minute*.

sepelit. Plutarch says he cremated the body and sent the ashes to the son of Marcellus.

§ **3**. **sagaciter**, 'the two sharp-witted leaders bestirred themselves.' Instead of an adjective with the subject, the quality of the subject is expressed by an adverb in the predicate. Weissenborn cps. c. 48. 11 *impotentius regi*.

§ **4**. **anulis**, 'signet ring.' The use of the plural for a single ring is curious and does not appear to occur elsewhere.

signi errore, 'mistake or deception arising from the use of this signet.' The genitive is used to denote the sphere ('in the matter of,' 'in respect of') in which the *error* might take place.

PAGE 45

§ **5**. **Salapiam.** See n. on c. 1. 1.

si quo, etc., 'if in any direction,' i.e. 'for any movement that might be necessary.' Cp. 26. 9. 9 *alii offerunt se si quo usus operae sit*, and see n. on c. 14. 6.

qui...erant. The indicative is used since the clause, being a remark of the historian, is not affected by the oblique.

§ **6**. **ab ira.** See n. on c. 17. 5. This causal use of *ab* gives the motive or source of feeling. It is also used to express the external cause of a state or act 'in consequence of,' e.g. 2. 14. 4 *inopi tum urbe ab longinqua obsidione*.

defectionis, objective genitive, '(anger) at the revolt.' **equitum interfectorum.** Salapia and its Carthaginian garrison of 500 Numidian cavalry were handed over to Marcellus through the machinations of one of the leading citizens, Blattius. The cavalry fought till only one-tenth of them remained alive (*pugnantes ad ultimum occubuerunt*). Hannibal felt their loss very severely and Livy says *nec deinde unquam Poenus, quo longe plurimum valuerat, equitatu superior fuit*. See 26. 38. 11 f.

§ **7**. **ut sine arbitro.** This clause refers not to *remisso nuntio* but to *oppidanos...disponunt.* The townspeople were not to be trusted. *sine arbitro,* 'without a witness,' cp. 2. 37. 3 *arbitris remotis. Arbiter* probably meant originally 'one who comes to (two disputants as witness or arbitrator),' cp. *testis* = **tristis,* 'a *third* man who *stands* (besides two disputants).'

in stationibus. See n. on c. 2. 11.

§ **8. intentius,** 'very carefully,' cp. c. 24. 9.

quod roboris. See n. on c. 14. 5.

§ **9. quarta vigilia,** i.e. the last three hours in the early morning when the watch would most likely be slack.

§ **10. ad vocem...excitati.** In this common use of *ad* ('to meet,' 'at,' 'in face of') the original terminal force is often still slightly felt, as here with *excitati,* but the usage is much extended. Cp. c. 40. 11 *ad famam hostis,* 25. 37. 13 *ad haec...referunt pedem.*

moliri, 'toiled to open,' i.e. made a show of effort. *molior* is regularly used of moving a heavy mass with effort; cp. 6. 33. 11 *molientesque obices portarum,* 25. 36. 13 *foribus quas nulla moliri potuerant vi.* So usually *moliri portam* means 'burst open a gate.' But in this case the defenders merely pretended to be labouring to raise the portcullis.

cataracta, 'portcullis,' καταρράκτης, i.e. 'a dasher down,' from ῥάσσω. The spelling with one *r* would be from κατ-αράσσω. English 'cataract' is like the use in καταρράκτης ὄμβρος, 'dashing rain.' **clausa,** sc. *porta.*

§ **11. cum ruunt.** See n. on c. 20. 12.

§ **12. Salapitani alii...alii,** distributive apposition.

ex itinere, 'straight off the march,' 'just as they had been marching.' **ut,** 'under the impression that they were, etc.,' cp. the use of ὡς in Gk.

§ **13. ita,** 'accordingly.'

quam...oppugnabat. *obsidionem oppugnare* does not seem possible Latin for 'push a siege.' We should expect *urbem* as object. We must therefore understand *urbis* with *Locrorum* as the antecedent of *quam.* The parallels usually cited are rather easier than this case, inasmuch as they consist of adjectives equivalent to a substantive in genitive (or other case) which would be the logical antecedent, e.g. 2. 53. 1 Veiens *bellum exortum* quibus *Sabini arma coniunxerunt* (*Veiens* = *cum Veientibus*). See Notes on Text.

obsidionem...oppugnabat. Livy frequently distinguishes *obsidere* and *oppugnare.* The latter is general, 'attack,' 'assault,' the former 'invest,' 'blockade,' regularly implies surrounding the town with siege works. Cp. c. 39. 11 *obsidet magis quam oppugnat*, 5. 12. 5 *oppida nec oppugnata nec obsessa sunt.*

PAGE 46

§ **15. quantum accelerare posset,** 'with all possible speed.' *quantum potest* alone in colloquial language often means 'as quickly as possible,' cp. Plaut. *Most.* 758 *dare volt uxorem filio quantum potest*, Cic. *ad Att.* 4. 13. 1 *velim scribas ad me quantum potest.*

§ **16. adventare.** Livy uses frequentative verbs rather freely in the sense of the simple verbs. This was no doubt a usage of conversation in all periods of Latin. We find it in Plautus and it emerges again in Romance (e.g. French *chanter*, '*cantare*').

magis quia fecerat quam quod...esset. As usual the indicative is put for the real reason, the subjunctive in the rejected or alleged reason. If the reason rejected is a fact, though irrelevant as a reason, Cicero puts it in the indicative, but Livy's usage varies.

§ **17. quatiebant,** conative, 'were endeavouring to shake.'

CHAPTER 29

§ **2. prae gravitate.** In Classical Prose *prae* causal is only used of the preventing cause, i.e. with negatives and virtual negatives (here, *vix*). In early Latin the usage is freer, cp. Plaut. *Stich.* 215 *prae maerore... consenui.*

vulnerum patiens. A number of present participles are used freely as adjectives and so may lose their verbal construction by analogy, cp. *rei gerens* as well as *res gerens*, *cupiens tui* as well as *cupiens te* etc.

§ **3. nec...et.** See n. on c. 6. 4. **de Tarento sollicitus.** Part of the garrison had been withdrawn, c. 26. 4.

§ **4. Sex. Iulius Caesar.** If this is the same man as the Sex. Iulius Caesar elected praetor for 208 B.C. (c. 21. 5) and assigned to Sicily (c. 22. 3) it would appear that Sicily was temporarily without a praetor or propraetor.

§ **5. in agro Romano.** See n. on c. 5. 15.

profectus esset. On the ambiguity of this tense in oblique, see n. on c. 5. 18.

Q. Claudium = Q. Claudius Flamen, elected praetor (c. 21. 5) and assigned to Tarentum (c. 22. 3). **inde,** from Tarentum, where he was in command.

PAGE 47

§ 7. **tramisit.** See n. on c. 5. 9.

Clupeam, 'Shield,' Gk Ἀσπίς, so named from the shape of the hill on which it stood (λόφος Ἀσπὶς καλούμενος ἀπὸ τῆς ὁμοιότητος). Cp. *Drepanum* from the sickle-shaped promontory (δρεπάνη). *Clupea* lay near the N.E. corner of the Carthaginian territory. Polybius tells of its siege and capture by the Romans in the first Punic war.

§ 9. **eadem aestate,** a mistake. See Introduction II.

Philippus. Philip V, king, 230 B.C.–179 B.C. **Achaeis,** the Achaean League. For the position of affairs in the East and the chronology see Introduction I and II.

Machanidas, tyrant of Sparta, 210 B.C.–207 B.C. On the death of Lycurgus, the successor of Cleomenes, this adventurer seized the power. He was slain by Philopoemen, general of the Achaean League, at Mantinea in 207 B.C.

quos bello urebat, 'was harassing sorely.' The original force of this military *uro,* 'lay waste by burning,' is seen in 36. 31. 5 *cum iam ager...passim ureretur*; thence it is easily extended to cases like c. 39. 9 *belli quo* Italia *urebatur,* and so, as here, with transference to personal object, 10. 17. 1 eos *bellum urebat.*

Rhion, properly the promontory on the S. side of the entrance to the Corinthian Gulf. Cp. Thuc. 5. 52. 2 τειχίσαι ἐπὶ τῷ Ῥίῳ τῷ Ἀχαϊκῷ.

§ 10. **Attalum.** See Introduction I.

summum magistrum, the office of *Strategus* of the League. In the case of Attalus the leadership was nominal. Cp. c. 30. 1 *absente Attalo.*

CHAPTER 30

§ 1. **ob haec,** etc. in 210 B.C.

ad Lamiam, a town in the south of Thessaly, famous in the war between the Greeks and Antipater after the death of Alexander.

praetor = στρατηγός.

§ 2. **a P. Sulpicio.** See c. 22. 10.

mille hostium. The genitive dep. on *mille* in the singular is common in Livy but it is only used when *mille* is nominative or accusative. **admodum,** 'quite,' 'fully.' The use with numerals is unciceronian.

§ 3. **Phalara,** used as the harbour of Lamia which was 6 or 7 miles inland from the Malian Gulf.

PAGE 48

tutasque circa stationes. *circa* adverb = *quae circa erant.* See n. on c. 1. 10. *Stationes* here means 'places of anchorage for ships,' 'roadsteads.' Cp. 20. 2. 6 *circumagi navis in stationem tutam*, and *infra* § 11 *classem* stare *ad Naupactum audivere.*

§ **4**. **Ptolomaeo.** Cp. c. 4. 10, Ptolemy Philopator (222–205 B.C.), a weak and profligate monarch. He sought to remain on friendly terms with Rome and sent them large quantities of corn from Egypt. **Rhodiis**, an important maritime power. **Atheniensibus.** Athens was independent but had little power.

pacificator, 'as peace maker.' **Amynander.** Cp. Bk 38. cc. 1–3. **Athamānum.** Their country lay N. of Aetolia.

§ **5**. **ferociori...gente,** a nation 'too warlike to suit the instincts of the Greeks' (Stephenson). See Notes on Text.

grave libertati, 'a serious menace to liberty.'

§ **6**. **in concilium,** 'for (or 'till') the meeting of the League.' The regular meetings were in autumn and spring.

indutiae, 'truce,' 'armistice,' perhaps derived from *in* 'not' and *dū* with the same root as *bellum* (O.L. *duellum*).

§ **7**. **Chalcidem Euboeae,** 'Chalcis in Euboea.' This variety of the possessive genitive expressing the *sphere* to which a place belongs is called by grammarians the 'chorographic' or geographical genitive. Cp. 36. 20. 5 *navis Cenaeum Euboeae petierunt*, Thuc. 8. 14 *προσβαλόντες πρῶτον Κωρύκῳ τῆς ἠπείρου.*

litorum appulsu, 'landing,' cp. *appellere* (sc. *navem*), 'put in.' The genitive is equivalent to a prepositional phrase *ad litora.* The name 'objective genitive' strictly applies only to cases where the verb corresponding to the abstract substantive on which the genitive depends would take an accusative, but the usage is freely extended. Cp. 1. 24. 1 *nominum error.* Cic. *de Nat. Deor.* 1. 12. 29 *in deorum opinione turpissime labitur*, *Tusc.* 1. 12. 27 *excessu vitae*, *ad Fam.* 6. 10. 2 *aditus de fortunis tuis agendi* (= *ad agendum*); similarly in Greek *συνουσία κακῶν.*

§ **8**. **si...traiecisset.** See n. on c. 14. 6.

§ **9**. **curatione,** 'administration,' 'presidency.' **Heraeorum,** the festival held at the Argive Heraeum, the most famous seat of the worship of Hera. Argos was the special centre of the cult of the goddess. From Argos it passed to Aegina where there was also a

Heraean festival, and to Samos, settled according to tradition by Epidaurus and then by Argives (Virg. *Aen.* 1. 15 f. *quam Iuno fertur terris magis omnibus unam posthabita coluisse Samo*). Perhaps also the Heraeum at Olympia had an Argive origin (see Bury, *Nemean Odes of Pindar*, p. 257).

Nemeorum. The Nemean games held in the cypress grove attached to the temple of Zeus in the vale of Nemea between Cleonae and Phlius. The presidency belonged originally, it appears, to the people of Cleonae (cp. Pind. Κλεωναῖος ἀγών), later the Argives claimed it.

suffragiis populi, sc. *Argivorum*.

ex ea civitate oriundos. The *Argead* kings of Macedonia sought to establish their Argive origin in order to be allowed to compete at the Olympic games. Cp. Hdt. 5. 22 Ἀλέξανδρος δὲ ἐπειδὴ ἀπέδεξε ὡς εἴη Ἀργεῖος, ἐκρίθη τε εἶναι Ἕλλην καὶ ἀγωνιζόμενος στάδιον συνεξέπιπτε τῷ πρώτῳ. 8. 137 ἐξ Ἄργεος ἔφυγον ἐς Ἰλλυριοὺς τῶν Τημένου ἀπογόνων τρεῖς ἀδελφοί...ἐκ δὲ Ἰλλυριῶν...ἐς τὴν ἄνω Μακεδονίην ἀπίκοντο. Cp. Thuc. 2. 99. 3 Τημενίδαι τὸ ἀρχαῖον ὄντες ἐξ Ἄργεος. According to another account Karanos, son (?) of Pheidon of Argos, was the founder of the Macedonian dynasty.

Aegium, Αἴγιον or Αἴγειον, one of the original 12 cities of the Achaean League. The shrine of Zeus Amarios close to it was now the meeting place of the League which originally had been at Helice.

sociorum, i.e. the Achaean League, or rather the larger league under Macedonian presidency of which the Achaeans were a part. Cp. *socios* in § 14.

§ 11. stare. See n. on § 3 *stationes*.

§ 12. eae legationes, cp. § 4. **vocati,** sc. *Aetoli*.

fidem = πίστις, 'pledge.' **conventionis,** 'agreement.'

tempore indutiarum, 'done during the time of the truce,' ablative of time 'within which,' corresponding to Gk genitive, cp. c. 15. 2.

§ 13. Atintania, "a people of northern Epirus, who had been declared free allies of Rome by the Romans after their defeat of the Illyrians B.C. 229; since then, in consequence of the desertion of Demetrius the Pharian and his alliance with Philip, the district had been lost to the Romans." (Stephenson.)

Scerdilaedo, a king of Illyria, who some years previously had received help from Rome against Philip. The **Ardiaei** lay north of Atintania and their country, which was part of Scerdilaedus' kingdom, had been taken by Philip. **Pleuratus** was the son of Scerdilaedus.

§ **14.** **enimvero.** See n. on c. 16. 14. **ultro,** 'actually.' **ferre,** 'offer,' 'propose' = *offerre*, cp. 2. 13. 2. The use of the simple verb for the compound is especially common in Livy and Tacitus. Cp. *ponere* = *proponere*, *mitto* = *omitto*, *ferre* = *auferre*, *moliri* = *amoliri*, etc.

PAGE 49

§ **15.** **ita,** 'accordingly,' cp. c. 28. 13. **infecta.** *in* 'not' is not used to form verbal compounds except in the participle which is the meeting point of the substantive and verb, cp. *indictus* and *indiciens*, *inficiens*, *inopinans* as adjectives, but not *indico*, *inficio* or *inopinor* in the corresponding sense.

dimisit, i.e. as president. At this time Philip had the Achaean League 'in his pocket.'

§ **16.** **nuper,** cp. c. 15. 7. **ab rege Prusia,** Prusias I, king of Bithynia, Philip's ally. See Bk 28. c. 12.

lacessere, 'challenge' (cp. *elicere*, etc.), with *proelio*, *bello*, etc. = 'assail.' *proelio* is instrumental ablative; cp. the construction with *invitare*, Cic. *Verr.* 2. 4. 11 *qui tecto ac domo non invitet*, and Greek προκαλεῖσθαι, Hom. *Il.* 7. 285 αὐτὸς γὰρ χάρμῃ προκαλέσσατο πάντας ἀρίστους.

iam diu potentes, since 211 B.C.

§ **17.** **Nemeorum tempus,** i.e. Midsummer every second year. Formerly it was thought that the Nemean Games were held in winter and summer alternately but it has been proved that the winter Nemea belonged to the later imperial times. **celebrari praesentia sua,** '*held* under his *distinguished* patronage.' *celebrari* here combines its two senses of 'be distinguished' and 'be attended.' Cp. the double sense of English 'celebrated' as (1) 'famous,' (2) 'held,' 'attended.'

CHAPTER 31

§ **1.** **ab Naupacto.** See n. on c. 17. 8.

§ **2.** **palatos** = *palantes*. Cp. 35. 51. 4 *palatos passim aggressus*. The past participle in *-to-* was originally timeless. Cp. *tacitus*, *iratus*, *maestus*, Gk πιστός, etc. The past sense in combination with *sum* is a development (chiefly in the Italic languages) which led to the participle also acquiring past sense. There are numerous traces in Latin of the older timeless use. These are seen especially in the case of deponent verbs which have the present participle parallel in the same voice, cp. Ter. *Eun.* 64 *iratus rogitas?* Virg. *G.* 1. 339 *sacra refer Cereri laetis* operatus ('sacrificing') *in herbis*, Hor. *Sat.* 2. 8. 40 *invertunt Allifanis vinaria tota Vibidius Balatroque* secutis omnibus. See also n. on c. 43. 3. Similarly *ratus*, *recordatus*, *comitatus*, etc.

§ **3.** **laeta praeda.** *laeta* goes with *classis*; *praeda*, instrumental ablative, 'with booty,' is construed with *laetus* as with *gravis* (§ 2) or *onustus* (1. 4. 9). If it were construed with *redit* we should expect *cum praeda*.

celebritatem. See n. on c. 30. 17. **quantaecumque**, 'insignificant'; *-cumque* added to *qualis* and *quantus* regularly gives depreciatory force, cp. the use of *ὁστισδήποτε* in Gk.

§ **4.** **populariter**, 'to please the crowd,' 'in democratic fashion.' **capitis insigni**, 'diadem.'

§ **5.** **maritas domos**, a poetical use of the substantive as an adjective.

§ **6.** **summittendo se**, 'lowering himself,' 'condescending,' cp. Gk *συγκαθιέναι*. **in privatum fastigium.** *fastigium* means 'point,' 'top,' 'gable' (*fasti* for **farsti*, cp. Eng. 'bristle'), 'sloping side' (c. 18. 6). Hence in metaphorical usage it usually denotes 'height,' 'high level' of rank, etc. Cp. c. 19. 6.

PAGE 50

vanam ostendisset, 'presented a show of liberty.'

verterat. The pluperfect tense does not here express priority to the time of the subordinate verb, as it usually does. It merely emphasises the 'aoristic' character of the action, 'lo and behold! he (had) monopolised'; cp. 32. 12. 3 *postquam...recepere se regii*, verterat *periculum in Romanos*, Virg. *Aen.* 2. 257 *flammas cum regia puppis* extulerat. Probably the pluperfect had originally no force of 'priority,' but as its form shows was an *s*-aorist. In Old Latin there are very numerous instances of this aoristic pluperfect. See also n. on c. 32. 8.

§ **7.** **flagitiis**, 'open guilt.' *flăgitium* is commonly used of 'crime of passion.' Augustine (*de doctr. Chr.* 3. 10) says '*quod agit indomita cupiditas ad corrumpendum animum et corpus suum flagitium vocatur. quod autem agit ut alteri noceat facinus dicitur.*' The Romans probably connected the word with *flăgrare*, but it is more probably to be attached to *flāgitare* (cp. Eng. 'a crying shame').

viris, 'husbands, cp. Germ. Mann and Scotch 'guid man'=husband.

§ **8**. **Arato**, son of the famous Aratus of Sicyon.

§ **9**. **per haec flagitia**. This seems to be an extension of the *temporal* use of *per*, 'during' (e.g. *per triennium*), which shades off into the meaning 'on the occasion of,' 'on' in phrases like *per eandem occasionem* (2. 37. 6), and so *per* comes to be used, as here, of the attendant circumstances. The *local* use of *per*, 'through,' gives rise to the sense of agency (e.g. *per me fit*) and a weakened instrumental readily comes to denote attendant circumstances. We might therefore say that phrases like *per haec flagitia* lie between the temporal and the instrumental use.

sollemni. The neuter of the adjective *sollemnis* is used freely by Livy and Tacitus as a substantive and may have other adjectives added to it, e.g. 9. 34. 8 *antiquissimum sollemne*, 40. 10. 3 *sollemne lustrale*, etc.

§ **10**. **summa imperii**, i.e. he was *Strategus*.

ad Dymas, 'at D.,' 'in neighbourhood of D.' *Dymae* or *Dyme*, in the W. of Achaea, was one of the 12 original Achaean towns and along with *Patrae* started the revival of the Achaean League. **Eliorum**, but **ab Eleis** in § 9. *Ēlēi* and *Ēlĭi* both occur as forms of the ethnicon.

a ceteris Achaeis. The Eleans were on the side of their kinsmen the Aetolians and were not members of the Achaean League at this time. In 191 B.C. they were induced by T. Quinctius Flamininus to join the League along with Messenia, Sparta having joined in 192 B.C. *a ceteris Achaeis* seems to be a translation of ὑπ' ἄλλων 'Αχαιῶν.

movisse, 'stirred,' 'caused,' cp. πόλεμον κινεῖν. *bellum facere* can mean either 'cause a war' (πόλεμον ποιεῖν) or rarely 'wage war' (πόλεμον ποιεῖσθαι).

CHAPTER 32

§ **1**. **urbem**. Elis, cp. § 7 *urbe Eliorum*. **obequitando**, 'riding in front of' or 'up to.'

§ **2**. **Cyllenen**, a port in the W. of Elis, not the Arcadian mountain sacred to Hermes.

§ **3**. **improvisa res**, 'the surprise.' **cognovere**, sc. the Achaeans and Philip.

§ **4**. **cohortem**. See n. on c. 13. 7.

PAGE 51

§ **6.** **pugna**, 'his fighting,' 'the king himself fought gallantly.'

§ **8.** **compensaverat.** See n. on c. 31. 6. Note that frequently with this pluperfect there is a pluperfect in the subordinate clause, *ostendisset* in c. 31. 6, *acciderat* in c. 33. 7, *fuerat* here; perhaps in such cases we have an illogical attraction of tense as in English 'I should have liked to have gone.'

quod ignominiae, 'the measure of disgrace he had suffered.'

§ **9.** **Lychnidum.** *Lychnidus* or *Lychnis*, the capital of the Dassaretii, was a fortified town on the interior of Illyricum. **Dardanos**, inhabitants of the country in Upper Moesia extending from Illyricum along the borders of Macedonia.

§ **11.** **Demetriadem**, at the head of the Gulf of Pagasae in S. Thessaly. At this time it was one of the most important towns in Greece, though it was less than a century since its foundation by Demetrius Poliorcetes.

decumis castris, 'ten days' march.' Weissenborn notes that this use of *castra* applies properly only to the march of Romans who encamped each night.

CHAPTER **33**

§ **1.** **tumultum**, 'disturbance,' 'rising.' See n. on c. 1. 10. **Orestidem**, the district of the Orestae (cp. Thuc. 2. 80), on the Macedonian borders. The name is derived from Orestes, who is said to have fled thither after slaying Clytaemnestra. **Argestaeum campum**, not otherwise known.

celebrem esse, 'was bruited abroad.'

§ **2.** **expeditione ea**, cp. c. 31. 2.

pugnavit...praefregit. These tenses are equivalent to pluperfects. Livy merely states the past facts and leaves the priority of the acts to be gathered from the context. Cp. 25. 29. 9 *quosque fors* obtulit, *irati interfecere*, and the similar use of the aorist in Greek, especially in ἐπειδὴ clauses where the context shows the priority very clearly.

cornu, projecting horns worn on the helmet as special *insigne* by the successors of Alexander.

praefregit, 'broke off.'

§ **3.** **interfecti regis.** See n. on c. 5. 14 and cp. § 7.

PAGE 52

§ **6.** **exitu huius anni.** See Introduction II and n. on c. 35. 3.

alii...alii. In c. 29 Livy leaves it an open question whether Crispinus went to Tarentum or not. See §§ 2, 6.

§ **7.** **reliquerant.** See n. on c. 32. 8.

§ **8.** **ludos magnos.** See n. on c. 6. 19. In 1. 35. 9 Livy speaks of *ludi Romani* and *ludi magni* as the same. After the establishment of the annual *ludi Romani* the *ludi votivi* continued and were known as *ludi magni*. **quos...in quinquennium voverat.** This took place 10 years previously in 217 B.C. The praetor was given charge of the vow for the state *quoniam Fabium belli cura occupatura esset.* See 22. 10. 2 and 22. 9. 10. The condition of fulfilment was *si bellatum prospere esset respublicaque in eodem quo ante bellum fuisset, statu permansisset.* As the vow was for five years ahead, it must have been renewed in 212 B.C. or 213 B.C. For other instances of *ludi magni* and the conditions of the vow, see 4. 27. 1 (fulfilled 5. 31. 2), 36. 2. 2 f. (fulfilled 39. 22. 1).

§ **9.** **ceterum,** a good instance of the resumptive use of *ceterum* after a parenthetic passage. See n. on c. 1. 3.

omnibus aliis, 'all other things.' The use of the neuter adjective or pronoun as a substantive in cases where the form is the same as the masculine (gen. dat. abl.) is generally avoided in Latin on account of the ambiguity. Livy, however, has numerous instances like *omnibus, omnium, his, horum, eorum* etc.

primo quoque tempore. See n. on c. 5. 12.

potissimum emphasises *eos*, cp. c. 45. 10, 2. 13. 10 *eam aetatem potissimum*; so regularly with demonstrative pronoun to mark selection from a number.

quorum virtus, 'who were possessed of qualities that would be proof against Hannibal's stratagem,' i.e. qualities like those of Fabius who '*unus homo nobis cunctando restituit rem.*'

§ **10.** **cum...tum,** 'both...and particularly,' with *cum...tum* equivalent to *et...et* the *cum* clause naturally goes into the accusative and infinitive in oblique. See n. on c. 18. 8. *fuissent* however has better MSS. authority. See Notes on Text.

necopinatam. In this word we have a survival of the old use of *nec*=*non*; cp. *nec recte dicere* in Plautus.

CHAPTER **34**

§ **1.** **facerent,** 'seek to elect,' or 'get elected,' cp. § 15 and see n. on c. 17. 7.

C. Claudius Nero. He had been in command of one of the armies at Capua and afterwards in Spain in 211 B.C. In the previous year (209 B.C.) he was legate under Marcellus (c. 14. 4).

et...quidem. See n. on c. 2. 3.

PAGE 53

§ **2.** **quam postularent.** The expression is condensed, i.e. = *promptiorem* (*esse*) *quam is esset quem tempora postularent*, cp. 3. 16. 5 *maiore quam venerint silentio abituros*. The subjunctive is due to the oblique relation after *ducebant* ('they thought he was'), cp. 38. 55. 6. In ordinary comparative clauses the mood in the dependent clause is regularly indicative and here the direct form would be *promptior est quam tempora postulant*, cp. (in similar abbreviated comparisons) 3. 50. 3, 26. 20. 11. There is another class of comparative sentences with the subjunctive which must be distinguished from these. When two actions are compared with *citius*, *potius*, *prius* followed by *quam*, the second clause containing the rejected alternative is in Livy regularly put in the subjunctive as denoting purpose or result. Livy frequently writes *quam ut* in such cases, cp. 32. 21. 13 *cur igitur nostrum ille auxilium absens petit* potius quam *praesens nos*...tueatur. Instances occur commonly in oblique (but the subjunctive is not due simply to the oblique relation, as in *quam postularent*) e.g. 24. 3. 12 *morituros se affirmabant* citius quam...verterentur, Tac. *Ann.* 13. 42. In Cicero the infinitive is the usual construction in the *quam* clause, if the leading verb is in the infinitive, cp. *ad Fam.* 2. 16. 3 *nonne tibi affirmavi quidvis me* potius *perpessurum* quam *ex Italia*...exiturum?

§ **4.** **M. Livius erat.** *M. Livius Salinator*, consul 219 B.C. with L. Aemilius Paulus. They waged war with the Illyrian pirates and defeated their leader, Demetrius of Pharos. An accusation was brought against them of having made an unfair division of the booty and Livius was condemned. Aemilius narrowly escaped (*ex damnatione collegae ex qua prope ambustus evaserat*). Livius was censor in 204 B.C. with Claudius Nero. The name *Salinator* ('Salter') was due to his having imposed a tax on salt, in revenge, it was thought, for his condemnation by the tribes. See 29. 37. 3 f.

erat, 'there was,' cp. 7. 26. 2 *M. erat Valerius tribunus...qui.*

ex consulatu, 'straight after,' cp. c. 28. 12 *ex itinere.* **populi iudicio.** Out of 35 tribes only the Maecian did not vote against him (29. 37. 13).

migraret...caruerit. See n. on c. 16. 7 on the sequence of tenses in consecutive clauses and the use of the perfect subjunctive as a secondary tense. Where the imperfect and the aoristic perfect are contrasted, the former is descriptive and gives the process, the latter sums up and gives the resultant fact, e.g. 24. 40. 12 *inde tantus terror pavorque omnes occupavit ut non modo alius quisquam arma* caperet *aut castris pellere hostem* conaretur, *sed etiam ipse rex...ad flumen navesque* perfugerit. 5. 45. 4 *adeo nihil miseriti sunt, ut in agrum Romanum incursionem* facerent...*Veios in animo* habuerint *oppugnare* (*facerent* continuous, *habuerint* completion of process), 8. 36. 7, 24. 16. 1. Sometimes, however, it is difficult to see a difference of meaning. In this passage the Puteanus MS. has *careret.* See Notes on Text.

§ **5.** **ferme.** See n. on c. 15. 2.

prae se ferens, 'exhibiting.' **habitu.** See n. on c. 16. 8. Here it probably means 'bearing,' 'port' rather than 'dress.' Cp. σχῆμα in Gk e.g. Luc. *Timon,* c. 54 οὗτος ὁ τὸ σχῆμα εὐσταλὴς καὶ κόσμιος τὸ βάδισμα. **insignem,** 'striking,' 'noticeable.'

§ **6.** **tonderi,** 'get himself shaved.' **squalorem deponere.** *squalor* like *sordes,* is regularly used of mourning guise, cp. 29. 16. 6 (suppliant envoys) *obsiti squalore et sordibus* and *sordes suscipere,* 'put on mourning.'

coegerunt. Attendance of senators was obligatory and they could be fined for non-attendance. Cp. Cic. *Phil.* 1. 5. 12 *de supplicationibus referebatur, quo in genere senatores deesse non solent; coguntur enim non pignoribus, sed eorum de quorum honore agitur, gratia; quod idem fit cum de triumpho refertur; ita sine cura consules sunt* ut paene liberum sit senatori non adesse.

§ **7.** **verbo,** i.e. without getting up and making a formal speech. When called upon a senator usually rose (*surrexit*), cp. *stantem.*

pedibus in sententiam ibat. After debate the president put the question and took a division (*discessio*) and the senators walked to opposite sides of the house, cp. *discedere in sententias.*

donec. The construing order is *donec causa* (nom.) *cognati hominis M. Livi Macati...eum coegit* etc. **Macati...fama.** See c. 25. 1–5.

§ **8.** **indigno,** used absolutely, 'one who did not deserve it,' 'innocent.' **id quod**, 'the fact that,' rather than *id* in apposition to *magnam iniuriam factam* and *quod* 'because.'

tam gravi bello, instrumental ablative of attendant circumstances or locatival ablative of time, not dative with *usa esset* ('used for').

duos patricios...non liceret, since 366 B.C. See 6. 35. 5 *con sulumque utique alter ex plebe crearetur.*

§ **10.** **in T. Manlio,** 'in the case of T. Manlius,' cp. c. 1. 9. **praeterquam quod,** 'besides the fact that.' See n. on c. 6. 5.

§ **11.** **egregium par,** 'an excellent pair,' cp. *par nobile fratrum, centum pares* ('100 pairs of gladiators') etc. In their censorship Nero and Livius could hardly be called *egregium par*. See Bk 29. c. 37.

nec mentionem...aspernatus, 'when this was mooted the people took it up.'

§ **12.** **levitatem,** 'changeableness.' **sordidati rei,** cp. 2. 54. 3 and n. on § 6 *supra.*

eodem...congeri, 'piled on the same individual.' See n. on c. 1. 13. *congerere* is used in both friendly and unfriendly sense.

§ **13.** **si...ducerent...damnassent.** The *recta* would be *si ducitis...damnavistis* (aoristic). According to Prof. Conway's rule (see n. on c. 9. 3), Livy would usually turn this by *si...ducant... damnaverint.* Similarly **comperissent...crederent** represent *comperistis* (aoristic) and *creditis.* The first **ita**='as they did,' the second **ita**='as they were doing.' **male,** 'with unfortunate results.'

PAGE 54

§ **14.** **M. Furium,** i.e. Camillus. For the story see Bk 5. cc. 32–49 (exile, c. 32. 8 f., recall, c. 46. 7 f., desertion of Rome, c. 40, deliverance of Rome, c. 49).

sede sua, with *pulsam.* Note the effective alliteration in *restitutum restituisse, patriam pulsam, sede sua.*

§ **15.** **fecerunt.** See n. on § 1 *facerent.*

CHAPTER 35

§ **1.** **post diem tertium eius diei,** 'two days after that day.' The genitive defines as giving the starting-point of the period. This genitive is sometimes regarded as a development of the partitive genitive but seems more akin to the possessive genitive here, cp. Cic. *ad Att.*

3. 7. 1 *post diem tertium eius diei*, Caes. *B. G.* 1. 48 *postridie eius diei.* Cicero uses this genitive only with words denoting time (where indeed the expression seems clumsy), but later it is extended to other words, cp. Tac. *Ann.* 1. 62. 1 *sextum post* cladis *annum*; Plin. *Ep.* 6. 10. 3 *post decimum* mortis *annum*, just as though in English we were to say 'in the tenth year of his death' on the analogy of 'in the tenth year of his reign.'

magistratu abierunt, 'resigned office.' The consuls for 208 B.C. were both dead but the year was nearly over when *Crispinus* died (c. 33. 6), and no *consules suffecti* had been elected.

§ **2.** **C. Terentius.** See c. 24. **C. Hostilius,** Tubulus. See c. 22. 4 and c. 24. **ut iret,** 'with the proviso that he should go.'

§ **3.** **et L. Manlius.** See Notes on Text. If *L.* is right, the man meant is probably L. Manlius Acidinus whom we find serving against Hasdrubal in the following year (cp. c. 50. 8). Weissenborn suggests that it would be possible for him to fulfil his mission to Greece and get back in time for the Metaurus battle.

iret...viseretque, 'was to go and see,' past jussive parallel with *ut...iret*, see n. on c. 7. 9. The legation of Manlius must have taken place considerably earlier in the year than the events mentioned in § 1, for 208 B.C. was nearly at an end when Quinctius died (c. 33. 6 *exitu huius anni*), and the Olympic Games were held in August 208 B.C. (Ol. 143. 1 = Aug. 208—July 207 B.C.). Livy finding the mention of this mission under Ol. 143. 1 puts it in at the end of 208 B.C. leaving *ea aestate* which *ought* to refer to the summer of 208 B.C. in a context which makes it refer forward to 207 B.C. If Livy had said 'Manlius *had been* sent on a commission etc.,' referring to an appointment earlier in 208 B.C., the chronology would have been correct and *futurum erat* would suit this as past prospective, expressing time future to the time of the appointment but past in relation to the events which L. is mentioning. Had L.'s chronology of Greek events been otherwise correct, one would be tempted to suppose that he wrote: *habu*ERAT. ⟨ERAT *et L.*⟩ *Manlius trans mare legatus* ⟨*ut*⟩ *iret viseretque* or *habuerat. Et L. Manlius trans* MARE ⟨ERAT⟩ *legatus* ⟨*ut*⟩. *iret viseretque.*

simul, quod Olympiae ludicrum, etc. Weissenborn takes *quod futurum erat* as causal 'because,' as giving the second reason for Manlius' mission, and *quod celebraretur* as relative ('which would be held' (?)). But the point of the remark *maximo coetu celebraretur* is that Manlius would probably find there a number of fugitive Sicilians and Tarentines. Therefore *quod...celebraretur* is to be taken as causal and the subjunctive as the oblique of *quod celebratur*. Then *quod Ol. ludicrum* is a relative clause thrown forward and rather clumsily caught up by *adiret id concilium*.

per hostem, 'if the enemy allowed him to do so with safety.' *per* has not its ordinary local meaning ('through the enemy'), but the derived sense, 'unhindered by,' which is an easy extension of 'through' in the sense 'by reason of' or 'by aid of.' So commonly *per me* = 'as far as I am concerned,' Cic. *ad Fam.* 7. 32 *trahantur per me pedibus omnes rei*.

§ **4.** **domos,** 'to their homes.' See n. on c. 16. 2. **scirent,** 'learn,' 'be made aware.'

sua omnia iis. See n. on c. 5. 4, and cp. 29. 1. 17 *suas res Syracusanis restituit*, 37. 32. 14 *urbem agrosque et suas leges restituit*. **iis,** 'to all such persons.'

reddere, 'is restoring.' The announcement would be *populus Romanus reddit*. The present is used here either of what was actually being done or vividly for the future. See n. on c. 2. 2.

§ **5.** **praesciscere,** 'ascertain beforehand.'

quisque, used of two persons, for *uterque*, as frequently in Livy with *suus*, cp. 10. 26. 6 *ut suae quisque provinciae sortem tueretur*.

haberet, 'was to have,' 'would have' (= future). The periphrastic subjunctive is regularly used to represent the future (here, *habiturus esset*), but there are numerous exceptions, (1) where, as here (*volebant praesciscere*), the future relation is made clear by the leading verb (verbs of hoping, expecting, willing, etc.) or otherwise, e.g. 8. 35. 4 *in discrimine fuerunt an ulla* post hanc diem *essent*, Tac. *Hist.* 2. 34 intentique...*quando hostis inprudentia rueret* (= 'would rush,' direct, *ruet*); (2) where the subjunctive is deliberative. We have an instructive example in 35. 28. 4 *quem locum ipse* capturus esset, *cogitando aut quaerendo exsequebatur, aut quot armatis*,...usurus; *quo impedimenta...* reiceret, *quanto...praesidio* custodiret *et utrum pergere...an repetere* melius esset. Here *capturus esset, usurus* (*esset*) represent future indicatives (*capiam, utar*), while *reiceret, custodiret* represent deliberative subjunctives (*reiciam custodiam*) and *melius esset* represents *melius est* (or *sit*). (3) In other cases the imperfect subjunctive may represent a present indicative used vividly for a future, e.g. 2. 55. 9 *incerti quatenus Volero exerceret victoriam* ('how far is he pushing?').

§ **7.** **inimicitiae nobiles,** 'a notorious feud.' **indigniores fecerat,** 'made L. feel it more deeply.'

sua refers to the logical subject *Livio*, as frequently.

in ea fortuna, i.e. when suffering the *ignominia* described above.

PAGE 55

§ **8.** **timentes,** 'if (or 'so long as') they were apprehensive.' **crescendi ex se,** 'rising at his expense.' *ex* with *crescere* is used of the root or material from which growth takes place, cp. 35. 19. 5 *aliam materiam crescendi ex me quaerant.* **inimico** goes with *collegae* rather than with *se.*

§ **9.** **vicit ut.** See n. on c. 11. 11, and cp. 9. 26. 5 *vicit tamen sententia ut mitterentur.*

auctoritas senatus, 'the influence of the Senate,' not in the technical sense. See n. on c. 6. 6.

§ **10.** **provinciae...decreta.** *decreta* agrees with the nearer subject, *Gallia.*

permixtae regionibus. Ordinarily if Italy was assigned as province to both consuls the *provincia* of each extended over the whole, cp. c. 22. 2. **diversae,** 'in opposite directions.'

§ **11.** **addito urbano.** This does not mean that the consul was to have either the Gallic or the Etrurian army *plus* the urban, but 'with the urban army added as a third possible choice.' Against the former interpretation are (1) the necessity to take *quem* = *utrum*, (2) the fact that each consul had two legions only (cp. c. 36. 12). On the other hand *novis legionibus urbanis scriptis* (§ 12) shows that the choice of the consul who got *Gallia* would in any case mean the displacement of the old *urbanus exercitus.* We must therefore suppose that if his choice fell upon the Gallic or the Etrurian army, the urban was to replace it. Livy, however, does not say this clearly.

§ **12.** **consulum prioris anni,** i.e. the army of Marcellus at Venusia and that of Crispinus at (?) Tarentum.

§ **13.** **Q. Fulvius,** cp. c. 22. 3.

§ **14.** **C. Hostilio,** cp. § 2.

CHAPTER 36

§ **1.** **in dies.** See n. on c. 24. 6.

§ **2.** **quia...diceretur.** The subjunctive is due to the oblique. Distinguish this from the illogical attraction of an indicative *dicebat*, etc. into the subjunctive of virtual oblique in a causal clause, e.g. *rediit paulo post quod se oblitum nescioquid diceret.*

§ **3.** **ducibus,** 'guides,' cp. 17. 17. **hospites,** 'friends,' combines the meanings of Eng. 'guest' and 'host'; *guest* is the same word as *hostis*, originally 'stranger,' and *host*=*hospes*, which is **hosti-potis*.

§ **4.** **pro comperto,** 'as ascertained fact,' *pro*='for,' 'as good as.' Cp. Eng. 'for certain.' *habere* in such phrases gets the meaning of 'know,' like Eng. 'I *have* it on good authority that....'

PAGE 56

nisi quod, cp. c. 7. 17.

§ **5.** **inauguratus.** See n. on c. 8. 4. **rex sacrorum.** See n. on c. 6. 16.

§ **6.** **lustrum conditum.** *lustrum condere* or *facere* is used of the performance of the great purificatory rite by the Censors at the conclusion of their duties.

§ **7.** **numerus.** Ten years previously the number was nearly twice as great, viz. over 270,000 (Periocha 20).

§ **8.** **comitium tectum,** i.e. awnings were stretched over the *comitium* as protection from the sun and rain. The *comitium* was the end of the Forum away from the Capitol. Editors suppose that the games mentioned were held in the lower Forum instead of in the *circus maximus*, and that the more distinguished people watched them from the *comitium*.

§ **9.** **biduum instauratum,** an unusual expression for *ludi per biduum* (or *biduum*) *instaurati*. See n. on c. 6. 19. *biduum* may be taken as nominative or as the usual accusative of time with *instauratum* impersonal. In either case *ludis* is probably dative rather than ablative ('at the games'). See Notes on Text.

ad Cereris. See n. on c. 6. 19. **dederunt,** 'dedicated.' See n. on c. 6. 19.

Iovis epulum...ludorum causa. Where Livy mentions the *Iovis epulum* it is regularly in close connexion with the *ludi plebei*, cp. 25. 2. 10, 31. 4. 7, 33. 42. 10 etc. The *Iovis epulum* took place on Nov. 13 in the middle of the *ludi plebei* between the *ludi scenici* and the *ludi circenses*. It was held in the Capitol and the Senate joined in it. There was also an *epulum Iovis* held in the middle of the *ludi Romani* on Sept. 13.

§ **11**. **C. Hostilio,** sc. *Catoni*. See c. 35. 1.

§ **12**. **trium et viginti**. See n. on c. 22. 11.

§ **14**. **primis quattuor,** i.e. the 24 tribunes of the legions regularly commanded by the consuls. See n. on c. 12. 14. Livy mentions this as an innovation. In 362 B.C. the people obtained the right to elect 6 of the tribunes (7. 5. 9), and in 311 B.C. the number was raised to 16 (9. 30. 3).

CHAPTER 37

§ **1**. **proficiscerentur**. See n. on c. 8. 11.

novendiale sacrum, i.e. *sacrum per novem dies factum*. So regularly when a stone-shower fell, cp. 1. 31. 4 *mansit sollemne, ut, quandoque idem prodigium nuntiaretur, feriae per novem dies agerentur*.

lapidaverat. Cp. 43. 13. 4 *Reate imbri lapidavit*. Also used in the impersonal passive *lapidatum est* (29. 14. 4). The more usual expression is *pluere lapidibus* or *lapides*.

§ **2**. **sub...mentionem**, 'following close upon the announcement.' *sub* with accusative 'to under,' gets the meaning '*close* up to,' e.g. *sub muros* (place), *sub vesperum* (time, 'just before'); then the idea of *proximity* is easily extended to mean 'close upon,' 'just after.' Cp. 25. 7. 1 *sub haec dicta*, 24. 25. 7 *sub hanc vocem*.

PAGE 57

Maricae, a Latin nymph, mother of Latinus by Faunus, worshipped by the Minturnenses in a grove on the Liris in S. Latium near their town.

sanguinis rivum, cp. 24. 10. 7 *Mantuae stagnum Mincio amni cruentum visum; et Calibus creta et Romae in foro bovario sanguine pluvisse*.

§ **4**. **Armilustro**, on the Aventine. A festival called *Armilustrium* was held there in October. The ceremony is said to have been performed by armed men, but we know nothing of its nature.

§ **5**. **nuntiatum**. The subject of *turbavit* is *nuntiatum...esse*. The whole phrase becomes the equivalent of a substantive. This may be regarded as a development of the construction noted on c. 5. 14. Thus *haec nuntiata turbaverunt* (= 'the announcement of these things disturbed') produces from *nuntiatum est infantem natum esse* a parallel *nuntiatum infantem natum esse turbavit* where the accusative and infinitive clause is felt to correspond to the substantive or pronoun in the former case (see n. on c. 2. 12). Cp. c. 45. 4 auditum *modo in acie...alterum consulem advenisse...victoriam facturum*, 7. 22. 1, Tac. *Hist.* 1. 51 *accessit callide* vulgatum, *temere* creditum *decumari legiones*. Virg. *Aen.* 5. 6 *dolores*...notumque *furens quid femina possit...ducunt*. And on the other hand the development of the substantival use of the participle with retention of verbal functions (e.g. *perperam factum* 'a wrong deed,' see n. on c. 3. 2) made easy the passage to instances where there is no dependent clause, e.g. 7. 8. 5 *diu non* perlitatum *tenuerat dictatorem* ('the fact that for long the sacrifice was not successful'), 1. 51. 1 *degeneratum* 'his degeneracy.'

quadrimo parem. Similar prodigies are reported in the inscriptions recording the wonderful ἰάματα ('cures') in the temple of Aesculapius at Epidaurus. *quadrimus* lit. 'four *winters* old,' cp. *bimus* = *bi-hĭmus, Dialectal Eng. *twinter*, 'a beast two years old.'

ut Sinuessae, cp. c. 11. 5.

incertus, 'indeterminate,' ἄκριτος, cp. 31. 12. 6, 30. 35. 9 *Italicos incertos socii an hostes essent*. When *incertus* is used objectively of the thing that causes uncertainty, if there is a dependent interrogative clause, the impersonal construction (*incertum est de*...) is more usual.

§ 6. **ex Etruria.** See n. on c. 4. 15. When Etruria failed them in matters of religious difficulty, the Romans had to send to Delphi, cp. 5. 15. 1 (during war with Veii) *quia hostibus Etruscis, per quos ea procurarent, haruspices non erant.*

§ 7. **novenae**, 'a group or set of nine maidens.' Dr Postgate (*Class. Rev.* Nov. 1907) has shown convincingly that the so-called distributive numerals are really in origin collectives, and their use as distributives ('nine each' etc.) is a development. Relics of the original sense are seen in their use (1) as cardinals in poetry, (2) as multiplicatives, *ter novenae* = 'thrice a group of nine,' (3) with words like *castra* which have not a corresponding singular. Note the ritual *ter*.

Iovis Statoris, 'Juppiter the Stayer of Flight'; according to tradition the temple was vowed by Romulus in battle with the Sabines, cp. 1. 12. 6.

conditum, 'composed,' 'put together,' (con + do = τίθημι). Cp. Milton's 'build the lofty rhyme.'

Livio, *Andronicus*, a Greek or Samnite who came to Rome after the fall of Tarentum in 272 B.C. as the slave of Livius. Having obtained his freedom and taken the name of Livius, he started a school, and to provide text-books for his pupils he translated into Latin the Odyssey and several Greek tragedies and comedies. The first performance of a play by him took place, we are told, in 240 B.C.

§ **8**. **divam** = *deam*, a usage mostly archaic and poetical.

§ **9**. **aedilium**. The aediles had charge of the temples in virtue of their functions as *curatores urbis*. They had the right of issuing proclamations dealing with matters within their jurisdiction. **intra decimum lapidem.** Normally the authority of the aediles extended only one mile from the walls.

§ **11**. **ab decemviris**, sc. *sacrorum*. See n. on c. 6. 15. In addition to the charge of the Sibylline books the decemvirs had certain administrative duties.

Carmentali, called after the nymph Carmentis, mother of Evander, who had an altar at this gate. This temple of Apollo lay outside the Servian walls in the *prata Flaminia*, close to the *porta Carmentalis*, cp. Dionys. 1. 32 ὑπὸ τῷ καλουμένῳ καπιτωλίῳ παρὰ ταῖς Καρμεντίσι πύλαις.

§ **13**. **indutae**, 'wearing,' 'clothed in,' only here in Livy with the accusative in imitation of the poets. The accusative is the same as that used with middle verbs in Greek. Three uses of the accusative of different origin are frequently confused in Latin, (1) accusative of 'respect' (*accusativus Graecus*), very limited in strict prose, but much extended by Virgil and the Augustan poets, e.g. *tremit artus*, *Cressa genus*; (2) the object accusative after middle verbs, e.g. *inutile ferrum cingitur*; (3) the object accusative retained in the passive, e.g. *inscripti nomina regum flores*. The usages come very close together, and with the past participle it is often difficult to distinguish between (2) and (3). In Greek too when the construction of the accusative of 'the whole and part' is turned into the passive, the accusative of 'the part' remains and is felt as an accusative of respect, although in the active it may have been an object accusative.

in Iunonem, 'to Juno,' 'in honour of Juno,' cp. 4. 20. 2 *in eum*.

PAGE 58

forsitan, 'it may be,' used parenthetically without influence on the construction, and so equivalent to an adverb, cp. 9. 11. 13 *et illi quidem, forsitan et publica, sua certe liberata fide...redierunt, Praef.* § 12 *cum forsitan necessariae erunt.* Usually *forsitan* has a subjunctive dependent on it, *fortasse* being used adverbially.

rudibus ingeniis, 'when men's mental powers were uncultivated.' We may call this an instrumental ablative of circumstances or a locatival ablative of time. It is also possible to construe it as a dative of the person judging.

abhorrens, used absolutely, 'harsh.' **inconditum,** 'rough.'

si referatur. The apodosis of the ideal condition (*sit*) is implied, though *nunc abhorrens et inconditum* is of course a fact apart from any condition, cp. 36. 32. 5 *erat Quinctius, si cederes, placabilis* which is *est si cedas* thrown into the past.

§ **14.** **Iugario vico,** 'by way of the *vicus Iugarius.*' See n. on c. 2. 10. This road led from the *porta Carmentalis* to the *Forum.*

per manus, i.e. in order to help them to keep time. **modulantes,** 'keeping the measure with their foot beat.' The processional dance was as important an element as the words; hence Livy says 'keeping the sound in tune by the beat of the foot'; cp. Pind. *Ol.* 3. 5 Δωρίῳ φωνὰν ἐναρμόξαι πεδίλῳ.

§ **15.** **vico Tusco,** etc. "all lying on the route from the *Forum* to the Aventine, which was approached by the *clivus Publicius,* a paved road, ascending from the *porta trigemina* and forming the regular access to the Aventine from the quarter of the *Forum*" (Stephenson).

perrectum, 'they proceeded to,' impersonal passive, cp. Hor. *Sat.* 1. 9. 35 *ventum erat ad Vestae.*

CHAPTER 38

§ **1.** **intentius.** See n. on c. 24. 9.

§ **2.** **iuventutis,** 'men of military age.' Technically *iuniores* were men between 17 and 46. Normally the levy was confined to these, but in emergencies the *seniores* (men from 47 to 60) were called out for service in the field. **unde,** see n. on c. 1. 13.

§ **3.** **colonos maritimos.** The *coloniae maritimae* were colonies of Roman citizens, such as Ostia or Antium, established as coast guards. The inhabitants of *coloniae civium Romanorum*, to which class the *coloniae maritimae* belonged, were as Roman citizens of course liable to service in the army, but the *coloni maritimi* had a special exemption at ordinary times, no doubt in consideration of the garrison duty they performed for the guarding of the coasts. In 191 B.C. they made an appeal against service in the fleet, but the Senate decided unanimously to disallow it. See 36. 3. 4 f.

sacrosanctam. This epithet is applied to any person or thing protected by a *lex sacrata* the violation of which made the offender *sacer* ('devoted to gods') and as such liable to be slain with impunity. See a discussion of the term in Bk 3. c. 55. The compound is explained as 'consecrated by a sacred penalty' or 'a sacred rite.' Dictionaries give *sacrōsanctus*, treating *sacro* as an instrumental ablative, but the first element might be the stem *sacrŏ-*, cp. *Ahenobarbus*, the archaic spelling being naturally preserved in technical terms of religion and law and in proper names. See n. on c. 1. 2.

cogebant, 'were for compelling.'

in diem certam ut, 'for a specified day.' The expression is slightly peculiar. We should expect *diem edicere* or else *in diem edicere* with an accusative (*senatum, concilium*, etc., cp. c. 6. 2), instead of the *ut* clause.

§ **4.** **Alsiensis,** the people of Alsium, an old Etruscan coast town near Caere. It became a colony after the 1st Punic War. **Senensis,** the people of Sena on the Umbrian coast, not Sena in Etruria, which was also a Roman colony. See n. on c. 46. 4.

§ **5.** **cum...recitaret.** With *cum* temporal *recitasset* might have been expected, but the imperfect is descriptive, 'as each read.' This is better than taking *cum* as adversative, 'although.'

praeter Antiatem Ostiensemque, i.e. *praeter vacationem Antiatum* etc. In the case of these two towns the coast garrison duty was particularly important for the protection of Rome and Latium.

iuniores. See n. on § 3 *iuventutis*.

iure iurando adacti, lit. 'compelled with an oath,' i.e. 'compelled *to take oath* that,' and so governing an accusative and infinitive like *iurare*. In the common active form, *sacramento adigere*, used of the person who tenders the oath, the ablative is instrumental, and in the passive (*sacramento adigi*), where the subject is the person or persons taking the oath, it is an easy transition to the meaning 'forced (to promise) under oath,' in which the ablative ceases to be so purely instrumental. Livy extends the usage of the case still further in putting it with the active of a veib applying to the taker of the oath, *sacramento dicere* (e.g. 4. 43. 2 and often), instead of the normal *sacramentum dicere*.

§ **6.** **Etruriam erectam**, cp. c. 21. 6 and c. 24.

§ **7.** **occupandum**, 'must be kept engaged.' *occupare*, as regularly, has the sense of anticipating or forestalling, i.e. 'must be engaged...to prevent his....' Cp. c. 39. 2 *qui...occuparet.* So with the infinitive 1. 14. 4 *occupant bellum facere*, 'begin war first.'

PAGE 59

provinciarum, i.e. *Etruria* and *Gallia.* See c. 35. 11.

§ **8.** **collegam habere**, sc. *reputabat.*

tertio cui...praeesset, cp. c. 36. 13. But according to c. 35. 12 this is not true. Nero had the choice between the armies of Marcellus and Crispinus. The two legions which Q. Claudius Flamen commanded *circa Tarentum et Sallentinos* (see c. 22. 2, 3 and c. 36. 13) were distinct from the army of Crispinus (see c. 29. 6). Weissenborn supposes that Livy has taken this statement from a different source, but it may be that he has here confused the choice of armies for 207 B.C. with that for 208 B.C. See c. 22. 2, where the two legions commanded afterwards by Q. Claudius are one of the three armies from which the consuls are to choose.

intuleratque mentionem, 'and indeed he had made a proposal for the recall.' *mentionem inferre*, like *mentionem facere*, used of individual senators means 'mention a fact' in debate, usually with a view to a motion (*relatio*) on the subject. Cp. 4. 8. 4 *mentio illata apud senatum est rem operosam...magistratu egere*, 30. 21. 6 *mentio...ab senioribus facta est segnius homines bona quam mala sentire.*

de volonibus revocandis. *volones*='volunteers.' Cp. Macrob. *Sat.* 1. 11. 30 *servi pro dominis pugnaturos se polliciti...et volones quia sponte hoc voluerunt, appellati.* The reference is to a body of 8000 slaves enrolled after Cannae in 216 B.C. Cp. 22. 57. 11 *octo milia iuvenum validorum ex servitiis, prius sciscitantes singulos vellentne militare, empta publice armaverunt.* They were freed by their commander Gracchus in 214 B.C. after the battle of Beneventum, cp. 24. 16. 9 *omnes eos liberos esse iubere.*

§ **9.** **senatus fecit.** This is a new order substituted for the arrangements mentioned in c. 35. 11 f.

§ **10.** **volones in undevicensimam**, etc. Livius evidently drew very largely from the two Etrurian legions and it was necessary to fill up the blanks with *volones* to such an extent that in the following year these legions are called *duas volonum legiones* (28. 10. 11).

§ **11.** **de legione**, 'legionary.' The singular means perhaps 'from a (single) legion,' but, as Weissenborn says, we should expect the number of the legion to be mentioned.

mixtos agrees with the sense of *equitum mille.*

CHAPTER 39

§ **1.** **L. Porcio**, praetor of Gallia Cisalpina, cp. c. 36. 11.

§ **2.** **occuparet**. See n. on c. 38. 7.

§ **3.** **contineret**, 'hold within bounds,' 'keep in check,' cp. Tac. *Agr.* 18 *victos continuisse.*

§ **4.** **in eam rem**, 'for that object.' See n. on c. 3. 9. **nunc...nunc.** See n. on c. 3. 8. **exhausisset**, 'he had undergone,' cp. *laborem exhaurire.*

PAGE 60

§ **6.** **Arverni**, mod. Auvergne.

§ **7.** **per munita pleraque**. See n. on c. 17. 9. For *munita* as opposed to *invia* cp. *viam munire*, 'make a causeway.' **ducebat.** See n. on c. 17. 8.

duodecim annorum, i.e. from 218 B.C. to 207 B.C.

adsuetudine, an exaggeration. There were not other crossings of the Alps between Hannibal's passage and that of Hasdrubal.

inter mitiora, etc., 'he found the tribes he passed through had now become more civilised.' *iam* goes with *mitiora*; see n. on c. 3. 8.

§ **8.** **invisitati...alienigenis** means 'not seen outside their own country' rather than 'not visited by.' For the dative see n. on c. 8. 6.

primo, 'on the first occasion,' i.e. when Hannibal came; **deinde**, 'afterwards,' at Hasdrubal's passage.

§ **9.** **urebatur**. See n. on c. 29. 9.

opibus, 'power.'

§ **11.** **quod...profectum erat**, 'the advantage gained.' **ad Placentiam**, 'before Placentia.' On the approach of Hannibal in 218 B.C. large bodies of colonists were hastily sent to occupy Placentia and

Cremona, on opposite sides of the Po, in order to keep the Gauls quiet and assist the praetor's army.

obsidet magis quam oppugnat. See n. on c. 28. 13.

§ **12.** **campestris oppidi** = *oppidi in campo et plano siti*, cp. *campestre iter*.

nobilitas, 'the name and fame.'

§ **13.** **spe sua**, 'than he himself (Hannibal) had expected.' See n. on c. 35. 4. **celeriorem.** See Notes on Text.

§ **14.** **quippe**, with participle (cp. ὡς in Greek), is rare before Livy (cp. Lucr. 3. 190 *quippe volubilibus parvisque creata figuris*). The addition of adverbs to show the nature of the clause to which a participle is equivalent (temporal, causal, etc.) is not common in classical Latin, and the more frequent occurrence from Livy on is perhaps due to Greek influence. Thus L. appears to imitate the use of ὡς with future participle by using *tamquam* in 37. 23. 6 *classis tamquam eo die pugnatura*.

frustra...temptasset. After Trebia Hannibal attacked a fortified post in the neighbourhood of Placentia but was repulsed by the Roman legions who were wintering at Placentia. See 21. 57. 6 f.

CHAPTER 40

§ **1.** **duo pariter bella**, 'two simultaneous wars,' cp. 6. 4. 1 *trium simul bellorum* and see n. on c. 1. 10.

§ **2.** **simul...simul.** See n. on c. 3. 2. The repetition of *cura* in *angeret cura* is rather clumsy. The *simul* clauses do not give an explanation why their anxieties were divided (*distenderant curas*) but a description of the various grounds for anxiety.

quos...fore. The rhetorical question is reported in the accusative and infinitive, as regularly, cp. 26. 35. 10 *unde paraturos*.

PAGE 61

utrubique, 'at both points.'

§ **3.** **adhuc**, 'up till now,' 'so far,' cp. § 8 and see n. on c. 20. 4. *adhuc* is unnecessary here and may possibly be a gloss on *ad id tempus*.

pensando, modal ablative, 'while one set off successes against defeats.' The unexpressed agent is indefinite, 'one' or 'they' rather than 'the gods.' **rem**, 'the war.'

Romana res, 'the power of Rome had been suddenly brought low, but her fallen fortunes had been raised again by successes.' For **praecipitasset** intransitive see n. on c. 16. 4.

§ 4. **alia super aliam**, 'one *on the top of* another'; *super* gives the cumulative effect more vividly than *post*. This picturesque use of *super* in phrases denoting repetition is quoted from Early Latin and reappears in Livy. It was no doubt a colloquial usage at all periods. Cp. 9. 23. 3 *cum...alii super alios nuntiarent*.

duobus...ducibus, the two Scipios. See n. on c. 18. 1. **delesset** = *delevisset*. See n. on c. 6. 8.

multa secunda...gesta, 'many successes.' See n. on c. 8. 12. *gesta* is substantival.

excepisse. Stephenson takes this as a nautical metaphor, 'had harboured the weather-beaten ship of the state.' This suits *quassatam*, but the preceding *praecipitasset*, *prolapsam*, *erexisse* suggest that the metaphor of a fallen building or column is continued and that *excepisse* means 'held up,' 'steadied,' 'supported.' Cp. Cic. *labentem excepit*, etc., and see also n. on c. 27. 3.

§ 6. **circumstare**, 'threatened.' *circumstare* is frequently used of dangers surrounding a thing.

§ 7. **terrebat**, 'caused great apprehension.' The subject is not merely *annus* but the whole sentence *proximus...funeribus*. See n. on c. 5. 12.

§ 8. **adhuc** = *etiam tum*. See n. on § 3.

§ 9. **ex civibus victis** = *ex caede civium*. See notes on c. 5. 12 and c. 35. 8.

§ 10. **priusquam...perveniret**, 'before he could reach.' See n. on c. 8. 11.

agri Larinatis. The geography is confused here. We do not know where Hostilius Tubulus was. He had been appointed to Tarentum (c. 35. 4) and then transferred to Capua (c. 35. 14 and c. 36. 13), and was probably on his way to the latter place (cp. § 13). Hannibal was in Bruttium (c. 29. 1, c. 35. 10, c. 38. 7, c. 39. 13) The territory of the Sallentini lay in S. Calabria, while Larinum was a town of the Frentani close to the N. border of Apulia (c. 43. 10) and therefore far to the north of Hannibal's direct route. It seems likely that Livy found somewhere in one of his authorities the mention of a march by Hannibal to N. Apulia and tried unsuccessfully to fit it in with his movements in the south. In § 12 Hannibal is suddenly in the *ager Tarentinus.* Madvig seeks to get out of the difficulty by reading *Uriatis.* This would suit the rest of Livy's account, for Uria lay between Tarentum and Brundisium.

§ **11.** **Q. Claudius.** See c. 36. 13. **per urbes...castra disposita** means 'had his army in quarters in the various towns.' Cp. 6. 6. 13 *in urbe castra habere.*

PAGE 62

§ **14.** **utroque exercitu.** Nero had been empowered to choose either of the two consular armies of the previous year (c. 35. 12). Then he and Livius were permitted to select soldiers from any of the armies as they thought fit (c. 38. 9). According to Livy Nero interpreted this permission in the widest sense, for from the numbers given—40,000 foot—he must have taken over practically the whole of both armies. The *reliquiae* left to Fulvius (cp. c. 35. 13) could not have amounted to more than one or two thousand men. Kromayer declares that Livy's figures are incredible and thinks that Nero had about 20,000 men.

CHAPTER 41

§ **1.** **ad Grumentum,** cp. 25. 22. 14 *ad Brundisium flexit iter* and see n. on c. 17. 8. Grumentum was W. of Metapontum in the centre of Lucania.

defecissent. The subjunctive expresses the thought of Hannibal implied in the phrase *spe recipiendi* ('hoping that he might recover').

§ **2.** **exploratis itineribus,** 'carefully reconnoitring the ground as he advanced.'

§ **4.** **castra...interiacebat.** *interiacere* does not occur in prose before Livy. It may be construed with a dative of the person or thing concerned or with an accusative of extent governed by the *inter* in the compound, cp. 7. 29. 6 *in planitiem quae Capuam Tifataque interiacet.* Various attempts have been made to identify the scene of the battle. The latest is that of Kromayer (*Antike Schlachtfelder* III. 1, p. 415 f.). He sets the camp of Hannibal ½ a mile to the W. of the site of Grumentum near the mod. Saponara, and takes the *campus* to be the plain to the north of the stream Agri, the spot behind which the ambush lay being a small hill in front of Madonna di Monserrato.

nudi, 'bare of trees,' 'without cover,' cp. c. 42. 6 *via nuda*.

neutris suspecti. See n. on c. 8. 6.

nihil...neque. See n. on c. 8. 14; instead of a second *nihil* with *latebrarum* we must understand *quidquam*.

§ **5.** **ab stationibus.** See n. on c. 2. 11. **certamina serebant.** See n. on c. 12. 9.

evadere, 'get away,' cp. c. 1. 15 and see n. on c. 18. 15.

§ **6.** **ingenio hostis usus**, 'adopting a strategy similar to Hannibal's.'

quo minus. In comparative sentences *quo minus* is normally followed by *eo magis* or some other comparative (or word implying comparison), but Livy frequently omits the correlative *eo* (e.g. 2. 51. 5 *quo plures erant maior caedes fuit*) and sometimes, as here, leaves out the comparative expression altogether in the latter clause; cp. 23. 15. 14 *quo frequentior mecum fueris, senties eam rem tibi dignitati atque emolumento esse*, Tac. *Hist.* 1. 14 *quo suspectior sollicitis, adoptanti placebat.* Tacitus sometimes substitutes a positive for the comparative, cp. *Ann.* 1. 74 *quantoque incautius efferverat, paenitentia* patiens *tulit absolvi reum*.

cohortes, 'allies.' **manipulis**, 'Roman legionaries.' See n. on c. 13. 9.

aversis, 'in valleys lying behind the hills,' i.e. on the side of the hills away from the Carthaginians.

§ **7.** **socium** = *sociorum*. See n. on c. 1. 2.

mittebat. Note the imperfect tense ('was sending') marking the continuance involved in the action resulting; so in Greek ἔπεμπον is used idiomatically where English would employ an aoristic tense. The writer's 'thoughts follow the motion,' cp. Hdt. 1. 69 ὁ Κροῖσος ἔπεμπε ἐς Σπάρτην ἀγγέλους, Thuc. 8. 39. 4 ἐντεῦθεν δὴ ἀγγελίαν ἔπεμπον.

PAGE 63

§ **8.** **signum** means 'a signal that there was to be a battle that day.' The regular sign for this in the *Roman* camp was the flying of a red ensign over the general's tent.

pedes...portis...palati...properare. The alliteration is probably intentional here. See n. on c. 11. 1. **portis ruere**, 'rush out by the gates' (instrumental ablative of route), not 'rush out from the gates' (true ablative).

§ **9**. **tribuno militum.** The six tribunes commanded the legion in turn.

quanto. *quanto maximo* (or *maxime*) *impetu posset* is Livy's regular usage for the ordinary *quam maximo impetu posset.*

§ **10**. **toto campo.** See n. on c. 8. 6.

CHAPTER 42

§ **1**. **cum...audivit.** See n. on c. 27. 10.

§ **2**. **equestris terror,** 'panic caused by the cavalry.'

legio et ala...inibat. The singular verb is used probably because *legio* and *ala* are regarded as a fighting unit.

§ **3**. **crescit...augetur.** *crescit* refers to the intensity of the conflict, *augetur* to its extent.

in vetere exercitu et duci, etc., 'in the case of a veteran army *and* for a veteran general.' *et* is not to be taken as 'even.'

§ **5**. **minorque caedes,** '*but* the slaughter was less' (i.e. than might have been expected). Note **que** 'and indeed,' where we should expect an adversative conjunction. This adversative use of *que* is most common when a negative clause precedes, cp. 23. 7. 11 *ne quid eo die seriae rei gereret diemque et ipse adventu suo festum...celebraret.* For an instance with a positive clause preceding, cp. Caes. *B. G.* 2. 33 *ex proximis castellis eo concursum est; pugnatumque ab hostibus ita acriter* etc.

quia...enim. *quia* gives the reason why the slaughter was smaller than it might have been; *enim* gives the reason why it might have been greater.

§ **6**. **trānsversa.** See n. on c. 18. 15. **secundis collibus,** 'down the hills,' 'with the slope of the hills in their favour' (lit. 'with the hills following'), an easy extension of phrases like *secundo vento* or *secundo amni* where the wind or current may be said actually to 'follow' one who goes with them. The opposite meaning is given by *adversus,* e.g. c. 48. 12 *in adversum collem,* 21. 31. 2 *adversa ripa* etc.

nuda, cp. c. 41. 4.

§ **7**. **supra.** See n. on c. 14. 14.

§ **8**. **circa**=*circiter,* cp. 45. 34. 6 *oppida circa septuaginta.* This use with numerals is unciceronian.

§ **9**. **insequentibus continuis diebus,** 'on several days following without a break.'

PAGE 64

§ **10**. **inferre signa**. See n. on c. 15. 18.

quae pars = *in ea parte quae. pars* is attracted into the relative sentence, cp. 40. 31. 9 *quae pars maxime...conspici poterat, iniecit ignem* (= *ei parti quae*).

relictis goes with *ignibus tabernaculisque* as well as with *Numidis*.

petere intendit, 'hastened to march towards.' *intendo* in this sense is frequent in Livy for the Ciceronian *contendo*.

§ **11**. **ex composito**. See n. on c. 1. 3.

paulisper, 'for a while,' lit. 'through(out) a little'; the second part of the word is the postpositive *per*, as in *parumper*, and *paulis-* may be for **paulius*, a comparative like *magis*.

§ **12**. **obambulaverant**, 'walked in front (of ramparts and gates).

§ **13**. **dum...discurrunt**. As Weissenborn notes, *dum* here = 'so long as' (*quamdiu*); cp. Sall. *Cat.* 36. 1 *paucos dies commoratus... dum...exornat.* When used with the historic present it more usually means 'while' and the action of the main clause is not completely coextensive in time with that of the *dum* clause.

receptui cecinit, 'sounded a retreat'; *receptui* dative of purpose, frequent in military phrases; cp. 21. 53. 11 *locum insidiis circumspectare coepit.* See n. on c. 6. 15.

§ **14**. **procul Venusia**. See n. on c. 1. 4.

§ **15**. **tumultuaria pugna**. See n. on c. 27. 10.

§ **16**. **Hanno**, son of Bomilcar, an able officer, distinguished at Cannae where he commanded the right wing. He had been defeated by Gracchus at Beneventum in 214 B.C.

§ **17**. **Fulvium**. See c. 40. 14.

CHAPTER 43

§ **1**. **Placentiae**. See c. 39. 11.

PAGE 65

emensi, 'after traversing,' a word chiefly used in poetry.

§ **2**. **Q. Claudium**. See c. 36. 13 and c. 40. 11.

§ **3**. **incertis implicantes responsis**, 'after seeking to mislead him by vague replies.' Livy uses the present participle here to express attempted action; the *time* of the action (i.e. prior to *edocuerunt*) is not given by the participle but by the temporal adverb *primo*. On the other hand *cum implicassent* would have expressed the time relation but not the kind of action (conative). Participles in Greek and Latin were originally 'timeless.' See n. on c. 31. 2 *palatos* and cp. Hom. *Il.* 7. 115 σὺ μὲν νῦν ἵζευ ἰὼν μετὰ ἔθνος ἑταίρων, Soph. *Ant.* 1192 ἐγὼ παρὼν ἐρῶ, Thuc. 2. 29 Νυμφόδωρον...οἱ Ἀθηναῖοι πρότερον πολέμιον νομίζοντες πρόξενον ἐποιήσαντο, where the present participles ἰών, παρών, and νομίζοντες all express action *prior* to that of the main verb.

ut, 'when.'

§ **4**. **sicut erant signatis**, 'just as he got them, with the seal unbroken.' Cicero would write *sicut erant signatae*.

§ **5**. **per interpretem**. The despatch would of course be in Punic.

§ **6**. **ordinariis** seems to mean 'according to regulation,' i.e. keeping to the prescribed sphere. Though the consuls had been given wider powers than usual with regard to their armies (c. 38. 9), their *provinciae* were expressly separated (c. 35. 10 *provinciae iis non permixtae regionibus sicut superioribus annis, sed diversa extremis Italiae partibus*).

tempus quo gereret, 'a crisis such that....' *gereret* is consecutive subjunctive.

§ **7**. **audendum ac novandum**, 'he must adopt a bold and original line of action.' *novare*, more commonly in bad sense. See n. on c. 24. 7.

coeptum...perpetratum, 'at the outset...if it were carried through successfully.'

verteret, sc. *cives*.

§ **8**. **pararet, edocet...arcessant**. The historic present may have either primary or secondary sequence. The shift from one to the other is seen frequently in clauses of 'double subordination,' e.g. *monent ut edoceat quid pararet*.

§ **9**. **ad Narniam**. Narnia in Umbria was an important strategic position, commanding the Flaminian Way to Rome. The town was situated on a high and precipitous hill with the deep ravine of the river Nar guarding it on two sides; cp. c. 50. 6 *faucibus Umbriae*.

exercitum urbanum. See c. 35. 11, 12. The legion from Capua and the newly enrolled soldiers were to form the new urban army.

§ **10**. **senatu**. The 4th declension dative in *-u*, which is the regular form in neuters, occurs not infrequently in masculines also, and is paralleled in the Italic dialects. Gellius quotes Caesar's authority for it as the proper form. These forms in *-u* are best explained as locatives.

Larinatem. See n. on c. 40. 10. These districts lay along the Adriatic between Apulia and Umbria. The geographical order is *Larinates, Frentani, Marrucini, Praetutii.*

paratos ad vescendum, 'cooked ready for eating.'

§ **11. quod roboris.** See n. on c. 14. 5.

PAGE 66

§ **12. flexit in Picenum,** 'directed his course towards Picenum.' *flectit=flectit se* or *flectit iter.* See n. on c. 47. 3.

quantis maximis. See n. on c. 41. 9. **ducebat.** See n. on c. 17. 8.

CHAPTER 44

§ **1. biennio ante.** This is an error. Hannibal's march on Rome in the attempt to raise the siege of Capua took place in 211 B.C., i.e. *four* years before the Metaurus. See Bk 26. cc. 9, 10 (c. 10. 3 *ipse cum duobus milibus equitum ad portam Collinam usque ad Herculis templum est progressus atque unde proxime poterat, moenia situmque urbis obequitans contemplabatur*).

castra Punica. Hannibal encamped on the Anio three miles from Rome.

constabat animis, 'they were not at all sure in their minds whether to....' *animis* is generally taken as an extension of the usual dative of the person with *constare* (lit. 'it was not fixed for their minds'), but the analogy of phrases like *constare apud animum* (30. 28. 1) makes it likely that *animis* was felt by the Romans to be an ablative as in *animo agitare.*

laudarent vituperarentne. This use of *-ne* in the second member of a double question for the usual *utrum...an* or *-ne...an* is not common and seems to be confined to cases where, as here, single words are contrasted. Cp. c. 47. 3 *semel bisne*, 9. 23. 4 *victi victoresne essent.* See also n. on c. 13. 7 *an.*

§ **2. famam habiturum,** 'would be praised or censured.'

roboris...floris. See n. on c. 14. 5. **fuerit** represents *fuit* (aoristic) of the *recta*. See n. on c. 16. 7. The direct form of the other tenses in this sentence would be *detractum est* (true perfect), *ostendit* (true perfect), *petat*, *ignoret* or perhaps rather *ostendit* (aorist), *peteret*, *ignoraret*. See n. on c. 9. 3.

ostendisse iter, 'pretended he was marching,' cp. 4. 59. 4 *oppugnationem ostendit*; different from c. 46. 10 *aperire in Galliam iter*.

§ **3. nulla alia re tutiora**, 'with no better protection than the erroneous impression in the mind of the enemy.' The expression is somewhat confused. We should expect either 'more secure by...than by anything' or 'by nothing else so secure as by....' See n. on c. 6. 5.

§ **4. futurum**, infinitive in rhetorical question, cp. c. 40. 2.

sine imperio, sine auspicio, 'without military authority, without religious sanction for action.' "*imperium* was the consular power viewed in its civil and military, *auspicium* the same viewed in its religious aspect" (Stephenson). As Weissenborn points out, this is a rhetorical exaggeration. The general's representative could hold his powers.

§ **5. veteres...terrebant.** These words are a piece of narrative inserted in the middle of the oblique, but yet the succeeding clauses of the oblique are dependent on the verb of thinking implied in *terrebant*. It would have been more regular if the sentence had run on, *veteres fuisse e. b. clades, duos consules p. a. interfectos, et ea omnia* etc. For a similar inserted remark of the historian cp. 9. 31. 13 *sed quem esse iam virtuti Romanae inexpugnabilem locum? Fregellana arx Soranaque, et ubicumque iniquo successum erat loco, memorabantur.* There, however, it is easier as coming at the end of the speech.

§ **6. gemina victoria**, the defeat of the two Scipios in 211 B.C. See Bk 25, c. 34 and c. 36.

§ **8. hunc**=*Hasdrubalem*. *hic* is often vividly retained in oblique like *nunc* for *tum*, cp. 5. 2. 3 *hoc illud esse*. Here it is kept because of the contrast with *ille*.

in iis locis quibus. The preposition is usually omitted with the relative when it has the same construction as the antecedent.

PAGE 67

§ **9. in saltu deprensus**, etc. Nero had been praetor in 212 B.C. In the following year he was despatched to Spain. Marching against

Hasdrubal, he succeeded in shutting him up in a difficult pass. Hasdrubal offered to deport the whole Carthaginian army from Spain if he were allowed to escape. The negociating of the terms was spun out and each night some of Hasdrubal's soldiers slipped away. The remainder finally got off under cover of a thick morning mist *vacuaque hostium castra conspexerunt Romani*. An excellent example of *Punica fraus!*

frustratus elusisset. This phrase is echoed in c. 47. 6 (*frustratione elusum*), when Nero outwits Hannibal as Hasdrubal had outwitted him.

§ **10.** **vero,** 'than they actually were,' an example of *comparatio compendiaria*. See n. on c. 1. 3.

praesidia, used generally, 'fighting resources,' 'forces.'

metu interprete, 'since fear is always apt to make men take the more pessimistic view.'

CHAPTER 45

§ **1.** **tantum intervalli...fecerat,** 'had put such a distance between himself and the enemy.'

§ **3.** **ad quod bellum...eo,** etc. The sentence is difficult and variously interpreted. The MSS. reading is *eo ipsos quantumcumque* etc. Madvig's emendation *eo ipsi si quantumcumque* is generally accepted. With this reading, *quantumcumque* is an indefinite pronoun ('if they should add *ever so small* a force to the Roman side of the scale'), *eo* is an adverb (=*ad id bellum*, cp. c. 22. 9) and goes with *addiderint*, while *ipsi* is also drawn forward out of its clause for greater emphasis. But the MSS. reading might be retained with Weissenborn and *eo* interpreted as=*eo bello*, 'in this war,' not=*ad id bellum* with *inclinaturos*.

momentum. See n. on c. 9. 1.

rem omnem inclinaturos, 'will change the balance of things completely,' i.e. 'will prove the determining factor in the struggle.'

§ **4.** **auditum modo,** 'the mere announcement on the field of battle that....' The subject of *facturum* is the whole clause *auditum... advenisse*. See n. on c. 37. 5 *nuntiatum*.

daturum, sc. *se*.

§ **5.** **gloriae...fructum,** defining genitive, 'the fruits (consisting) of the glory.'

§ **6**. **traxisse** carries on the metaphor of *parva momenta*. *traho* is used of the weight in the scale pan which 'draws up' the weight in the other scale. ἕλκειν and ἄγειν are similarly used in Greek.

quo concursu, etc., 'the admiring and enthusiastic crowds that line their route.'

§ **7**. **per instructa omnia**, 'everywhere through regular lines.' See n. on c. 17. 9.

§ **8**. **faustum**...**felix**, regularly combined in the formula *quod felix ac faustum sit*. *faustum* means 'favoured of heaven,' 'blest,' *felix* 'successful' ('fruitful,' cp. *fetus*, *fecundus*).

ex hostibus, 'over the enemy,' goes closely with *victoria* sc. *reportata*. See n. on c. 11. 9.

PAGE 68

damnarentur votorum, 'condemned to pay the vows.' *voti damnare*, 'condemn (in the matter) of a vow,' means 'to bring about the event for the accomplishment of which the vow is made.' The 'judicial' genitive of the punishment or the crime in Latin and Greek is usually explained as dependent on *crimine*, δίκῃ etc. understood, but this is unnecessary. The genitive denotes the sphere of the action. For the use with *voti* cp. C. I. L. 1. 1175 *semol te orant se voti crebro condemnes* and Virg. *Aen*. 5. 237 *voti reus*.

§ **10**. **benigne**...**cumulata**, 'with the most lavish generosity.'

§ **11**. **modestia certare**, sc. *cum iis*, 'the soldiers were as moderate as they were pressing, refusing to take etc.' (Stephenson).

⟨**abscedere**⟩. See Notes on Text.

§ **12**. **noctu**...**nocte** are both locatival forms. The 4th declension stem **noctu* survives in Latin only in this adverbial case but a parallel form in Sanskrit is declined throughout.

CHAPTER **46**

§ **1**. **tessera**, derived from Gk τέσσαρα. *tesserae* were four-sided wooden tablets circulated to the officers and soldiers on duty with the watchword for the night inscribed on them. Hence *tesseram dare* comes to mean 'send an order round,' since in many cases an order or announcement would accompany the watchword; cp. 7. 35. 1 *tesseram dari iubet armati convenirent*.

§ **2**. **tendentium**. See n. on c. 17. 17.

§ **3**. **nomina dantes**, the regular phrase for giving in one's name for the army list.

§ **4**. **ad Senam**, 'near Sena.' See Introduction III. Sēna or Sena Gallica was an Umbrian coast town, settled by the Gallic tribe of the Senones and after their defeat colonised by Rome in 283 B.C.

quingentos...passus. As this seems unusually close quarters, Weissenborn suggests that a larger number preceding *quingentos* has fallen out.

§ **5**. **L. Porcius**, praetor of Gallia, cp. c. 36. 11.

PAGE 69

§ **6**. **transitum**, sc. *hosti* (or *hostis*).

carperet agmen, 'harass the enemy's army on the march.' *carpere*, 'pluck off,' is used here of frequent attacks inflicting slight losses on parts of the main body. So *carptim pugnare* is used of skirmishing attacks. An old translator renders 'by frequent skirmishes and falling sometimes on the Enemies' Rear, and by and by goring them on the flanks.'

§ **9**. **errore velut torpentem**, 'in a kind of lethargy in consequence of his delusion.' *torpere errore* is a curious phrase. Mental *torpor* is usually a state of sluggishness induced by fear, wonder, success or the like. Possibly, however, *errore* may be taken with the whole sentence *nec...adgredi nec...intendisse*, rather than with *torpentem* only.

iter intendisse, 'pushed forward.' **rediri**, impersonal passive, 'a return march could be made.'

§ **11**. **abutendum**, not 'abuse,' but 'use to the full,' 'take full advantage of'; cp. ἀποχρῆσθαι in Greek.

§ **12**. **signum proponitur**. See n. on c. 41. 8.

CHAPTER 47

§ **1**. **attulit**. The subject is the *quod* clause, 'the fact that H. marked.'

ante signa. See n. on c. 18. 2. *ante signa* here obviously means 'in front of the whole army.' Similarly in c. 18. 18 and in c. 48. 5, where the elephants are placed *ante signa*, it appears that the *signa* of the troops behind the elephants were placed *in front of* those troops. On the other hand passages like 8. 11. 7 *caesos hastatos* *principesque, stragem et ante signa et post signa factam*, imply that the standards were at the rear of the front line.

vetera, 'travel-stained.' **strigosiores**, 'in poor condition,' 'with their ribs showing' (lit. 'striped,' from the same root as *stringo*, cp. *striga* 'a stretch' or 'swathe of grain'). For the comparative see n. on c. 13. 13.

solita, sc. *multitudine*, i.e. greater than the (particular) number he had been accustomed to during the time he had been encamped near Livius. *maior solito* would be general, 'unusually great' (for a Roman army).

§ **2**. **receptui**. See n. on c. 42. 13. **misit**. See n. on c. 26. 5.

aquabantur, sc. *Romani*.

excipi, 'caught.' See n. on c. 27. 3.

adustioris coloris, 'sunburnt,' 'tanned.' **ex recenti via**, 'fresh from a march,' cp. c. 28. 12 *ex itinere*.

§ **3**. **circumvehi iubet...ut attendant**. Livy frequently follows up an infinitive after *iubeo* with an *ut* clause.

PAGE 70

semel bisne. See n. on c. 44. 1.

signum canat. *signum* might be taken as object, cp. the passive use of *cano* in 26. 6. 7 *receptui cani iussit*, or as subject with *cano* intransitive. The latter is more probable. See n. on c. 5. 9. The *signum* in question was probably the one given at the conclusion of the evening meal.

§ **4**. **castra nihil aucta**, 'the fact that the camp was not enlarged.' See n. on c. 5. 12.

quo latius tenderetur, 'to give more space for tents.'

§ **5**. **duos profecto**. This clause is not dependent on *cura angebat*, but is in oblique as expressing Hasdrubal's thought, cp. § 7 *profecto haud...ausum*.

§ **6**. **frustratione elusum**. See n. on c. 44. 9. **tantae rei...ut**. The expression is somewhat condensed; instead of 'outwitted in a serious matter to such an extent,' we have 'outwitted in such a serious matter that....'

castra collata. See n. on c. 12. 9.

habuerit. For the reading see Notes on Text, and for the use of the perfect subjunctive see notes on c. 9. 3 and c. 44. 2. *habuerit* is the oblique of *habuit*. Thus *ignorat ubi sit cum quo habuit* ('has had') becomes *suspicatus...ut ignoraret ubi esset cum quo habuisset* ('had had,' Ciceronian) or *habuerit* (Livian). *cum quo haberet* would represent (*ignorat ubi sit*) *cum quo habet* which is not true, whereas *minime id quod erat suspicari* in the leading clause implies that what is dependent is a statement of the facts as they really are, not what Hannibal thought they were.

§ 7. **profecto haud mediocri**, etc., 'it must indeed have been no ordinary disaster that had made him afraid to pursue.'

vereri, credere, sc. *Hasdrubal*, historic infinitives.

ne venisset, 'lest it should prove that he had come too late.'

§ 9. **duces**, 'the guides,' cp. c. 17. 17.

nota, 'which he knew of,' not 'well known.'

infrequentia, 'but thinly attended,' proleptic use of the adjective.

fessique somno, 'overcome by sleepiness,' 'heavy with (lack of) sleep.'

§ 10. **dum...ostenderet**, 'until the light should show.'

ripa, 'along the bank,' 'by way of the bank'; cp. c. 37. 14 *vico* and see n. on c. 2. 10.

errorem volvens, a poetical expression, 'wandering in circles.' Weissenborn suggests *orbem volvens*, 'marching in circles.'

ubi...ostendisset, etc., 'meant to cross as soon as the dawn...should show.' *ostendisset* represents *ostenderit* (fut. perf.) and depends on Hasdrubal's thought implied in *transiturus erat*. Weissenborn adopts Putsch's suggestion to insert *substitit* before *ubi* and omit *erat*. But this does not go well with the sentence that follows.

§ 11. **quantum**, accusative of extent. For the combination *quantum...tanto* with comparative cp. 5. 10. 5 *quantum augebatur numerus, tanto maiore pecunia in stipendium opus erat.*

CHAPTER 48

PAGE 71

§ 2. **carperent**. See n. on c. 46. 6.

§ 3. **itineris modo**, 'in marching formation.'

§ 4. **sed ubi, etc.** *sed* is not very strongly adversative here. It seems to contrast the action when the forces are combined with the separate movements described in the previous sections.

§ 5. **ante signa**. See n. on c. 47. 1. **circa eos**, 'on either side,' 'to right and left of them.' Livy seems to mean, however, that the elephants were in advance of the line and extended along a *part* of the left wing where the Gauls were stationed, cp. § 6 *post elephantos positi.*

haud tantum...quantum credebat, 'rather because he believed they were dreaded by the enemy than from any confidence he had in them.' *credebat* instead of *credens* (*opponit*) parallel to *fidens.*

§ **7**. **longior quam latior.** *latior* refers to the width of the front from left to right, *longior* to the depth inwards (*introrsus*) from front to rear. Polyb. τὸ βάθος αὐξήσας τῶν τάξεων. The meaning is 'rather deep than wide' (*longa potius quam lata*, cp. 33. 8. 14), not 'with greater depth than breadth.' This illogical usage of two comparatives where two qualities of the same subject are compared (instead of *magis* or *potius quam* with positives) is common in Livy and occurs rarely in Cicero. Greek has the same construction. The grammars say that the second clause is 'attracted into the comparative.' Why should it be so 'attracted'? I think the explanation is that the construction is due to the common use of the comparative in an absolute sense ('in a rather great degree,' see n. on c. 27. 3). Thus *longior...latior* can mean 'rather deep'...'rather wide,' and a mixture of this with the relative meaning *longior* (*quam*), 'deeper (than)' leads to *longior quam latior* 'rather long than (rather) wide.' Then by analogical extension the construction came to be used also where the meaning was 'with greater depth than breadth.' But it is important to notice that the stock method of bringing out the relative force of the first comparative 'with greater...than' often leads to a mistranslation as in the present instance. Cp. Cic. *Pro Sestio*, 32. 70 *citius quam tardius confici malebat*, where a translation 'with greater haste than slowness' would be absurd.

§ **8**. **ea frons** = *ea pars frontis.*

dextra omnis acies, i.e. the Roman right.

§ **9**. **caedes edebatur.** See n. on c. 14. 10.

§ **10**. **ibi...et Ligures.** This is inconsistent with § 6 where L. says the Ligurians were in the centre behind the elephants. Polybius XI. 1. 3 says Hasdrubal commanded the centre but he also says that he attacked the left wing of the enemy. We may explain the discrepancy by regarding the right wing and the centre as one division of the Punic army, to which the elephants were attached. See Henderson in *Eng. Hist. Rev.* 1898, p. 435. **versi**, sc. *sunt.*

antesignanos. See n. on c. 18. 2.

§ **11**. **impotentius iam regi**, 'were no longer under effective control.' See n. on c. 28. 3 *sagaciter moti.*

haud dissimiliter navibus. The adverb is construed with the dative on the analogy of the adjective. See n. on c. 7. 6 for the constructions of *similis*.

PAGE 72

§ **12.** **in adversum collem signa erigere,** 'march his companies up the face of the hill.' See n. on c. 2. 5.

§ **13.** **postquam...non videbat posse.** *non* goes with *posse*. *postquam* with the imperfect usually denotes an attempted action or one which continues and overlaps the time of the principal verb, e.g. 6. 30. 7 *postquam...afferebatur et apparuit.* The imperfect *videbat* here expresses the gradual realisation of the impossibility. The rather clumsy combination of the *cum...postquam* clauses is partly due to Livy's desire to gain an effect by throwing forward the *quid ergo* clause. **ubi** = 'where,' not 'when.'

stationem segnem, 'it would be rather a case of standing idle in their position than fighting.'

§ **14.** **inopinantibus.** See n. on c. 30. 15. **in sinistrum,** a mistake on Livy's part. It should be *in dextrum*, as many editors read. Pittaluga's defence of *in sinistrum* is not convincing.

§ **16.** **intolerantissima laboris corpora** refers to the Gauls; cp. the description in 38. 17. 7 *si primum impetum, quem fervido ingenio et caeca ira effundunt, sustinueris, fluunt sudore et lassitudine membra, labant arma; mollia corpora, molles ubi ira consedit, animos sol pulvis sitis, ut ferrum non admoveas, prosternunt.*

§ **17.** **hiantes,** 'gasping for air,' 'panting,' cp. Eng. 'yawn' and Gk χάσκω.

adfatim, 'to weariness,' 'to satiety.' The adverb is used here in its original sense. *fatim* is the accusative of an old substantive *fatis* 'weariness,' cp. *fatiscor*, *fatigo* etc. For the formation of the adverb cp. *admodum*, *adamussim* etc.

CHAPTER 49

§ **1.** **fabrile scalprum,** 'a carpenter's chisel.'

magister, i.e. each individual driver.

quanto maximo. See n. on c. 41. 10. **adigebat,** 'drove it in.'

§ **2.** **ubi...sprevissent,** subjunctive of indefinite frequency. See n. on c. 17. 8. It might be explained as virtual oblique for *spreverint* after ***inventa erat*** giving the thought in the mind of the originator. For the reading see Notes on Text.

§ **3. fessos abnuentesque,** 'worn out and refusing to fight by reason of weariness and toil.' Madvig suggests *taedio laborem* in order to provide an object for ***abnuentes***, but *certamen* (c. 4. 1) or *pugnam* is easily understood.

nunc...nunc. See n. on c. 3. 8.

§ **4. nomen,** 'his name and fame.'

PAGE 73

§ **5. reddita aequa,** etc. 'in respect of the slaughter, whether of the leader or of the army, a disaster was inflicted that fully repaid that suffered at Cannae.' For *reddita* cp. 24. 20. 2 *reddidit hosti cladem.*

§ **6. quinquaginta sex,** 56,000 slain! Polybius says 10,000 and puts the Roman loss at 2,000. Roman writers naturally wanted to make it appear *aequa Cannensi clades.*

§ **7. quattuor.** See Notes on Text.

id solacii fuit. See n. on c. 14. 5.

§ **8. ut postero die...inquit.** Although *ut* precedes, *inquit* is thrown in out of construction for the sake of making the description more vivid, cp. 4. 28. 3 *poenas rebellionis dedissent, ni Vettius Messius...inquit.* The Puteanus MS. omits *inquit.*

§ **9. supersint.** See Notes on Text.

CHAPTER 50

§ **1. ⟨profectus⟩.** A participle is required to go with *ea nocte* on account of the *die sexto* following. Madvig suggests *regressus.*

die sexto. See Introduction III.

§ **3. nam,** elliptical, '(I describe the transports of joy along the march) for of the state of feeling at Rome no adequate description is possible.' **incerta** goes with *civitas.*

§ **5. suppliciis,** archaic for *supplicationibus.* It occurs combined with *precibus* in 22. 57. 5. The derived sense of 'punishment' (which one *kneels* to receive) is the regular meaning in classical prose.

§ **6. civitati...accidit,** dative of personal recipient, instead of the colder *ad.*

in castra quae. Nero had advised the despatch of the urban legions to Narnia to cover the approach to Rome. See c. 43. 9. They had evidently been sent under the command of L. Manlius Acidinus (§ 8).

PAGE 74

opposita, sc. *hostibus*; cp. c. 43. 9 *hosti opponant.*

§ **7. magis auribus quam animis**, 'they heard but scarce believed.'

§ **9. tribunal**, the raised platform at the end of the *Comitium* on which the *praetor urbanus* sat to administer justice. In later times it was in one of the *basilicae* surrounding the Forum. The despatch was brought to the praetor as representing the supreme authority in the absence of the consuls.

curia, sc. *Hostilia*, the regular meeting-place of the Senate. It was at the N. end of the *Comitium* facing the tribunal. **rostris**, at the S. end of the *Comitium* where it joined the lower Forum.

§ **10. summoti**, 'removed.' *summovere* is the word regularly used of the action of the lictors in clearing the way before a magistrate.

dispensari, 'the glad tidings could be conveyed by due degrees to minds which could not contain themselves for delight.' *dispenso* means 'pay out,' 'distribute shares of money etc.,' and the metaphor is that of a bailiff doling out money or rations in order. "*laetitia* is used both subjectively and objectively in the same sentence; as subject to *potuit* it is the news which raised the feeling of joy, in *eius* it is the feeling they were powerless to control" (Stephenson).

§ **11. aliis certum gaudium**, 'some rejoiced without further question, others said they would not believe until they should hear etc.' *nulla futura erat*, 'were not going to believe.'

CHAPTER 51

§ **1. tum enim vero.** See n. on c. 16. 14.

omnis aetas, 'people of all ages'; **obvii** is construed according to the sense with *aetas*. Cp. *pars caesi* etc.

primus quisque...cupientes may mean 'desiring each one to be the first to...' or 'one after another desiring.' See n. on c. 5. 12.

§ **2.** **Mulvium pontem.** The Mulvian bridge carrying the *via Flaminia* over the Tiber was two miles from Rome.

continens, 'uninterrupted.' See n. on c. 17. 3.

§ **3.** **P. Licinius Varus**, *praetor urbanus* in the previous year, cp. c. 22. 3. **Q. Caecilius Metellus** (curule aedile c. 36. 8), and **L. Veturius Philo** were made consuls in the following year, cp. 28. 10. 2.

§ **5.** **summota turba,** ablative absolute.

§ **6.** **traducti,** for the regular *producti* see n. on c. 7. 4 and Notes on Text.

Page 75

animis caperent, 'could contain.'

§ **7.** **grates.** See n. on c. 13. 2. **domos.** See n. on c. 16. 2.

§ **8.** **pro contione.** See n. on c. 19. 11.

§ **9.** **amplissima veste,** 'in their gayest attire.'

§ **10.** **statum,** 'position of affairs,' cp. c. 1. 1. **movit**, 'altered,' 'affected,' cp. 25. 16. 4 *nulla tamen providentia fatum imminens movere potuit.* See Notes on Text.

res contrahere, 'enter into business transactions.'

mutuum and **creditum** go with *argentum*, 'on loan...borrowed.' *argentum*, 'money,' not a common prose usage, but cp. *argentum multaticium*.

§ **11.** **ut erant**, cp. c. 43. 4.

§ **12.** **agnoscere se fortunam**, 'recognised the fate.' Editors quote Horace, *Od.* 4. 4. 70 f. *occidit occidit spes omnis et fortuna nostri nominis Hasdrubale interempto.*

§ **13.** **Bruttios**, 'to Bruttium,' in apposition to *angulum*. The preposition is usually repeated in such cases.

suae dicionis, 'under his control.'

APPENDIX

NOTES ON THE TEXT

Among the large number of MSS. containing Book 27, by far the most important authority for the text is a Paris MS. called *Codex Puteanus* (P) from the name of its former owner Claudius Puteanus. It dates from the 7th or the beginning of the 8th century and until about 50 years ago it was thought to be the source of all the later MSS. It has been shown, however, that we must recognise a second family of MSS. originating from a codex parallel with P and differing from it, but derived from the same 6th century archetype. Apart from an early Palimpsest T (*Codex Taurinensis*), the earliest of this family is the MS. known as the *Codex Spirensis*, but with the exception probably of a single leaf found some forty years ago at Munich by Halm (*Folium Monacense*, 11th century, M), this codex has disappeared. However a large number of readings (S) from it are preserved in a 16th century Livy (2nd edition published by Froben at Basle in 1535), edited by Sigismund Gelenius, and especially in the *Annotationes* of Beatus Rhenanus prefixed to this edition. August Luchs has compared these readings with the other extant MSS. and has made it clear that a number of the latter belong to the same family as the *Codex Spirensis*. For Book 27, however, none of these are entirely independent of the P family. To denote the probable reading of the parent MS. of the *Spirensis* family the symbol Σ is used. For the determination of such readings some of the more important of these later MSS. are the following:

H = Codex Harleianus 2684 (15th century).

λ = Codex Laurentianus LXIII 21 (13th century) copied from a copy of P, but corrected in the 13th century from a MS. of the S family (L).

V = Codex Vaticanus Palatinus 876 (15th century).

F = Codex Florentinus Laurentianus LXXXI inf. 1 (15th century).

The consensus of a group of MSS. α, β (two 15th century MSS. in London), γ (14th century in Venice), δ, ε (two 15th century MSS. in Florence) is denoted by Luchs by R.

Wb = Weissenborn.

Mdg = Madvig.

c. **1.** § 8. **pugnantium** VR, *oppidantium* P, *trepidantium*, Gronov, *necopinantium* Sauppe, *spectantium* Friedersdorff. See Commentary.

§ 9. **in Fulvis** P, *in Cn Fulvii* V. Madvig says *in similitudinem increpare* is not Latin. See Commentary.

§ 10. **ante.** See Commentary.

c. **2.** § 6. **stetit.** ⟨ut⟩ Mdg. ⟨*ubi*⟩ *diu...stetit*, Wb.

§ 11. **tumultuosa magis proelia.** There is a lacuna in P from this point to c. 3. 7.

c. **3.** § 4. **incenderent** MSS. ⟨*ut*⟩ *incenderent* is generally read. *incendere* (Wb.) would also be correct Latin and *incendere centum* might easily have become *incenderent centum.*

c. **5.** § 4. **neminem Siculum, qui,** etc. Mdg. transposes the relative clause and reads *neminem Siculum non esse; qui fugati metu inde afuerint, omnes* etc.

§ 9. **atque in** Σ. *et ad* P, retained by Mdg. and Wb.

§ 14. **dictatore...dicto** Σ, *dictatorem...dici et* P.

c. **6.** § 3. **ni se** Drakenborch, *nisi* MSS.

§ 8. **exemplaque** Σ, *exemplumque* P. The plural is regular in distributive apposition. See Commentary.

§ 15. **factus...Crassi** (at the end of the §) bracketed by Mdg. as spurious, but the repetition of the words is quite natural in a formal list.

§ 19. **magnifice apparatos** Σ, *magnifici apparatus* P. Either reading might stand.

c. **7.** § 3. **obsistentem,** an early correction of MSS. *subsistentem.* With *subsistere* in the sense of 'withstand' Livy uses the accusative, cp. 1. 4. 9 *feras subsistere.*

§ 6. **quod** P, *sed* Σ.

§ 16. **placere** omitted in P.

c. **8.** § 3. ⟨**rem**⟩ I. F. Gronov, omitted in MSS. See Commentary.

§ 4. **decemvirum** P. Mdg. reads *decemvir* which might have been corrupted to *decemvirum* by the two words in *-um* which precede.

§ 8. **ei**, an emendation of Mdg. for *et* of MSS.

c. **9.** § 13. **diu iactassent** RFL, *dimastassent* P, *diu agitassent* V.

quod novi Mdg., *quid novi* MSS.

c. **11.** § 2. **lacus** P, *locus* Σ, *lucus* Crévier, *ostium lacus* Luterbacher.

§ 3. **aedis**, bracketed by Luchs.

c. **12.** § 3. **nec quod** Wesenberg, *nec quid* MSS.

remorandi P. *morandi* the reading of some later MSS. is preferred by Mdg. on the ground that *remorari* is not used intransitively in prose.

c. **13.** § 7. **ademisset** TVRF, *abstulisset* P, Wb. Livy does not elsewhere use the phrase *signa auferre*.

§ 9. **destitui et** Gronov, *destitui iussit et* P, *destituit* VR.

c. **15.** § 15. **illo** P, *illi* Σ.

c. **16.** § 7. **aequaverint** P, *aequarent* Σ. See Commentary.

§ 8. **interroganti** VRL, *interrogatis* P. **scriba** Drakenborch, *scribae* MSS. See Commentary.

§ 11. **constiterat** VRF, Mdg., *constituerat* P, Wb.

c. **17.** § 7. ⟨**et**⟩ Alschefski, and § 10. ⟨**ut**⟩...⟨**ac**⟩ Alschefski, omitted in MSS.

c. **18.** § 6. **faciliori ascensu** Mdg., *facilior in ascensum* PVRF. There does not seem to be any parallel for *facilior in ascensum* = 'easier to ascend,' 'easily ascended.' Mdg. suggests that the scribe taking *crepido haud facilior* together changed the superfluous *-i* into *in* and then *ascensu* into *ascensum*.

§ 11. **per aspreta** S, *per aspera* PVRF.

c. **19.** § 6. **alto** VR, *magno* PF.

c. **20.** § 3. **in cetera exsequenda belli.** See Commentary.

§ 4. **provinciae regione.** See Commentary.

§ 12. **obicerent** VRFL, *decernerent* P.

c. **22.** § 2. **utrisque consulibus** P, *utrique consulum* Σ.

§ 6. **additae ei ad** Σ, *additum et ad* P, *additum ei et* Gronov, *additum et aliud* Mdg. (Em. Liv. p. 397), *additum etiam* Wb.

§ 12. **compleret** Σ, *inpleret* P.

c. **23.** § 2. **Casini.** See Commentary.

c. **24.** § 2. **forum** Duker, *foro* MSS.

§ 3. **biduum ad considerandum tempus** MSS., 'vel *bidui* legendum vel *tempus* pro glossa delendum.' Duker.

§ 9. **praecavisset** Σ, *cavisset* P.

c. **25**. § 8. **duobus diis** Wb., *duobus* P, *amplius quam uni deo* Σ.

§ 14. **in aciem exire** adopted by Gronov. P has *inacieheare*, other MSS. *milites in aciem exire* (or *exciere* or *excire*). *in acie stare* Mdg.

c. **26**. § 1. **habebat** Gronov., *haberet* MSS.

c. **27**. § 3. **ab suis quisque latebris** Σ, *ab utrisque lateribus* P.

§ 8. ⟨**L.**⟩ omitted in best MSS.

§ 11. **iam enim maior** VR, *maior iam enim* P.

§ 13. **memoriam** Luchs, *ordinem* MSS. In support of *memoriam* Luchs quotes 21. 28. 5 *variat memoria actae rei*. Other suggested corrections of *ordinem* are *rationem*, *seriem*, *originem*, *narrationem*, *recordationem*. The two most likely guesses seem to be *rei memoriam* and *rei recordationem*. If these became *reimoriam* and *reiordationem*, *rei ordinem* would be a natural correction.

c. **28**. § 4. **anulis**. See Commentary. Two later MSS. have *anulo*.

§ 13. **quam ⟨L.⟩ Cincius** Sigonius, *quam urbem L. Cincius* Wesenberg. See Commentary. The MSS. omit the praenomen.

c. **29**. § 10. **proximo concilio**. The reading of P is *proximo anno concilio*, from which Wb. conjectures *proximo annuo concilio*.

c. **30**. § 5. **ferociori...gente** is Gronov's suggestion for *ferocioris...gentis* of the MSS. It seems more likely that Livy wrote this than *ferocioribus...gentis* (Ascensius), which is an easier correction (*-is* for *-ibus* is a common mistake), but does not give so natural a construction.

§ 9. **ferunt** Perizonius, *referunt* MSS.

c. **32**. § 5. **super caput** Mdg., *per caput* MSS.

c. **33**. § 7. **ita** Wb., *id* MSS., *ad id* Mdg.

§ 10. **fuisse**. See Commentary. *fuissent* is the reading of the Aldine edition of 1521 and probably also of the palimpsest T.

c. **34**. § 4. **migraret** MSS., *migrarit* Gelenius. *careret* P, **caruerit** Σ. See Commentary. As Rhenanus read *caruerit* but left *migraret*, no doubt Gelenius' *migrarit* is not derived from Σ.

c. **35**. § 2. **Quintius consul habuerat et L.** VRF, omitted in P. See Commentary.

c. **36.** § 9. **plebeis ludis** MSS., *plebeii ludi biduum instaurati* Wesenberg. See Commentary.

c. **37.** § 2. **Minturnis,** § 3 **Minturnenses** Σ, *Menturnis...Menturnenses* P, Wb. Similarly in c. 38. 4.

§ 6. **extorrem.** Mdg. reads *extorre* with P.

c. **38.** § 9. **⟨et⟩**, omitted in MSS. **quo,** Madvig's correction of *quos,* the reading of P.

c. **39.** § 13. **oppugnatione** Rhenanus, *oppugnatio* P.

celeriorem MSS., *celerioris* Luchs. If *celeriorem* is right it goes with *famam,* but Luchs' suggestion *celerioris* is attractive.

c. **40.** § 10. **Larinatis** MSS., *Uriatis* Mdg. See Commentary.

c. **41.** § 6. **vallibus** Σ. Mdg. reads *collibus* with P.

c. **42.** § 4. **decurrentium** Σ, *decursū* P.

§ 7. **septingentos** an early correction of *septingenti* P.

c. **43.** § 8. **edocet, ⟨et⟩ ut** Duker, Mdg., *edocet ut* P. If the reading of P is retained, *et ipse* means 'he himself also' (as contrasted with *litteris missis*). With Duker's emendation, which most edd. accept, *et...et* means 'both...and.'

c. **45.** § 3. **ipsi si** Mdg., *ipsos* MSS. See Commentary.

§ 4. **audiatur** Σ, *audiretur* P, Wb.

§ 11. **⟨abscedere⟩ ab signis** Wesenberg. *ab signis* MSS. *nec* before *subsistere* is omitted in several MSS. Madvig inserts *nisi* before *cibum* unnecessarily, I think. Other suggestions for the second infinitive required with *ab signis* are *abire* Wb., *discedere* Mdg. Gronov reads *nec ab signis absistere cibum capientes.*

c. **47.** § 6. **habuerit** P, *haberet* Σ. See Commentary.

§ 10. **errorem** MSS., *orbem* Wb. See Commentary.

ubi...erat. See Commentary.

c. **48.** § 5. **locat** Σ, Mdg., *conlocat* P, Wb.

§ 14. **sinistrum.** See Commentary.

c. **49.** § 2. **regentes sprevissent** Wb. The reading of P *regendispervicissent* is obviously corrupt. *regendi spem vicissent* Σ may possibly be what Livy wrote, and Mdg. and Luchs retain it, but Mdg. (*Em. Liv.*[2] p. 402, n. 2) says that it is curious Latin for *regiminis spem sustulissent* and approves Wb.'s conjecture. Luchs suggests *regendi spem incidissent.* Others adopt M. Müller's emendation *regentis imperium sprevissent.*

§ 3. **taedio ac labore** V, *taedio et labore* PRF, *taedio laborem* Mdg. (Em. Liv.[2] p. 402). See Commentary.

§ 7. **quattuor** is the reading of several MSS. P has ∞ ∞ ∞, and Mdg. and Wb. read *tria millia.* But cp. Zonar. 9. 9 Ῥωμαίους αἰχμαλώτους ἐς τετρακισχιλίους ἐν τῷ στρατοπέδῳ εὑρόντες, Oros. 4. 18 *quattuor milia civium Romanorum inter eos reperta.*

§ 10. **deleri supersint.** P has *delerique supersint* and a later MS. *deleriqui supersint.* Hence Gronov conjectures *deleri: quin supersint,* which is accepted by Mdg. and Wb.

c. **50.** § 1. **⟨profectus⟩** Sartorius. See Commentary.

§ 10. **inter impotentes.** P has *interponentis.* Hence Mdg. suggests (Em. Liv.[2] p. 403) *inter potentes.*

c. **51.** § 6. **traducti** PΣ, *producti* Sigonius. A later MS. and the Aldine edition have *introducti.*

§ 10. **movit ut** is omitted in P. *firmavit* is suggested by Mdg. (1882, vol. II, 2, p. ix) as more suitable to the context. *movere* usually denotes a change for the worse.

INDEX

(*The first number indicates the chapter, the second the section.*)

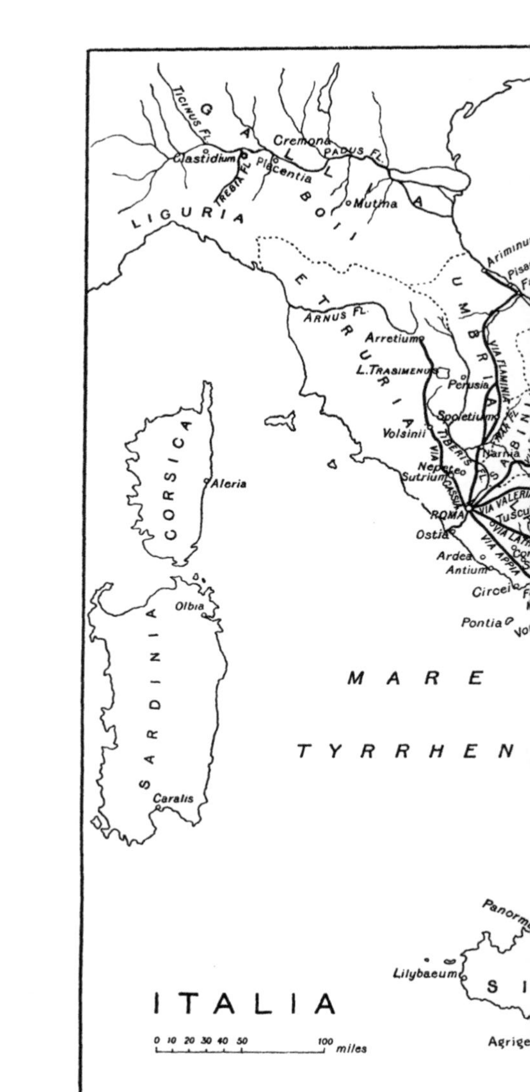

TICINUS FL.
GALLIA
Cremona
PADUS FL.
Clastidium
TREBIA FL.
Placentia
BOII
Mutina
LIGURIA
ETRURIA
ARNUS FL.
Arretium
L. TRASIMENUS
Perusia
UMBRIA
VIA FLAMINIA
Spoletium
Volsinii
TIBERIS FL.
VIA CASSIA
Nepete
Sutrium
Narnia
ROMA
Ostia
Ardea
Antium
Circei
Pontia
VIA APPIA
CORSICA
Aleria
SARDINIA
Olbia
Caralis
MARE
TYRRHEN
Lilybaeum
ITALIA
0 10 20 30 40 50 100 miles

MARE ADRIATICUM
Firmum
Hadria
VESTINI
FRENTANI
FUCINUS L.
Larinum
Arpi
Salapia
Luceria
Herdonea
Cannae
Canusium
AUFIDUS FL.
SAMNIUM
APULIA
Fregellae
Interamna
Casilinum
Capua
Calatia
Beneventum
HIRPINI
Venusia
Atella
Acerrae
Nola
Abella
Nuceria
Numistro
Bantia
LUCANIA
Paestum
Metapontum
Grumentum
Tarentum
Manduria
Uria
Brundisium
CALABRIA
SALLENTINI
SINUS TARENTINUS
BRUTTII
Thurii
Petelia
Croton
Lacinium Pr.
Caulon
Locri
Rhegium
Agathyrnum
Syracuse

For EU product safety concerns, contact us at Calle de José Abascal, 56–1°, 28003 Madrid, Spain or eugpsr@cambridge.org.

www.ingramcontent.com/pod-product-compliance
Ingram Content Group UK Ltd.
Pitfield, Milton Keynes, MK11 3LW, UK
UKHW020318140625
459647UK00018B/1930

* 9 7 8 1 1 0 7 6 2 0 0 2 5 *